D1624487

FINDING #1 STOCKS

FINDING #1 STOCKS

STOCKS

Screening, Backtesting, and Time-Proven Strategies

Kevin Matras

WILEY

John Wiley & Sons, Inc.

Copyright © 2011 by John Wiley & Sons, Inc. All rights reserved.

Published by John Wiley & Sons, Inc., Hoboken, New Jersey.
Published simultaneously in Canada.

No part of this publication may be reproduced, stored in a retrieval system, or transmitted in any form or by any means, electronic, mechanical, photocopying, recording, scanning, or otherwise, except as permitted under Section 107 or 108 of the 1976 United States Copyright Act, without either the prior written permission of the Publisher, or authorization through payment of the appropriate per-copy fee to the Copyright Clearance Center, Inc., 222 Rosewood Drive, Danvers, MA 01923, (978) 750–8400, fax (978) 646–8600, or on the Web at www.copyright.com. Requests to the Publisher for permission should be addressed to the Permissions Department, John Wiley & Sons, Inc., 111 River Street, Hoboken, NJ 07030, (201) 748–6011, fax (201) 748–6008, or online at http://www.wiley.com/go/permissions.

Limit of Liability/Disclaimer of Warranty: While the publisher and author have used their best efforts in preparing this book, they make no representations or warranties with respect to the accuracy or completeness of the contents of this book and specifically disclaim any implied warranties of merchantability or fitness for a particular purpose. No warranty may be created or extended by sales representatives or written sales materials. The advice and strategies contained herein may not be suitable for your situation. You should consult with a professional where appropriate. Neither the publisher nor author shall be liable for any loss of profit or any other commercial damages, including but not limited to special, incidental, consequential, or other damages.

For general information on our other products and services or for technical support, please contact our Customer Care Department within the United States at (800) 762–2974, outside the United States at (317) 572–3993 or fax (317) 572–4002.

Wiley also publishes its books in a variety of electronic formats. Some content that appears in print may not be available in electronic books. For more information about Wiley products, visit our web site at www.wiley.com.

Library of Congress Cataloging-in-Publication Data:

Matras, Kevin.
  Finding #1 Stocks: Screening, Backtesting, and Time-Proven Strategies / Kevin Matras.
    p. cm.—(The Zacks Series; 1)
  Includes index.
  ISBN 978–0–470–90340–7 (hardback); ISBN 978–1–118–05797–1 (ebk);
  ISBN 978–1–118–05798–8 (ebk); ISBN 978–1–118–05799–5 (ebk)
  1. Stocks. 2. Investments. 3. Investment analysis. I. Zacks Investment Research (Firm). II. Title.
  HG4661.M369 2011
  332.63'2042—dc22
                                                        2010050388

Printed in the United States of America

SKY10020850_082820

*To every trader and investor
who wants to be better.*

Contents

Chapter 4

Chapter 5

Chapter 6

Chapter 7

Chapter 8

Acknowledgments

I'd like to thank Len Zacks, CEO of Zacks Investment Research, who made writing this book possible through his breakthrough research in creating the Zacks Rank; Steve Reitmeister, Executive Vice President at Zacks, for giving me the opportunity to do so and for sharing his insights with me throughout the years; Meg Freeborn of John Wiley & Sons for all of her help and editorial expertise; and a very special thank you and acknowledgment to my wife Mary for all of her support while I was writing this book and every day.

Thank you.

Kevin Matras
Zacks Investment Research

Introduction

Let me congratulate you. Why? Because whether this is the first investment book you've ever read or the hundredth, the more you read, the more you learn, and the more you do, the better you'll become at something, whatever that something happens to be.

Finding #1 Stocks is about becoming a better trader and investor. My goal is to show you how to do this with the proven, profitable trading techniques used by Zacks, a leading investment research firm focusing on earnings estimates and stock analysis for the individual investor. In addition, you'll see plenty of my personal favorite trading strategies. And I'm also going to show you how you can create your own stock picking screens and trading strategies and how to test them to make sure they work.

Throughout this book, I will share with you real life, practical, and actionable information and strategies that you can start using immediately in your own trading, like how to identify stocks with the highest probability of success, when to sell to maximize your returns, and how to minimize your risk while doing so.

By developing the skills taught in this book, you can live the kind of life you want to live and have the kinds of freedoms and choices that greater financial success can give you. Best of all, you'll see that it's a lot easier than you think and you won't have to stay glued to your computer screen to do it.

While all of the screening ideas and trading strategies explained in this book were created and tested with Zacks' own stock picking and backtesting program called the Research Wizard, you can recreate many of these with your own screening program. Some screeners are more capable than others, but the information presented in this book can be applied to anybody's trading without any special tools or set-ups. (If you don't have a screening program, not to worry; go to page 287 in the back of the book for a free trial of the Research Wizard and follow along.)

So read on for some great stock picking screens and trading strategies.

Your investments are one of the largest, most important chunks of money you will ever be responsible for in your entire life. (And if it isn't now, it likely will be one day.)

In the pages that follow, we'll show you how to better take care of it.

Let's get started!

The Importance of Screening and Backtesting

O ne of the reasons why so many people are not seeing the kinds of returns they hope to see in their stock investments is because they don't know which stocks to buy and sell. They find themselves invested in mediocre stocks because they don't know of anything better to get into. For some, their knowledge or "universe" of familiar stocks is relatively small, and this limits their opportunity to invest in better ones.

Worse, when they finally do pick a new stock (likely an all too familiar one) and that doesn't work out as planned either, it discourages them even more from going out and finding others.

But it doesn't have to be that way.

Why Should I Use a Stock Screener?

With over 10,000 stocks out there to pick and choose from, we all need a way to find the good ones.

Aside from buying stocks that are talked about on TV, written about in the newspaper, or touted on the Internet (not to mention tips from a friend)— how else are you going to find stocks that meet certain characteristics?

Even if you don't use a screener now, most people still do their own screening in one way or another. You may hear that a stock has a certain growth rate or a certain P/E ratio or sales surprise or whatever. You then find yourself listening for or reading about or surfing the Internet for stocks that meet this criteria. Well, if you want to find stocks that meet certain criteria, certain characteristics, you can find them quickly and easily with a stock screener.

But just because you've narrowed down 10,000 stocks to only a handful, doesn't necessarily mean that you've picked the best stocks on the planet. You might have picked the worst ones.

> **Just because you've narrowed down 10,000 stocks to only a handful, doesn't necessarily mean that you've picked the best stocks on the planet. You might have picked the worst ones.**

But how will you know?

Backtesting!

Once you've created a screen, you can then backtest it to see how good or bad your screening strategy has performed in the past.

In other words, does your screening strategy generally find stocks that go up once they've been identified? Or does your screen generally find stocks that get buried once they've been identified?

This is good stuff to know. With backtesting, you can see how successful your stock picking strategy has performed in the past so you'll have a better idea as to what your probability of success will be now and in the future.

Of course, past performance is no guarantee of future results, but what else do you have to go by? Think about it. If you saw that a stock picking strategy did nothing but lose money year after year, trade after trade, stock after stock, over and over again, there's no way you'd want to trade that strategy or use that screen to pick stocks.

Why?

Because it's proven that it picks bad stocks. Sure, it may turn around and start picking winners all of a sudden, but it may also continue to pick losing stocks the way it always has. On the other hand, what if you saw that a strategy did great year after year, period after period, over and over again? You would, of course, want to trade that strategy.

Why?

Because it's proven to be a profitable stock picking strategy. And while it may start picking losers all of a sudden (now that you're using it—right?), it may also continue to pick winning stocks just like it had been doing over and over before.

Now, keep in mind that a screening and backtesting program isn't a box of magic, but it's a great way to see what works and what doesn't before you put your money at risk.

> **Backtesting is a great way to see what works and what doesn't before you put your money at risk.**

Unfortunately, too many people have no idea how to pick the right stocks. And this often leads people into staying in the wrong stocks too long or never getting into new stocks altogether.

I remember I had a conversation with a friend several years ago who was stuck in a losing stock:

Me: Why are you still in that stock if it keeps going down, losing you money?

Friend: I don't think it'll go much lower from here.

Me: Did you think it would go this low when you first bought it?

Friend: No.

Me: Do you think it will go up from here?

Friend: Probably not right away. It may still go down some more.

Me: You know, there are plenty of stocks going straight up. Why don't you get out of that one that keeps going down and losing you money and get into a better one?

Friend: I don't know of any better stocks to get into.

Me: What if you did know of a better stock to get into, would you do it?

Friend: Yeah! (Pause) But I'm not sure *how* to find better stocks.

And that last comment said it all. He was in losing stocks because he didn't know how to pick better ones. But if he had a proven profitable stock picking strategy, he could.

Don't get me wrong. Just because you have a great strategy for picking winning stocks, it isn't going to preclude you from ever having another losing trade. On the contrary, even some of the best strategies "only" have win ratios of 65% or 70% or 80%—not 100%.

But if your stock picking strategy picks winners far more often than it picks losers, you can quickly cut your losses once you find yourself in a losing trade and feel confident that your next pick will have a high probability of succeeding.

> **If your strategy picks winners far more often than losers, you can feel confident that your next pick will have a high probability of success.**

And that's why someone should use a screener and a backtester to pick stocks.

Chapter 2

Identifying What Kind of Trader You Are

Now that we know the importance of screening and backtesting, the next step is to identify what kind of trader you are (or want to be). This will make sure that you're getting into the right kinds of strategies and stocks *for you*.

The first step in identifying what kind of trader you are is to ask yourself some questions. What's interesting is that, often when I ask someone what kind of trader they are, they'll immediately say they're a growth trader or a value investor, and so forth. But when they stop and review the answers they've given themselves, it turns out they're completely different than the kind of trader they thought they were.

Here are three great questions to ask yourself to help you identify what kind of trader you are.

Question 1: What Kinds of Stocks Do You Want to Invest In?

This first question is intentionally broad, but it's a great place to start. Once you've indentified the kinds of stocks you'd like to trade, you can then learn about what style of trade these types of stocks fall into. And knowing what types of stocks you're looking for will make the process of finding them that much easier. So first things first.

Are you looking for:

- High flyers and fast movers?
- Stocks with big earnings momentum or aggressive growth?
- Maybe solid companies with dependable growth?
- Perhaps mature companies with income producing dividends?
- Or deeply discounted or undervalued stocks?

There are a lot of different types of stocks to choose from. I've listed just a few. But do your best at answering this first main question. Once you're done, then it's time to dig a little deeper.

Question 2: What Characteristics Do You Want Your Stocks to Have?

This is an extension of Question 1, but now we're getting into some of the details. And it's these details that help distinguish one type of stock from another. Go through the list below and expand on the characteristics as much as you'd like. This is actually a fun step and can be quite interesting because oftentimes some of the details people identify with are quite different than the types of stocks they identified as wanting to trade.

Ask yourself which characteristics are most important to you:

- Low valuations (e.g., low P/E ratios, or price to sales ratios, etc.)?
- Great management (as reflected by a strong ROE)?
- Stocks making new highs?
- Maybe big earnings growth or earnings surprises?
- Companies with a particular ranking (like the Zacks Rank)?

The number of possible characteristics is virtually endless. But there's no need to list them all. The characteristics you've probably already thought of are enough to better understand what kinds of stocks are right for you. Although, you might want to go back to the first question to see how closely aligned your answers to both 1 and 2 are to each other. Whether your answers are in perfect synch (good for you) or all over the map (don't worry about it for now), this is all part of the identification phase. And so is the next question.

Question 3: What Do You Want Your Stocks to Do for You?

Of course you want your stocks to make money. But how? How do you expect them to perform? Over what time period? And by how much? Answer this question and the ones that go along with it to better identify what type of trader you are.

- Are you looking to make fast money by getting in and getting out quickly?
- Or are you interested in finding long-term core holdings?
- Are you looking for stocks to generate income?
- Or would you prefer a medium-term trading strategy to actively pick stocks and grow a portfolio?

These are great questions to ask yourself. And there are other great questions as well. What are your investing goals? Have you ever achieved any of them? (If not, could it be that you've been focusing on the wrong stocks to achieve those goals?) What is your time horizon? What are you even trying to make this money for? Is this for fun? For your retirement? For your kid's education? In other words, what are you investing for?

You may be thinking that figuring out what kind of trader you are is no big deal. But it is. And it's absolutely imperative that you do. Why? Because if you find yourself trading a strategy or getting into stocks that are not in alignment with who you are and what you want, you're going to drop that strategy (no matter how good it's proven to work); you're going to drop that strategy the very moment it hits a rough patch.

Identifying the type of trader you are and what kinds of stocks you want to get into is a critical step to trading success.

You may also want to reflect on your current holdings and ask yourself if your answers are consistent with what's in your portfolio. Are your stocks consistent with who you are as a trader? Are they consistent with the kinds of stocks you want to be in? If they are not, you need to make a change.

Chapter

Defining the Basic Trading Styles

Once you've taken stock of yourself (no pun intended) and have a better understanding of what kinds of stocks you want to be in, the next step is to identify what trading style fits you the best. Each trading style has a unique set of characteristics that sets it apart from the others.

To make it easier to identify what kind of trader you are, let's define the four main fundamental trading styles: Momentum, Aggressive Growth, Value, and Growth and Income. And there's no need to worry if you don't fit perfectly into just one style. Many people have parts of each style in them, including myself. But it's still important to accurately identify what the different trading styles are and what stocks are best suited for each one.

Momentum Style

Momentum traders and investors look to take advantage of upward trends or downward trends in a stock's price or earnings. We've all heard the old adage, "the trend is your friend." And who doesn't like riding a trend?

Momentum style traders believe that these stocks will continue to head in the same direction because of the momentum that is already behind them. Momentum traders often fall into two categories, those who focus on price momentum screens and those who focus on earnings momentum screens.

Price Momentum

If you're looking at a *price momentum* screen, you're going to be looking at stocks that have been continuously going up, day after day, week after week, and maybe even several months in a row.

These are the kinds of stocks a momentum trader is after. And this, of course, also includes stocks making new 52-week highs. I point this out specifically because some people hate getting into stocks making new highs. We'll talk later about why I think that is. But it's important to know that there's a lot of evidence that shows stocks making new highs have a tendency of making even higher highs.

If you're uncomfortable buying stocks making new highs, that's okay. But the Momentum style of trade is probably not for you.

I should also mention that this style of trade will likely carry with it a higher degree of volatility, which is the rate at which a stock moves up or down. Although, the Momentum trader expects the gains made because of this to make it all worthwhile.

Earnings Momentum

The same momentum concept is true with earnings. If you're an *earnings momentum* trader, you're looking for companies whose earnings growth rate continues to accelerate, quarter after quarter after quarter. These are the kinds of companies that are going to fall into this category.

Another thing to keep in mind is that it is quite common for price momentum companies and earnings momentum companies to trade at higher valuations—like a higher P/E ratio, for example. Why? Because investors witnessing this momentum are usually willing to pay up for these stocks for fear that they'll get even more "expensive" if they wait.

It should also come as no surprise that these two types of momentum (price and earnings) will often go hand in hand. Companies with earnings momentum attract buyers. And more buying equals more demand, which in turn increases stock prices.

Aggressive Growth Style

Aggressive Growth traders are primarily focused on stocks with aggressive earnings growth or revenue growth (or at least the potential for aggressive growth). And you can expect volatility in this style of trading as well.

You'll often find smaller-cap stocks in this category because smaller-cap stocks are typically newer companies that are in the early part of their growth cycle. Of course, they don't all have to be small-cap stocks. They could be mid-cap stocks or even large-caps, too. For example, if there's a company that has been in existence for a while and they have a new product or service and they're lighting sales on fire, you may see some spectacular growth rates allowing that company to work its way into an aggressive growth style screen.

However, a word of caution: It's not as easy as just simply looking for stocks that have the highest growth rates. So don't go out and start looking for stocks with a 500% or 1,000% growth rate. While there will definitely be companies out there like that who do well, my studies have shown that those kinds of companies will typically underperform. In fact, oftentimes you'll see the companies with the highest growth rates perform almost as poorly as those with the lowest growth rates.

Why is that? It's because those levels of growth are unsustainable. And the stocks are often priced for perfection.

For example, let's say company XYZ just reported earnings of 1 cent. Now analysts are projecting next quarter's earnings to be 6 cents, which is a 500% growth rate. Weeks go by, and for whatever reason the analysts now revise their earnings estimates down to 5 cents a share. So, while 5 cents is still a 400% projected growth rate, it's also 100 points less than what was first expected for a −16% earnings estimate revision.

And if you're the person who just got into that stock the day before, you'll likely be scratching your head wondering why on earth a stock with a 400% growth rate is getting pounded. That's why.

Aggressive growth stocks are some of the most exciting picks out there. And they can be extremely rewarding. Just be sure to use your head when looking for those kinds of companies. And pay attention to the earnings estimate revisions. One of the best ways to find aggressive growth stocks is to screen for companies with growth rates that are meaningfully above the median for their industry, but not necessarily crazy high above it.

Value Style

Value investors and traders favor good stocks at great prices over great stocks at good prices.

This does not mean they have to be cheap stocks in price, though. The key is the belief that they're undervalued. That they are, for some reason, trading under what their true value or potential really is, and the value investor hopes to get in before the market "discovers" this and moves higher.

There could be many reasons why these stocks are being discounted by the market. Maybe they had disappointed in previous quarters and everybody just kind of lost interest. Maybe they don't have the kinds of exciting growth rates that can attract investor interest like an aggressive growth stock can. Maybe they're just in a boring industry. Who knows?

But the value investor is trying to find these kinds of stocks that have been ignored by the market. And normally you'll see these kinds of stocks showing up in your screens by looking at their valuations.

Understand though, the value investor will typically need to have a longer time horizon because, if that stock has been undervalued (i.e., "ignored" for a while), it may take a bit of time before that stock gets noticed and makes a move. So don't think that just because it showed up on your screen that it's immediately going to skyrocket. You may need a longer holding period for the rest of the market to catch up and reprice that company higher.

But keep your eyes out for their earnings estimates. There usually needs to be a catalyst for these unloved, underappreciated, overlooked companies to move. And I can think of no better way than to look at a series of upward earnings estimate revisions to put these stocks on someone's radar screen and to have them sit up and take notice.

Growth and Income Style

Growth and Income investors are looking for good companies with solid revenue that pay a good dividend.

Oftentimes these are more mature, larger-cap companies that generate solid revenue. These companies then pass that revenue along to their shareholders in the form of a dividend.

These are companies that may not have the kinds of spectacular growth rates like some of the younger or smaller companies have (or like they themselves had when they were younger and earlier in their growth cycle).

But it's not as if they're bad companies. They may be great companies, generating huge amounts of cash, but, because of their size, they may not have the growth opportunities they once had.

For example, let's say there was a small-cap company that does $100 million dollars in sales. And someone comes up with a great idea that will increase sales by an additional $100 million dollars. That's great news. And that company is now looking at a 100% growth rate. But apply that to a mid-cap company that does $1 billion in sales, and that $100 million dollar increase is now only a 10% increase in sales. Now apply that same $100 million dollar increase to a company that does $10 billion in sales, and that's only a 1% increase.

Simply put, for some companies, the law of big numbers makes it harder to grow at the torrent pace that a younger and smaller company is capable of. So instead of investing all of their earnings back into the company, they reward their shareholders by paying out a portion of their profits in the form of a dividend.

Like the value investor, the growth and income investors will also have a longer time horizon, especially since they'll want to hang onto their stocks long enough to receive the dividend. Usually, this kind of investor is looking to hold onto these companies for three to six to 12 months or longer.

"All Style" Style

Another style, which I alluded to at the top, that is equally as popular, or maybe even more so, is a combination style or "All Style" style as I like to call it. (It reminds me of "All-Star.")

This combines the best of some of the different trading styles or even all of the different trading styles into one screen. And this is the category that probably most people will fall into. They have a little bit of everything in their screen.

But don't think that when you're building your screens, you're going to find companies with a 100% growth rate that are also paying a 10% dividend. Those things are on the opposite ends of the spectrum.

Also, if you're looking at a value company—remember, these are the ones that are overlooked or ignored—don't expect to find many deep value stocks that are up 30%, 40%, or 50% over the course of the last few weeks, because that's the antithesis of being overlooked. Everybody's now on that stock.

I'm sure there are some value stocks out there like that, but those are probably the ones the value guy found several months ago that are now paying off. And those stocks are no longer trading at the same value as they once were when he first got into them.

Smartly combining the best of one or more styles that complement one another can make for a powerful strategy.

Technical Analysis

No discussion on trading styles would be complete without the inclusion of Technical Analysis (TA).

My favorite brand of technical analysis is chart pattern recognition. In addition to that, I also use moving averages and the relative strength index (RSI) oscillator among others.

Technical analysis is really just a study of price movement and volume and all the different ways of displaying and measuring that. I'll go into more detail on chart pattern analysis later in the book, but technical analysis can be applied to any and all base styles of trade.

Momentum style traders will typically monitor price trends and moving averages as well as volume changes and more—all forms of technical analysis. This is also true for Aggressive Growth traders as well. Value traders and Growth and Income traders also look at technical analysis, including charts and price patterns, in an effort to determine when a stock will move and in what direction.

Whether you consider yourself a fundamental trader or technical trader, each style has something to offer. In fact, even the most die-hard of technicians, while espousing the virtues of technical analysis, will still look at the fundamentals. And nowadays, even the strictest of fundamental traders will at least glance at a chart before getting in.

Winning in Style

Think about the last car you bought. Once you decided what kind of car you wanted, you probably saw them everywhere. They didn't just magically appear on the road. They were always there. You just became aware of them.

The same can be said for picking stocks. Once you've identified what kind of trader you are and the style of trade that fits you the best, it becomes easier to find stocks with those characteristics. When you know what you're looking for, it becomes easier to find. And the sooner you start finding the right stocks for your trading style, the more money you'll make.

4

Trading the Zacks Rank

One of the simplest and one of the best trading strategies is to simply buy the stocks that have a Zacks Rank #1 and sell them when they're no longer Ranked a #1 (which means a 2, 3, 4, or 5). Since 1988, this strategy has beaten the S&P in 20 out of the last 22 years.

The Zacks Rank versus the Market

The strategy of buying the Zacks #1 Ranked stocks and selling them a month later if they're no longer Ranked a #1 has shown an average annual gross return of 27.27% a year.[1] This is in stark contrast to the S&P 500's 8.86% average return.

Take a look at the returns and you can see that the Zacks Rank has increased by over three times that of the S&P. (See Table 4.1.)

But understand, if you're able to do this in a repeatable way, over and over again, that can add up to a lot more than just three times the S&P.

In fact, assuming you could realize the returns for each year as shown, the following chart illustrates how a portfolio could have grown in value. (Note: the compounded returns displayed do not include brokerage commissions and fees or potential price impacts due to trade execution or bid/ask spreads.) (See Figure 4.1.)

---

[1] For a complete explanation of how the performance of the Zacks Rank is calculated, please refer to page 285.

TABLE 4.1 Zacks Rank Performance Summary (Monthly Rebalancing)

Year	#1 Rank	#2 Rank	#3 Rank	#4 Rank	#5 Rank	S&P 500
1988	37.46%	29.69%	20.79%	19.13%	18.39%	16.20%
1989	36.09%	26.84%	15.85%	9.55%	−5.10%	31.70%
1990	−2.97%	−13.69%	−21.32%	−23.85%	−34.71%	−3.10%
1991	79.79%	56.80%	45.98%	36.60%	34.35%	30.40%
1992	40.65%	29.63%	18.04%	12.24%	17.31%	7.51%
1993	44.41%	26.86%	14.78%	8.59%	9.54%	10.07%
1994	14.34%	5.15%	−3.56%	−11.14%	−10.90%	0.59%
1995	54.99%	46.84%	30.63%	17.35%	9.11%	36.31%
1996	40.93%	28.60%	16.07%	7.71%	8.02%	22.36%
1997	43.91%	33.87%	22.93%	10.17%	3.05%	33.25%
1998	19.52%	12.92%	−3.47%	−8.77%	−14.84%	28.57%
1999	45.92%	35.53%	31.02%	18.46%	17.69%	21.03%
2000	14.31%	−1.47%	−17.75%	−19.52%	−3.95%	−9.10%
2001	24.27%	11.70%	14.09%	17.93%	20.20%	−11.88%
2002	1.22%	−14.51%	−19.39%	−23.50%	−17.59%	−22.10%
2003	74.74%	71.02%	66.69%	57.34%	55.99%	28.69%
2004	28.79%	23.26%	18.51%	11.92%	16.63%	10.87%
2005	17.97%	12.01%	6.54%	−1.31%	−5.08%	4.90%
2006	23.69%	26.63%	18.09%	15.17%	16.88%	15.80%
2007	19.91%	5.42%	−4.34%	−13.06%	−23.90%	5.49%
2008	−41.13%	−43.48%	−48.70%	−45.75%	−50.95%	−37.00%
2009	66.87%	82.46%	78.42%	59.91%	49.18%	26.46%
2010*	−1.71%	2.87%	−1.50%	−1.89%	−0.56%	−6.64%
Annual Average	27.27%	18.65%	9.70%	3.93%	1.70%	8.86%

*2010 returns are for the period of Jan. 1 to June 30, 2010.

What's interesting is that we've all heard people say that becoming a better investor can change your life. While it's a great catch phrase, I don't think anybody really stops to think about it or let alone believes it. But it's true. Becoming a better investor can change your life. Just ask the guy who's going to retire this year on $67,000 vs. the guy who's going to retire on $2.2 million and tell me that guy with $2.2 million isn't living a different life than the guy with $67,000. Becoming a better trader *can* change your life.

As you can see, implementing ways to consistently beat the market can quickly add up. Of course, there are over 200 Zacks #1 Ranked stocks at any given time, so narrowing them down to a smaller, more manageable list or portfolio is the next step.

FIGURE 4.1   Zacks #1 Rank Compounded Performance

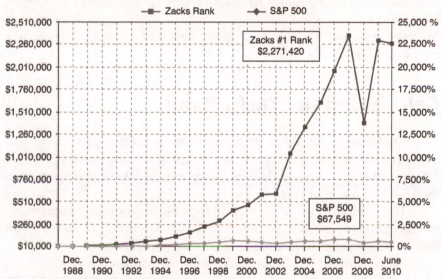

Zacks #1 Rank ($10,000 Starting Equity)

—■— Zacks Rank   —◆— S&P 500

Zacks #1 Rank
$2,271,420

S&P 500
$67,549

| | Dec. | Dec. | Dec. | Dec. | Dec. | Dec. | Dec. | Dec. | Dec. | Dec. | Dec. | June |
| | 1988 | 1990 | 1992 | 1994 | 1996 | 1998 | 2000 | 2002 | 2004 | 2006 | 2008 | 2010 |

See page 285 for a complete explanation of how these compounded returns are calculated.

But before we go any further, in order to fully understand why the Zacks Rank works so well, it's important to understand what the Zacks Rank is and how it's calculated.

About Len Zacks

The Zacks Rank was created by Leonard Zacks, the CEO and co-founder with his brother Ben Zacks, of Zacks Investment Research. Len, who has a PhD from MIT, spent many years on Wall Street testing statistical models to help uncover ways to beat the market. Len's research led to a breakthrough discovery: "Earnings estimate revisions are the most powerful force impacting stock prices."

"Earnings estimate revisions are the most powerful force impacting stock prices."—Ben and Len Zacks

His findings were first published in 1979 in the *Financial Analysts Journal* and entitled "EPS Forecasts–Accuracy Is Not Enough". From this seminal work emerged the now famous Zacks Rank stock picking system, which harnesses the power of earnings estimate revisions. And so began a long tradition of innovations by his now famous firm, Zacks Investment Research.

Len may be a PhD, but you don't have to be one in order to take advantage of the Zacks Rank.

Calculating the Zacks Rank

The foundation of the Zacks Rank has to do with earnings estimate revisions. Stocks with rising estimates, as a group, have outperformed the S&P 500 year after year. And stocks with falling estimates have underperformed the S&P 500 year after year.

This means that the stocks most likely to outperform are the ones whose earnings estimates are being raised. And the stocks most likely to underperform are the ones whose earnings estimates are being lowered.

Zacks (through the Zacks Rank), has made the process of identifying stocks with changing earnings estimates easy and very profitable. Since 1978, Zacks has been compiling and analyzing brokerage research for both institutional investors and individual investors.

Today, Zacks processes this information from roughly 3,000 analysts from over 150 different brokerage firms. At any given point and time, they're monitoring well over 200,000 earnings estimates and other related data looking for any change. The ability to gather, analyze, and distribute this information on a timely basis makes Zacks' research among the most widely used investment research on the Web.

Our performance, of course, is another reason. As I mentioned earlier, a portfolio constructed of just the Zacks #1 Ranked stocks has generated an average annual return of 27.3%.

Even during the bear market of 2000 to 2002, this strategy generated positive returns (see Table 4.2). In 2000, the S&P lost −9.10%, while the Zacks #1s picked up 14.31%. In 2001, the S&P had another tough year, closing down −11.88%, while the Zacks #1s gained a spectacular 24.27%. And in 2002, the S&P had its worst year of that three-year period, losing another −22.10%, whereas the Zacks #1 Ranked stocks actually added to their gains, picking up an additional 1.22%.

The compounded returns of the Zacks #1 Ranked stocks during that three-year bear period was 43.79%. The S&P 500 during that same bear move was −37.60%.

TABLE 4.2 Zacks #1 Rank, 2000–2002

Year	#1 Rank	S&P 500	#1 vs. S&P
2000	14.31%	−9.10%	+23.41
2001	24.27%	−11.88%	+36.15
2002	1.22%	−22.10%	+23.32

What about the worst bear market in recent history and the second-worst bear market of all time? (The period 2000 through 2002 only ranks as the seventh-worst bear market.) I'm talking about the financial crisis of 2007 through the first quarter of 2009 when the S&P 500 lost −57.7% in a year and a half.

By the end of 2007, the market was starting to show its cracks, but the S&P managed to hold onto a 5.49% gain, while the Zacks #1s were up 19.91%. The year 2008 was a different story as there was virtually no place to hide. The S&P 500 was down −37.00% while the Zacks #1s lost −41.13%. The worst performance in the history of the Zacks Rank and only the second time ever that the Zacks #1s underperformed the market. However, with over a 20-year track record at that point, those who remained confident that the Zacks Rank would soon outperform the market once again were well rewarded. In 2009, after the market hit its lows in March, the S&P rallied for a 26.46% gain on the year, but the Zacks #1s gained more than 2.5 times that with a 66.87% gain (see Table 4.3).

TABLE 4.3 Zacks #1 Rank, 2007–2009

Year	#1 Rank	S&P 500	#1 vs. S&P
2007	19.91%	5.49%	+14.42
2008	−41.13%	−37.00%	−4.13
2009	66.87%	26.46%	+40.41

The Zacks #1 Ranked stocks from the beginning of the collapse in 2007, through the worst of 2008, and into the subsequent rebound of 2009, generated a total compounded return of 17.80% vs. the S&P's −15.96%.

In fact, in any one of those bear market periods, had someone been on the negative side of that equation, that could have forced some people to postpone their retirement or, worse, changed how they planned on living out their retirement years altogether.

Of course, if you were on the winning side, what a great send-off.

What the Rankings Mean

The Zacks Rank is a proprietary quantitative model that looks at changes and trends in earnings estimate revisions and earnings surprises. We then use this information to classify stocks into five groups:

Zacks Rank #1—Strong Buy

Zacks Rank #2—Buy

Zacks Rank #3—Hold

Zacks Rank #4—Sell

Zacks Rank #5—Strong Sell

But don't confuse this with the average broker rating, as it couldn't be more different.

First, the Zacks Rank is proportionately applied to the approximate 4,400 stocks for which sell-side analyst estimates are available. By proportionate, I mean only the top 5% of the stocks assigned a Zacks Rank can receive the coveted position of a Zacks #1 Rank—Strong Buy. It's also important to know, and maybe even more important, that the same number of stocks (5%) are assigned a Zacks #5 Ranking, which is a Strong Sell (see Table 4.4).

TABLE 4.4 Zacks Rank, Distribution

Zacks Rank	Zacks Rank Universe (Approximate)	Recommendation
1	5%	Strong Buy
2	15%	Buy
3	60%	Hold
4	15%	Sell
5	5%	Strong Sell

This equality between Strong Buy and Strong Sell recommendations makes the Zacks Rank a much more reliable indicator than your typical brokerage recommendations, which are significantly biased toward "Buy" ratings with a terrible reluctance to say "Sell."

So what do these recommendations mean?

- Zacks Rank #1 or Strong Buy means it should outperform the market the most, i.e., more than the other Ranks. (By "market" we are referring to the S&P 500, which is one of the most commonly used benchmarks.)

- Zacks Rank #2 or Buy means it should outperform the market.
- Zacks Rank #3 or Hold means it should perform in line with the market.

Let me clarify what a Hold recommendation is not. Some people think that a Hold means that if they are in the stock, they are supposed to hold onto it. Or if they're not in it yet, they're supposed to hold off from buying it. That is not what a Hold recommendation means.

A Hold recommendation very simply means there is no compelling reason, one way or the other, for the stock to underperform or outperform the market in any meaningful way. It simply means it should perform in line with the market.

- Zacks Rank #4 or Sell means it should underperform the market.
- Zacks Rank #5 or Strong Sell means it should underperform the market the most.

As Table 4.5 shows, the Zacks Ranks are all performing on target. The Strong Buys have outperformed the market the most. The Buys outperformed the market. The Holds performed in line with the market. The Sells underperformed the market. And the Strong Sells underperformed the market the most.

TABLE 4.5 Zacks Rank, Meaning and Performance

Zacks Rank	Recommendation	Meaning	Average Annual Return
1	Strong Buy	Outperform the market (the most)	27.27%
2	Buy	Outperform the market	18.65%
3	Hold	Market perform	9.70%
4	Sell	Underperform the market	3.93%
5	Strong Sell	Underperform the market (the most)	1.70%

(1988–6/2010)
Average annual return for the S&P 500: 8.86%.

As you can see from the following list, the entire assignment of the Zacks Rank is like a bell curve—an equal number of buys and sells with a larger number of holds in the middle:

- 5% of the stocks are Ranked a #1 or Strong Buy
- 15% are Ranked a #2 or Buy
- 60% are Ranked a #3 or a Hold
- Then going back down the slope: 15% are Ranked a #4 or Sell
- And 5% are Ranked a #5 or Strong Sell

Adding up all of the Strong Buy and Buys: 20% of the ratings are bullish. On the other side of the spectrum, adding up the Sells and Strong Sells: 20% of the ratings are bearish for an even distribution (see Figure 4.2).

FIGURE 4.2 Distribution of Zacks Rank

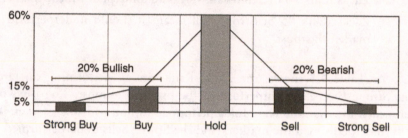

By contrast, if you look at the average broker ratings, as illustrated in the following list, they're quite lopsided:

- 19% of the stocks with a brokerage rating have an average Strong Buy rating
- 47% have a Buy rating
- 30% have a Hold
- 3% have an average broker rating of Sell
- Only 1% have a Strong Sell

Adding up the Strong Buys and Buys of the average broker ratings, a full 66% are bullish whereas the Sells and Strong Sells add up to only 4% being bearish (see Figure 4.3).

FIGURE 4.3 Distribution of Average Broker Ratings

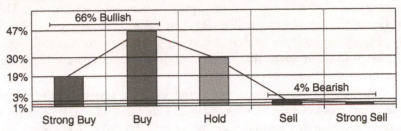

To be fair, the average broker rating can be quite useful, but I believe it's the change in the rating that carries the most value. (More on this later.)

While the analysts aren't that great at making subjective buy and sell predictions, they are good at providing estimates. This is why brokerage companies literally spend billions of dollars a year on analysts to research stocks. They must know something—and they do.

> **While analysts aren't that great at making subjective buy and sell predictions, they are good at providing estimates.**

Analysts are paid in aggregate, over $4 billion a year to analyze stocks. The typical analyst at a brokerage firm will work 80-hour weeks—devoting all his or her time to, at most, maybe 20 companies. And many companies are followed by 5 to 10 analysts or more. One of their main tasks is to determine what a company's earnings will be. This is where they excel. Not in their ratings, but in their earnings estimates.

The reason why earnings matter is because, at the end of the day, earnings give a stock its intrinsic value. And when trying to determine the future direction of a stock's price move, you really need to look at what a company will earn in the future. This is why earnings expectations or earnings estimates are so important.

> **It's the change in the earnings estimates (earnings estimate revisions) that have proven to be the most important.**

Why? Because stocks that receive upward earnings estimate revisions are more likely to receive even more upward revisions in the future. This is true because many analysts will revise their earnings slowly and incrementally. For example, if an analyst raised his earnings estimates last month, he is likely to do it again this month. And other analysts are likely to do the same.

Since stock prices respond to earnings estimate revisions, it's very profitable to buy stocks whose earnings estimates are being raised. By getting into stocks whose earnings estimates are being raised, you're likely getting into companies whose future earnings estimates will be raised as well, potentially influencing stock prices even more. As a result, *stocks receiving upward earnings estimate revisions tend to outperform over the next one to three months.*

Four Factors of the Zacks Rank

So *how* does Zacks use earnings estimates and earnings estimate revisions in the Zacks Rank? The Zacks Rank is calculated from four primary inputs:

Agreement: This is the extent to which all brokerage analysts are revising their earnings estimates in the same direction. The greater the percentage of analysts there are that are revising their estimates higher, the better the score for this component.

For example, if 40% of the analysts are increasing their earnings estimates for a stock whereas only 10% are increasing it for another stock, the higher the percentage of analysts making upward estimate revisions the better.

Magnitude: This is the size of the recent change in the current consensus estimate for the fiscal year and the next fiscal year.

For example; a 5% increase in the earnings estimate revision is better than a 2% earnings estimate revision and will thus get a better score for this component.

Upside: This is the difference between the most accurate estimate as calculated by Zacks and the consensus estimate.

A bigger difference between the most accurate estimate and the consensus estimate is better.

Surprise: The Zacks Rank factors in the last few quarters' earnings per share (EPS) surprise as well.

Since companies with a positive earnings surprise are more likely to surprise again (or miss again, if recently missed), this is looked at too.

Each one of these components is given a raw score and it's recalculated every night. These raw scores are then compiled into what is called the Zacks Rank and are made available to investors every day, helping them beat the market.

Beyond the Zacks Rank

While the Zacks Rank has proven to be one of the best rating systems out there, traders shouldn't stop at using only the Zacks Rank. Since there are over 200 stocks with a Zacks #1 Rank on any given day, it would be virtually impossible for most traders to trade them all.

So now it's time to narrow that list of stocks to a smaller, more manageable number of stocks for a real life portfolio.

Filtering the Zacks Rank

In good markets or bad, stocks with a Zacks #1 Rank continue to outperform the market. Since there are typically hundreds of stocks Ranked #1 by Zacks at any time, it's important to know what filters to apply to generate a smaller, more tradable list of stocks.

Two filters in particular, when applied to Zacks #1 Rank stocks, not only narrow the number of qualified stocks to a more practical portfolio size, but oftentimes increase its performance as well.

Let's take a look at what those filters are.

Parameters

The screen starts off with the Zacks Rank. And then the two additional filters are added to it.

- **Zacks Rank = 1**
  Strong Buys.

- **% Change (Q1) Est. over 4 Weeks > 0**
  Positive current quarter estimate revisions over the last four weeks.

- **% Broker Rating Change over 4 Weeks = Top # 5**
  Top five stocks with the best average broker rating changes over the last four weeks.

These two items, added to the Zacks #1 Rank, produce powerful results!

Methodology

Let's take a closer look at why.

- **Zacks Rank = 1**
  Once again, these are the best performing Zacks Rank stocks.

- **% Change (Q1) Est. over 4 Weeks > 0**
  The Zacks Rank already looks at earnings estimate revisions for the current year (F1) and the next year (F2). But this added component looks at the more immediate future, which is the current quarter (Q1).

  If a company's current quarter is seeing downward revisions, this is a potential warning sign that more downward revisions could follow. On the other hand, a company receiving upward earnings estimate revisions should see even more upward earnings estimate revisions, making it an attractive stock to buy.

- **% Broker Rating Change over 4 Weeks = Top # 5**
  We're looking for positive broker rating changes or upgrades over the last four weeks. And to limit the number of stocks that come through, we've constructed the screen to select the top five stocks with the best average broker rating upgrade.

  Since broker ratings are typically skewed to the upside, this makes sure that the brokers are getting more bullish, or at the very least, not getting less bullish (or even bearish) on the stock.

As I mentioned in the previous chapter, while I don't care so much for the actual broker rating per se, I do care about the change.

Results

I ran a series of tests on the Filtered Zacks Rank strategy *(Filtered Zacks Rank 5)* over each of the last 10 years (2000–2009) (see Figure 5.1). I rebalanced the portfolio every four weeks and started each run on different start dates so each test would be rebalanced over a different set of four-week periods. This is done to eliminate coincidental performance and to verify robustness.

FIGURE 5.1   Filtered Zacks Rank 5 Comparison

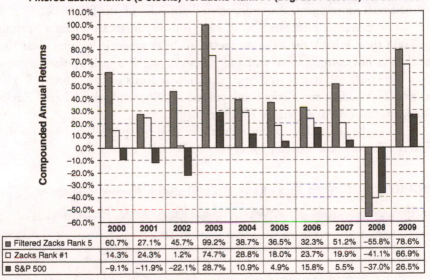

Filtered Zacks Rank 5 (5 stocks) vs. Zacks Rank #1 (avg. 200+ stocks) vs. S&P 500

	2000	2001	2002	2003	2004	2005	2006	2007	2008	2009
■ Filtered Zacks Rank 5	60.7%	27.1%	45.7%	99.2%	38.7%	36.5%	32.3%	51.2%	−55.8%	78.6%
□ Zacks Rank #1	14.3%	24.3%	1.2%	74.7%	28.8%	18.0%	23.7%	19.9%	−41.1%	66.9%
■ S&P 500	−9.1%	−11.9%	−22.1%	28.7%	10.9%	4.9%	15.8%	5.5%	−37.0%	26.5%

For 2000 through 2002, the Zacks #1 Ranked stocks stayed in the plus column even while the S&P 500 got progressively worse. The Filtered Zacks Rank strategy, however, outperformed both with an easily tradable portfolio of just five stocks.

In 2003, the market turned around and put in an impressive 28.7% performance. But the Zacks #1 Rank stocks did more than 2.5 times that with 74.7%. The Filtered Zacks Rank did even better with 99.2%.

For 2004 through 2006, the S&P produced respectable enough returns. Although, the Zacks #1 Rank stocks bested the S&P, while the five Filtered Zacks Rank stocks bested them all.

The end of 2007 marked the beginning of the financial crisis and the stock market collapse. And while the S&P still managed to end the year in the positive, the Zacks Rank strategies were far more robust with the Filtered Zacks Rank strategy up 51.2%.

The next year, 2008, was a strange year. It was one of the worst one-year drops for the S&P 500 and was the Zacks Rank's worst performance. The Filtered Zacks Rank didn't fare any better. How could this be? It's quite interesting. As the market turned from typical bear to all out panic, people seemed to be willing to get out at any price in an effort to go to cash. (And "any price" is where they indeed got out.) When so many stocks were all of a sudden trading for fractions of what they used to trade at, one of the only ways to raise cash was to sell even your best holdings. I believe that's one of the reasons why the Zacks Rank took such a drubbing. The Filtered Zacks Rank underperformed even more due to the concentrated portfolio of just five stocks.

However, the phenomenon of even top-notch stocks taking a beating in 2008 took a backseat to saner views in 2009 when it became clear the world was not coming to an end and investors raced to pick up the bargains they were only too happy to dump just a few months earlier. The S&P 500 gained 26.5%. But the Zacks Rank gained 66.9%, while the Filtered Zacks Rank trumped them all with a 78.6% return.

Over the entire 10-year time span, the total compounded return for the Filtered Zacks Rank 5 strategy was 1,774.4% (see Figure 5.2).

FIGURE 5.2 Filtered Zacks Rank 5 (2000–2009, 4-week rebalance)

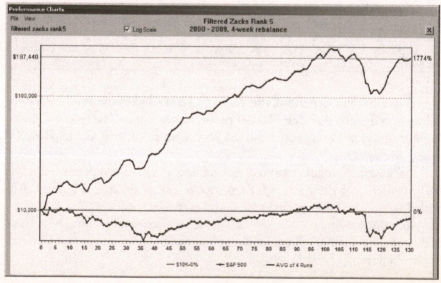

Once again, let me point out that these backtested results do not include commission costs or fees. In contrast, a person trading this strategy in real life would incur transaction costs, which would make his or her results lower than what is displayed in a backtest. And a trader with a smaller account would be impacted even more by the costs associated with trading. This is important to understand and can make a difference between the actual results an investor can achieve and a backtested return. All of that being said, the returns are still quite impressive and significantly beat the market.

This strategy can also be traded on a weekly basis. Rebalancing it every week is ideal for those who want to be more active, although this will also increase your transaction costs.

Nonetheless, the returns are even more impressive. And rebalancing it once a week will allow you to take advantage of some of the newer stocks coming through the screen each week.

How did it do? Over the last 10 years (2000–2009), it produced a total compounded return of 20,101.1% for an average annual return of 69.7%. (See Figure 5.3.)

FIGURE 5.3 Filtered Zacks Rank 5 (2000–2009, 1-week rebalance)

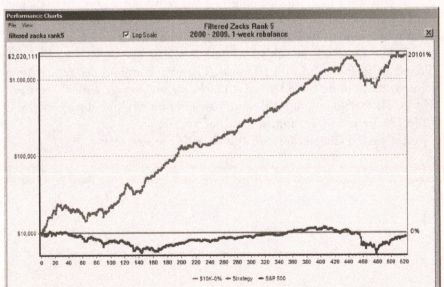

Regardless of how often you trade it (once a week, every two weeks, or every four weeks, etc.), trading five stocks at a time is a lot easier than 200 stocks.

So for a great and reliable way to trade some of the best Zacks #1 Rank stocks, try the Filtered Zacks Rank and trade fewer stocks for even bigger returns.

How Many Stocks Are Right for You?

While the Filtered Zacks Rank 5 strategy was specifically created to produce no more than five stocks at a time, those with larger portfolios might prefer to hold 10 stocks or more at a time.

Either way, with this screen (and with the others we'll demonstrate in the coming chapters) you can limit or expand the number of stocks coming through to whatever is right for you.

For example, let's take the last item in the Filtered Zacks Rank 5 screen, which reads: "% Broker Rating Change over 4 Weeks = Top # 5."

We used the operator "Top #" and then put in the number 5. By changing that from the Top # 5 to the Top # 10, you're now telling the screen to find the stocks that meet all of the other parameters but limit them to just the 10 best stocks with the highest average broker rating upgrade percentage.

If you want more stocks, plug in a larger number. Less stocks? Use a smaller number. And you can apply this type of operator and value logic to virtually any kind of item for virtually any kind of screen.

While we're on the subject of more (or less) stocks, let's see how the Filtered Zacks Rank did with 10 stocks. The total compounded return using a four-week holding period was 1,135.9% for an average annual return of 28.1%. The total compounded return using a one-week holding period was 7,286.7% for an average annual return of 53.5%.

Let's go to Chapter 6 to see *how* to trade the strategies.

How to Trade the Strategies

Trading strategies like the Filtered Zacks Rank we talked about in the previous chapter or any of the other strategies we present in this book are easy to implement.

You will find that some strategies work better when traded or rebalanced once a week. Others perform better when they are traded every two weeks or four weeks. And still other strategies do better when traded every 12 weeks (like dividend paying strategies or even some value style strategies).

Either way, it only takes about 10–15 minutes to rebalance your portfolio, whether it's once a week, once a month, or once a quarter.

Once a Month

In the first study we did of the Filtered Zacks Rank, we used a four-week holding period. To do that, you would run your screen once a month (every four weeks actually). On the first week—Monday morning—buy all the stocks that make it through your screen. Let's use five stocks as an example.

Each stock should be purchased with an equal dollar amount. In other words, an equal amount of money would be put into each stock for an equal dollar weighted portfolio.

Then you'll hang on to those stocks for the duration of the holding period—which in this case is four weeks. Four weeks later, run the screen again and see what stocks come through. This time, you'll keep the stocks that still qualify, sell the ones that no longer qualify (whether it's a profit or a loss, you'll sell them) and buy any new stocks that come through. That's it.

So once again, for your very first period:

1. Run your screen on Monday morning.
2. Buy the stocks that come through, putting an equal amount of money into each one.
3. Hang onto those stocks for four weeks.

Then every four weeks:

1. Run your screen again.
2. Keep the previously qualified stocks that still qualify. Sell the stocks that no longer qualify. And buy any new stocks that newly qualify.
3. Hang onto those stocks for four weeks.

Four weeks later, do it again.

For example (see Table 6.1): Let's call your first week Period 1. In that first week, five stocks will come through. For illustration purposes, let's say it's AAPL, T, MCD, ARLP, and PCLN. You're going to buy those stocks in an equal dollar weighted manner. And you're going to hang onto those stocks for four weeks.

Four weeks later, let's call this Period 2, you'll run your screen again. If AAPL comes through again, you'll keep it in your portfolio. If T comes through again, you're going to keep it. If MCD comes through again, you're going to keep this one as well. But if ARLP and PCLN no longer come through, you're going to sell those two stocks. Once again, whether it be at a profit or a loss, you'll sell them. And in their place, you'll add the two new stocks that came through—let's say AMZN and NFLX. You'll then hang onto those five stocks for the next four weeks. And you'll do this every four weeks. It's that easy.

TABLE 6.1 4-Week Rebalance Example	
Period 1	Period 2 (4 Weeks Later)
buy AAPL	keep APPL
buy T	keep T
buy MCD	keep MCD
buy ARPL	sell ARLP
buy PCLN	sell PCLN
	buy AMZN
	buy NFLX

Once a Week

Trading the strategies once a week is done the same way, except you'll be rebalancing the portfolio once a week instead of once every four weeks.

As mentioned earlier, this is an active approach. And it really is great for spotting changes in your screening items early on so you can take advantage of the newest stocks right away.

But just because you're running your screen every week doesn't necessarily mean you're turning over your entire portfolio every week. All it means is that you're checking on your stocks more often to make sure they still qualify. If they still do, nothing needs to be done. If some don't, you're simply exchanging them for new ones that do—ones that *do* meet your stock picking criteria and that should have a higher probability of success.

When you're testing your strategies, be sure to check on the turnover ratio to see how often you'll be turning your portfolio over. (For more information on backtesting your strategies, see Chapter 15.)

Combining Holding Periods

Another way to trade this strategy (and the other strategies we'll be covering in this book) is by using a combination of both the four-week and one-week holding periods. This can also be a very effective approach. This is done by running the screen on a weekly basis, but holding those stocks for a four-week period.

Here's the process for a four-week and one-week combination holding period:

1. Run the screen at the beginning of the week.
2. Buy all of the stocks that come through the screen.
3. Hang on to those stocks for the next four weeks.
4. Then, next week, run the screen again.
5. Buy any new stocks that made it through the screen and be sure to hang on to those stocks for the next four weeks.

Each set of stocks will be held for four weeks. So if stock ABC for example came through in week 1, but did not come through in week 2, you'll still hang onto ABC. Why? Because you're holding onto each stock for at least four weeks. Only in week 5, if ABC no longer comes through your screen, will you sell it.

Also, do not overweight your portfolio with any one stock. If stock XYZ comes through in week 1 but then also comes through again in week 2, don't buy more XYZ stock. Just know that from that day, you're going to hang onto that stock for at least another four weeks.

Repeat steps four and five each week. Remember, each week a stock comes through the screen, a new four-week hold count begins. If a stock never comes through again, sell the stock in four weeks. So, even though a four-week holding period is being used, the screen is being run weekly and only a portion of the portfolio is being rebalanced each week.

One of the benefits to this trading plan is that if you're running a great screen, you are now participating in every start date, meaning you'll have the opportunity to pick up any and every new stock that comes through at the beginning of each period. But you won't have to sell them at the end of each week in order to make room for any new picks coming through. While this approach will have you holding onto more than just five stocks (you'll likely be adding one to two new picks each week for the first several weeks, for a portfolio size of roughly 10 stocks, until you start rebalancing in week 5), this strategy can help you generate sizeable returns while smoothing out your performance.

This is also a good approach if you have a larger amount of money and want to include more stocks in your portfolio at any one time.

Trading your strategies can and should be easy. One of the key points to trading success is being able to just do it. But if it's hard or time consuming, you'll find yourself not doing it. And even the best trading strategy, if you don't use it, won't make you any money.

Trading should be fun and profitable. And by eliminating the guess-work, it can be.

Winning Momentum Strategies

L et's take a look at some winning Momentum style stock screens and trading strategies and dig deeper into what this style is all about. Even if you've identified yourself as something other than a Momentum trader, be sure to check out the screens that follow anyway. Remember, most people do not fit squarely into one style; that's the idea behind the "All Style" style. And you're likely to pick up some good ideas in this chapter.

Once again, the Momentum style focuses on price momentum or earnings momentum or both. In this chapter we highlight five strategies that cover all aspects of the Momentum style including how to apply these methods for Sector and Industry analysis.

Big Money

Let's start off with one of my personal all-time favorite screening strategies. This screen is called Big Money. Actually I have several variations of this, but the one I use the most is called Big Money Zacks (it's the Big Money screen with the Zacks Rank added to it).

This is a straight-up price momentum screen. But it has a great value twist added to it as well. First let's take a look at the parameters. Then we'll take a look at the methodology.

Parameters

The screen starts off with the following items:

- **Zacks Rank <= 3**
- **Average Broker Rating < 2**
- **Price to Sales Ratio < .5**
- **Average 20-Day Volume >= 50,000**

From there it adds:

- **Percent Change in Price over 24 Weeks Top # 20**
- **Percent Change in Price over 12 Weeks Top # 10**
- **Percent Change in Price over 4 Weeks Top # 3**

Now let's take a look at what each one of these items does and why it's in there.

Methodology

- **Zacks Rank <= 3**
  By setting the Zacks Rank to less than or equal to 3, I'm allowing Zacks Rank 1s, 2s, and 3s (Strong Buys, Buys, and Holds) to get through. However, it specifically excludes 4s and 5s. (I'm not interested in Sells or Strong Sells.) 1s, 2s, and 3s put the odds in my favor, while 4s and 5s work against me, and so they are excluded.

- **Average Broker Rating < 2**
  Quite frankly, I'm not all that interested in the Average Broker Rating per se. But since I know that the average broker ratings are so skewed to the upside, I'd prefer to have the brokers on board. So this item looks for stocks that have Strong Buys or varying degrees of Buys/Strong Buys. In short, if the most bullish camp out there isn't that bullish, maybe there's a good reason for that. (Maybe.) Either way, I don't want to find out.

- **Price to Sales Ratio < .5**

  The Price to Sales ratio or P/S as it's commonly referred to, is a favorite valuation metric of many traders including myself. In fact, it is my absolute favorite item in trying to determine if a company is undervalued or overvalued.

  The P/S ratio is calculated as price divided by sales. If a stock has a P/S ratio of 1, that means you're paying $1 for every $1 of sales the company makes. If a stock has a P/S ratio of 2, that means you're paying $2 for every $1 of sales the company makes. As you can see, the lower the number, the better.

  If a stock has a P/S ratio of .5, that means you're paying 50 cents for every $1 of sales the company makes. And that's how we're using it in this screen. Paying less than a dollar for a dollar's worth of something is a bargain.

- **Average 20-Day Volume >= 50,000**

  This item makes sure there's enough volume to be tradable. Being able to get in and out freely is important. The stocks that make it through this screen will often have average trading volumes of several times this. But with our cut-off for this screen at 50,000, any lesser traded stocks will not come through.

Next we have the price momentum components.

- **Percent Change in Price over 24 Weeks Top # 20**

  This item narrows down the list of all of the qualified stocks that met the requirements from above to just the top 20 stocks with the best price performance over the last 24 weeks.

- **Percent Change in Price over 12 Weeks Top # 10**

  From that list of 20, this item then narrows it down even more to the top 10 stocks with the best price performance over the last 12 weeks.

- **Percent Change in Price over 4 Weeks Top # 3**

  And from that list of 10 stocks, this one then picks only the top 3 stocks with the best percentage price change over the last 4 weeks.

All of the preceding items play an important role in the success of this screen. But it's the price change elements that make this momentum screen what it is. Each stock that comes through is displaying impressive price performance which is exactly what a momentum trader is looking for.

Results

I specifically designed this strategy to be traded on a weekly basis. Over the past 10 years (2000–2009), this strategy has shown an average annual return of 82.8% for a total compounded return of 42,639.8% (see Figure 7.1).

FIGURE 7.1 Big Money Zacks (2000–2009, 1-week rebalance)

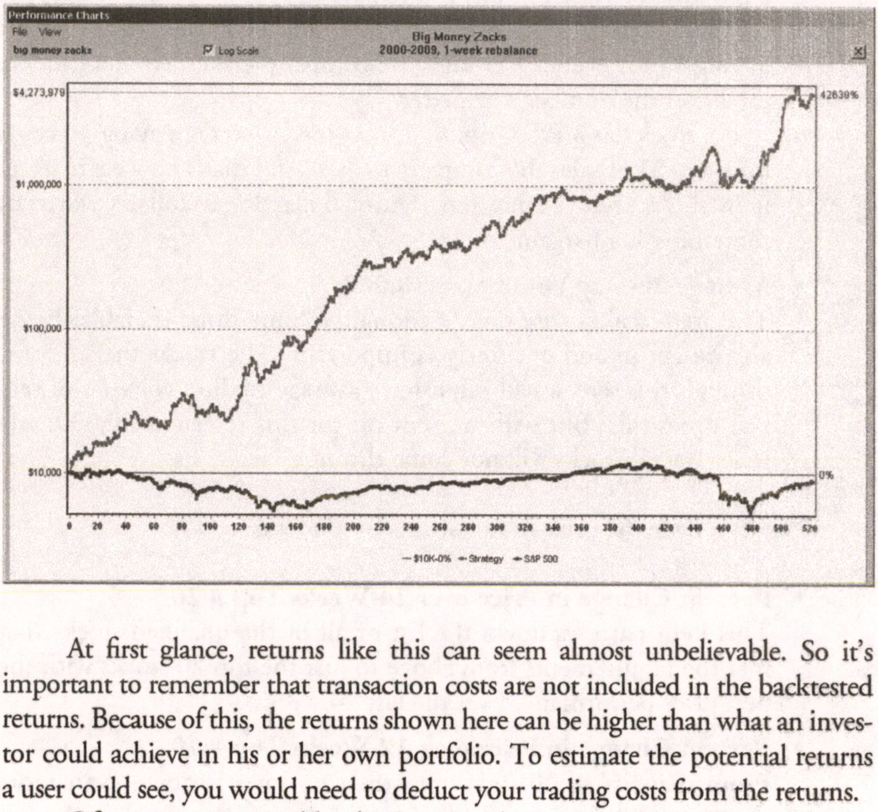

At first glance, returns like this can seem almost unbelievable. So it's important to remember that transaction costs are not included in the backtested returns. Because of this, the returns shown here can be higher than what an investor could achieve in his or her own portfolio. To estimate the potential returns a user could see, you would need to deduct your trading costs from the returns.

Of course, a strategy like this is not without its volatility. The maximum drawdown of this strategy was –46.1%. The maximum drawdown is defined as the largest drop in equity from a previous equity peak. This could mean a drop in profit or a drop in starting equity, depending on when you began. To put this in context, the S&P 500 during the same time span saw a maximum drawdown of –54.7%.

What's particularly impressive with this strategy is that it produced triple digit returns during the bear market of 2000–2002.

Most recently, it actually finished up in the bear market rout of 2008 with a 19.7% increase while the S&P was down –37%.

In 2009, it was one of the best performances for the market at 26.5%. One of the best performances for the Zacks Rank with the #1s, #2s, and #3s up 66.9%, 82.5%, and 78.4%, respectively. And needless to say, it was one of the best performances for the Big Money Zacks strategy with a spectacular 230.5% return.

I've personally created several iterations of the Big Money strategy as I'm always fascinated with its performance and the kinds of stocks it picks. One iteration I created didn't have the Zacks Rank as part of the screen at all. I'm pleased to say that the screen still did fantastic, producing an average annual return of 61.3%. (You'll remember that the Big Money with the Zacks Rank produced an 82.8% average annual return.)

Although, I should note that the Big Money with the Zacks Rank seems to hold up better during difficult periods, a clear testament to the power of the Zacks Rank.

But one item I would never do without (aside from the price momentum items—it wouldn't be a price momentum screen without them, would it?) is the Price to Sales ratio. Figure 7.2 shows the regular Big Money Zacks screen, which, of course, includes the P/S ratio (top line) and the Big Money Zacks screen with the P/S ratio removed (middle line). The difference in performance is not even close.

FIGURE 7.2 BMZ vs. BMZ no P/S ratio

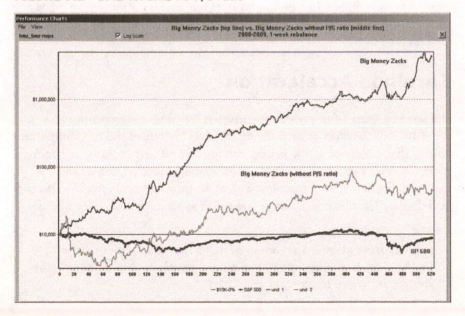

Since the Big Money Zacks screen was designed to find top performers, which includes trending stocks, explosive winners, and stocks making new highs, sometimes those types of stocks can get overheated (overvalued) as investors chase performance. But by adding the P/S ratio to it (specifically, the P/S ratio of less than .5), this valuation metric helps to make sure that these stocks, by and large, can still be considered good values.

I should also note that the Big Money Zacks screen performs well enough with a four-week holding period, but it's still superior with a one-week hold. This makes sense because it's a price performance screen. And with only three available spots (top three price performers), those are competitive positions. By running it more frequently, you can be sure that you'll get the most up-to-date price responders. If you only run it once a month, some of those stocks you might have added to your portfolio could get stale and no longer qualify as a top stock. So the shorter rebalancing times (more frequently you run it and check up on your stocks), the better.

For those looking for more than just three stocks a week, you can edit the screen to increase the number of stocks coming through. Just like we did with the Filtered Zacks Rank 5 strategy, you can change the parameter in the last item of the screen (in this case "Percent Change in Price over 4 Weeks") from Top # 3 to Top # 5 or Top # 7 or however many stocks you'd like.

I've tested the screen with 5 stocks, 7 stocks, and 10 stocks, and they have all been impressive. Indeed, I've probably tested this screen virtually every way imaginable. Just be sure to test your strategy after you've made any changes so you'll know the impact (positive or negative) your changes have had on the screen.

Earnings Acceleration

Let's switch gears from price momentum to earnings momentum.

In good markets or bad, strong earnings are one of the most important things that influence stock prices. But instead of just looking at the most recent quarter's earnings, try looking for earnings acceleration as well.

Studies have shown that almost all of the most successful stocks in the past had displayed accelerated earnings *before* their most impressive price moves.

Studies have shown that almost all of the most successful stocks in the past had displayed accelerated earnings *before* their most impressive price moves.

Sideways trending EPS growth rates (even if the earnings are good) or decelerating EPS growth rates (strong earnings or not) can potentially signal a period of consolidation (or slowdown), which in turn, can flatten out prices or send them lower.

But increasing EPS growth rates (consistently improving from the company's prior percentage of earnings growth) can often be the difference between good stocks and great stocks.

Parameters

In this screen, we're looking for the last two quarter over quarter % EPS growth rates to be greater than the previous periods' growth rates. And we also want the projected quarter over quarter % EPS growth rate to be greater than the previous period's growth rate.

- **EPS % Growth Q(0)/Q(–1) > EPS % Growth Q(–1)/Q(–2)**
- **EPS % Growth Q(–1)/Q(–2) > EPS % Growth Q(–2)/Q(–3)**
- **EPS % Projected Growth Q(1)/Q(0) > EPS % Growth Q(0)/Q(–1)**

I'm also adding in:

- **Price >= $5**
- **Average 20-Day Volume >= 50,000**

The naming convention for past, present, and future quarters in the financial industry can look peculiar at first glance, but it's quite simple once you understand it. See the following description for quick reference: Q(0) = the completed quarter. Q(–1) = the quarter prior to the completed quarter. Q(–2) = two quarters prior to the completed quarter, and so on. Moving in the other direction, Q(1) = the current quarter. Q(2) = the next quarter, and so on.

Methodology

Let's take a closer look at the quarterly growth items.

- **EPS % Growth Q(0)/Q(–1) > EPS % Growth Q(–1)/Q(–2)**
  The growth rate for the completed quarter (Q0) over one quarter ago (Q–1) has to be greater than the growth rate from one quarter ago (Q–1) over two quarters ago (Q–2).

- **EPS % Growth (Q–1)/(Q–2) > EPS % Growth (Q–2)/(Q–3)**
  The growth rate from one quarter ago (Q–1) over two quarters ago (Q–2) has to be greater than the growth rate from two quarters ago (Q–2) over three quarters ago (Q–3).
- **EPS % Projected Growth (Q1)/(Q0) > EPS % Growth (Q0)/(Q–1)**
  And the projected growth rate for the current quarter (Q1) over the completed quarter (Q0) has to be greater than the growth rate from the completed quarter (Q0) over one quarter ago (Q–1).

In tougher economic environments (like now, mid 2010 as I write this) fewer stocks will come through. Why? Stringing together accelerated growth rates for a meaningful period of time is no easy task. In better economic times, more stocks will come through. When that happens, you can add in additional growth periods to narrow that list down even more. For example, instead of just looking at the projected growth rates for one quarter and the historical growth rates for the last two, you can go further back (e.g., (Q–2/ Q–3) > (Q–3/Q–4) and etc.), until you've narrowed down your selection enough. Moreover, you can add in additional items as well, like the Zacks Rank and different valuation metrics.

I will typically use this screen more as a way to generate a watchlist of stocks for additional consideration and purchase rather than as a trading strategy per se. In particular, I'll look at not only those stocks that came through, but also their peers. This has produced some interesting picks for me in the past. The idea being where there's smoke, there's fire. And if a company is experiencing accelerated earnings growth, it's likely that at least some of that growth is attributable to the group that it's in.

So the next time a company reports earnings, take a look at their numbers, and then see how their current % EPS Growth Rate stacks up to their previous period's % EPS Growth Rate (and the period prior to that). Moreover, take a look at how their % Earnings Growth is forecasted in their next reporting period(s) as well. You just might find the next stock destined for greatness.

Increasing Earnings

Another screen I like running in regard to earnings momentum deals with increasing earnings (if not necessarily the percentage of earnings growth). But instead of just looking at the most recent quarter's earnings, or just a few quarters worth of earnings, try looking for a pattern of increasing earnings.

Steadily increasing earnings, in which each period improves upon the last, typically means the company is doing something right—and has been for a while. And that trend is likely to continue, especially when clearing these hurdles during economically challenging times.

Parameters and Methodology

In this screen, I'm looking for each of the last six quarters of earnings (that's right—six quarters) to be greater than the previous quarter's earnings:

- **Quarterly EPS Q(0) > Quarterly EPS Q(–1)**
- **Quarterly EPS Q(–1) > Quarterly EPS Q(–2)**
- **Quarterly EPS Q(–2) > Quarterly EPS Q(–3)**
- **Quarterly EPS Q(–3) > Quarterly EPS Q(–4)**
- **Quarterly EPS Q(–4) > Quarterly EPS Q(–5)**
- **Quarterly EPS Q(–5) > Quarterly EPS Q(–6)**

I also want this quarter's estimated earnings to be greater than last quarter's actual earnings. And I want next quarter's estimated earnings to be greater than this quarter's estimated earnings. That's another two more quarters of increased earnings bringing the number of quarters to eight:

- **Q(1) Consensus Estimate > Q(0) Actual EPS**
- **Q(2) Consensus Estimate > Q(1) Consensus Estimate**

In addition, I'm including:

- **Price >= $5**
- **Average 20-Day Volume >= 50,000**

You may see me adding in "Price >= $5" in screen after screen in this book. I do that largely because there are plenty of portfolio managers and institutional investors who won't even consider looking at a stock if it's under $5.00. And since these are the players that truly move the market, I want to ensure that these stocks at least have a chance of making it onto their radar screen. And while I will at times drop that price constraint to see what stocks below $5 come through (if any), in general, I tend to keep that $5 threshold in.

The thing that makes this screen so tough (i.e., a great stock picker), is that it demands a consistency of excellent performance from a company over an extended period of time.

> **The thing that makes this screen so tough (i.e., a great stock picker), is that it demands a consistency of excellent performance from a company over an extended period of time.**

In addition to finding stocks with fantastic earnings consistency, you'll also find that many of the stocks coming through this screen have a long history of positive surprises as well.

New Highs

Getting back to price momentum, this screen focuses on a powerful concept: buying stocks making new highs.

If somebody were to ask you what your best stocks are, you would likely name the stocks moving up the most in your portfolio. What about your worst stocks? You would say the ones going lower of course.

> **If somebody were to ask you what your best stocks are, you would likely name the stocks moving up the most in your portfolio.**

Simply put, the winners in your portfolio are the ones going up. Period.

If the stock is underperforming the market (or worse, going down), you'll quickly identify it as one of your worst holdings—and you would be right to do so.

Since the best stocks in your portfolio are the ones going up, it only makes sense that some of these will be making new highs along the way.

I know some are reluctant to buy stocks making new 52-week highs. But there's no reason to be. I suppose some may feel like they've already missed it. Or that now it has more room to fall. But if a stock is making a new 52-week high, that's a good thing. Just like a stock making a new 52-week low is a bad thing.

In fact, I'm pretty sure the person who dislikes buying stocks making new 52-week highs wouldn't be too upset if the stock he already owned broke out to a new 52-week high. And why should he? As I've mentioned before, statistics have shown that stocks making new highs have a tendency of making even higher highs. These are the stocks we all dream about. Getting in and watching it go up.

Of course, the fundamentals need to be there. And you should keep a watchful eye on valuations. But if you were in a stock making new highs and cheering it on, it seems silly to be afraid of one doing the same just because you haven't bought it yet.

One question I like asking myself just to put things into perspective is: If I was in it, would I be excited and would I still want to be in it? If the answer is "yes", then I'll look for the best opportunity to get in. If the answer is "no, I would be looking to take profits," then I'll move on.

This topic reminds me of a question someone asked me a while ago about a stock I was talking about that was at a new 52-week high. In fact, it was at a new 5-year high.

He said, "Aren't you worried about buying a stock at a 52-week high?" I said of course not. So it just made a new-52 week high. That's great news. Guess what—last year it made a new 52-week high as well. And the year before that. And the year before that. Can you imagine all the money you'd be leaving on the table if you were afraid of being in stocks every time they made a new high?

Parameters

There are 11 items that go onto this screen. Below is a list of each one to see the full scope of what goes into it. Then we'll dissect each one to see the *why* behind the *what*.

- **Stocks trading within 20% of their 52-week high**
- **Percent Change in Price over 12 Weeks > 0**
- **Percent Change in Price over 4 Weeks > 0**
- **Zacks Rank = 1**
- **Price to Sales <= Industry Median**
- **P/E using F(1) Estimates <= Industry Median**
- **Projected 12 Month EPS Growth >= Industry Median**
- **Current Avg. 20-Day Volume > Previous Week's Avg. 20-Day Volume**
- **Price >= $5**
- **Average 20-Day Volume >= 100,000 shares**

- **Percent Change in Price over 12 Weeks + Percent Change in Price over 4 Weeks = Top #5**

There are a lot of items in this screen. Now let's take a look at the methodology.

Methodology

- **Stocks trading within 20% of their 52-week high**
  The expression on most screeners would look something like this:

  Current Price / 52-Week High >= .80

  That means these stocks are either at a new 52-week high, or have just recently hit it, and they are still trading within 20% of it. Or they are climbing toward their 52-week high and are within a 20% striking distance.

- **Percent Change in Price over 12 Weeks > 0**
  Want to make sure the medium-term price momentum is moving up.

- **Percent Change in Price over 4 Weeks > 0**
  Want to make sure the short-term price momentum is moving up as well. (But wouldn't the % price change on these stocks automatically have to be greater than zero to be trading so close to the 52-week high? Not necessarily. They could be pulling back from it over those periods, and in that case, they would be excluded.)

- **Zacks Rank = 1**
  Only Zacks Strong Buys for this one.

- **Price to Sales <= Industry Median**
  As mentioned before, the Price to Sales ratio shows how much you're paying for every $1 of sales the company makes. For this screen, instead of assigning a value, we're requiring the P/S ratio to be less than the median P/S for its Industry. This is another effective way to use this valuation metric. Why? Because different industries will have different averages or medians for different items. A P/S of 1 is not such a great bargain if the median for its Industry is .7, but it's a great find if the Industry's median is 1.5. This parameter lets us focus in on discounted valuations germane to their Industry. And this allows these stocks to still be considered undervalued, even as their stock prices continue higher.

- **P/E using F(1) Estimates <= Industry Median**
  Just like the P/S ratio, we're looking for stocks whose P/E is below the median for their respective Industry. Including proven valuation metrics when using price momentum screens gives the trader a significant advantage.

- **Projected 12 Month EPS Growth >= Industry Median**
  While the P/S and P/E ratios searched for stocks with valuations below their Industry's median. This item is looking for stocks with projected growth rates above the median for its Industry. In order for a stock to continue to go higher, there needs to be a reason for it to do so. And strong growth of course is an important part of that.

- **Current Avg. 20-Day Volume > Previous Week's Avg. 20-Day Volume**
  This helps me find stocks where the volume has increased in the recent week vs. the previous week. If the price is climbing on increased volume, that shows increased demand or buying coming in. The more buying demand there is for a stock, the more it should climb.

- **Percent Change in Price over 12 Weeks + Percent Change in Price over 4 Weeks = Top # 5**
  I'm combining the percentage price change for both the 12-week and 4-week periods to select the top 5 stocks. Why? If the 12-week % price change is solid, but the 4-week change is relatively weak, that might mean the stock is retreating from its high rather than advancing toward it. On the other hand, if the 12-week gain came largely from just the last 4-weeks worth of gains, while that's impressive, it shows that the trend prior to the most recent period wasn't as robust. This item tries to find the best gainers on both time horizons in an effort to see that momentum carry forward.

Results

Over the past 10 years, this strategy has shown a compounded annual growth rate of 49.1% for a total compounded return of 5,432.2% (see Figure 7.3).

What's interesting is that, even though we're buying stocks near their highs, the risk/volatility (as defined by its maximum drawdown) was 16.4 points less than the S&P (−38.3% vs. −54.7%). That's nearly 30% less volatility than the market while generating a significantly better return.

FIGURE 7.3 New Highs (2000–2009, 1-week rebalance)

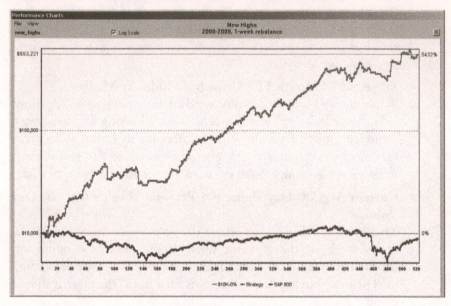

Further analysis of the backtest report shows that during bearish periods, there were fewer stocks (and sometimes no stocks) meeting the 52-week high requirement (let alone the Projected Growth Rate requirement), thus reducing the exposure of this strategy. In bullish periods, as you would expect, there were more stocks coming through (up to our maximum of course), allowing for greater participation when the market was up.

Using New Highs for Sector and Industry Analysis

While we're on the subject of new highs, here's a screen that I run quite regularly in an effort to see which sectors and industries are being favored. While I cover industry analysis in more detail later in the book (Chapter 11), this particular concept is rooted in the same "new highs" principle as the previous screen, making this the perfect place to include it.

Let me start by saying that since roughly half of a stock's price movement can be directly attributed to the group that it's in, it's important to stay on top of which groups are doing the best.

Half of a stock's price movement can be directly attributed to the group that it's in.

By definition, a strong sector or strong industry will have more of its companies moving higher than a weak sector or weak industry. If the majority of stocks are going down in an industry, it can't be a strong industry. Likewise, if more stocks are going up, it is a strong industry.

I've done numerous testing in the past, and interestingly found that, oftentimes just getting into an average stock in a strong group will outperform the best stocks in a troubled group.

Oftentimes just getting into an average stock in a strong group will outperform the best stocks in a troubled group.

This doesn't mean you can just pick anything and you'll make money. Far from it. But it illustrates how powerful the underlying group is to the success of your stock picking.

One of my favorite ways to find the top sectors is to look at the percentage of stocks trading within 10% of their 52-week highs. A lot of people like looking at the percentage price change over just the last 12 weeks or 24 weeks. That's fine, but I don't think that is sensitive enough.

Take the Oil and Energy sector in mid-2008 as an example. Based on its 12-week or 24-week price performance, it was continuously ranked as one of the top sectors using those metrics—even while it was collapsing. That was because the gains were so large in the first part of the 12- or 24-week periods, even a large pullback over a span of many weeks got lost within the larger run-up that preceded it.

By the way, this is one of the reasons why I'll typically include a shorter-term price change component (4-week % price change or 1-week % price change) when I use these longer-term ones as well—to spot the changes in trends early on.

But by checking their position in comparison to their 52-week highs, a simple 10% pullback from their highs will show up. And if more and more companies within that group are pulling back from their highs by more than 10%, it'll be reflected in that sector's ranking, and therefore, alert the investor that something systemic might be happening to that group as a whole rather than something that's just stock specific.

As I said earlier, since roughly half of a stock's price performance can be directly attributed to the group that it's in, it's important to be able to identify the best sectors quickly and accurately. You can probably do this manually with many screeners out there, but the basic steps are as follows:

1. First you need to identify the sectors.

2. Then determine the number of stocks within that sector.

3. And then determine the number of stocks trading within 10% of their 52-week highs.

4. Divide the number of stocks at their highs by the number of stocks in the group and you'll get your percentage.

5. Sort the sectors from highest to lowest to see which sectors are doing the best.

I use the Research Wizard, which allows me to script out all of these repetitive tasks down to a few simple mouse clicks. Here's a snapshot of my report once I export it to Excel (see Figure 7.4).

FIGURE 7.4 New Highs Sector Analysis Report

Sector	No. of "Highs" in Sector	No. of Stocks in Sector	% of "Highs" in Sector
COMGLOMERATES	21	40	53%
UTILITIES	122	253	48%
FINANCE	758	1974	38%
AUTO-TIRES-TRUCKS	34	94	36%
CONSUMER STAPLES	103	287	36%
BASIC MATERIALS	127	370	34%
AEROSPACE	26	84	31%
TRANSPORTATION	57	187	30%
OILS-ENERGY	147	548	27%
RETAIL WHOLESALE	116	433	27%
BUSINESS SERVICES	76	299	25%
INDUSTRIAL PRODUCTION	113	452	25%
COMPUTER AND TECHNOLOGY	354	1466	24%
CONSUMER DISCRETIONARY	113	512	22%
MEDICAL	173	972	18%
CONSTRUCTION	29	185	16%

This report shows me the sector name, the number of stocks making new highs (within 10% of their 52-week high), the number of stocks in the sector, and then finally, the percentage of stocks making new highs within that sector.

It's a great report. But regardless of how you do it, it's a powerful concept and worth the effort.

Additional Comments

Be sure to keep a record of your sector rankings. Seeing what new sectors have made it into the top positions is important. But so is tracking their movement—where they are now in comparison to where they've been.

Seeing a sector steadily move up the ranks, even if it hasn't reached the top spot yet, shows that group is becoming more and more in demand and making it a group you may want to put on your radar screen. The same is true for the ones moving down the list. Take note and act accordingly.

I also want to point out that, while the New Highs stock screen looks for stocks trading within 20% of their 52-week highs, the sector screen only counts those within 10% of the highs.

The reason for this, as I mentioned earlier, is I want the sector screen to be a sensitive measure. If a few stocks pull outside of that range, it should not materially affect the group. But if the majority are doing that (or a large percentage), it might mean more than a simple pullback or consolidation, but rather a retreat on its way even lower.

Plus with the stock screen, I'll also add in other factors as well, which allows me to give the individual stocks a little extra room. But when analyzing the group on just that one factor, I prefer to be a bit stricter. Nonetheless, when you see an increasing number of stocks moving in the same direction and making new highs—clearly something good is happening to that group. And the better the group the better your odds are of success.

Summary

Momentum stocks can be fun to trade as most uptrends exhibit some or all of the classic Momentum style characteristics. Seeing a stock take off from the moment you get in is one of the best parts of trading.

Of course, not every momentum stock turns out like that. But many do. And screening for them in the manner we just outlined is one of the best ways to find them.

Interestingly, you'll find that a lot Momentum style screens will often uncover aggressive growth stocks as well. This makes sense since earnings momentum often leads to aggressive earnings growth and both are great ways to get a stock's price to move.

In Chapter 8, we focus in on the Aggressive Growth aspect as our primary search. But don't be surprised if you see some momentum stocks pop up as well.

Chapter 8

Winning Aggressive Growth Strategies

Now let's take a look at some winning Aggressive Growth style screens and trading strategies. As I mentioned in the last chapter, even if you've identified yourself as something other than an Aggressive Growth trader, be sure to still check out the screens in this style. As you likely saw in the Momentum section, there were a lot of interesting ideas, many of which can be incorporated into any one of the other styles. And the same will be true for this style as well.

As the title suggests, we'll be looking for stocks with aggressive earnings growth or sales growth. And we'll be demonstrating this through four unique Aggressive Growth strategies. There's also a surprising performance study on market-caps that you'll want to see regardless of what style of trader you are. But first, let's take a look at some growth strategies.

Small-Cap Growth

When most people think of Aggressive Growth strategies, one of the first things that come to mind is small-cap stocks. Indeed, when I'm searching for Aggressive Growth stocks, I'll usually get plenty of small-cap stocks coming through regardless of whether I'm specifically looking for them or not.

So I set out to create an Aggressive Growth screen that did just that. And the results were amazing. So let's take a closer look at what went into it.

Parameters

The screen starts off with:

- **Market Value <= $1 Billion**
- **Zacks Rank = 1**
- **Price >= $1**
- **Average Dollar Trading Volume >= $500,000**
- **Estimated One Year EPS Growth >= 1.20 * the Industry Median, but Estimated One Year EPS Growth <= 50%**
- **P/E using F(1) Estimates <= Industry Median**
- **Price to Sales Ratio <= Industry Median**
- **Price to Sales Ratio = Bottom # 7**

Just by glancing at the items, you can probably tell that this is not your typical growth screen. Keep on reading for the rationale behind each item.

Methodology

- **Market Value (or Market Capitalization or Market–Cap) <= $1 Billion**
  This is the stock price multiplied by the number of shares outstanding. The definition of what a small-cap stock or a large-cap stock is seems to change every so often as the market changes. For now however, the generally agreed upon definition is as follows:
  Small-Cap <= $1 Billion
  Mid-Cap > $1 Billion and <= $5 Billion
  Large-Cap > $5 Billion

- **Zacks Rank = 1**
  This screen focuses only on the Zacks Rank #1s. Take note that the Zacks #1 Rank stocks will have a relatively larger selection of

small-cap to mid-cap stocks in it. Why? Usually small-cap stocks are newer stocks. And newer/younger stocks typically have less analyst coverage. If there are fewer analysts, it can be easier for an outstanding small-cap stock to score better on the "Agreement" portion of the four Zacks Rank components than an outstanding large-cap stock with more analysts following it. Remember, the "Agreement" factor looks at the percentage of analysts revising their estimates in the same direction. If two out of three analysts are making upward earnings estimate revisions on a company versus five out of eight for another company; that two out three (or 66.7%) is a better score than the five out of eight (or 62.5%), giving the advantage to the small-cap stock, at least on that component. Knowing this, I've chosen to only let the Zacks #1 Rank small-caps through on this screen.

- **Price >= $1**
I mentioned before that I generally like to find stocks trading over $5 in large part because of institutional interest and how many of them prefer stocks over $5. (Institutional investors are what typically move the market and thus I want to keep those stocks on their consideration list.) But small-cap stocks are a different story. And there can be an allure all of its own if the company is perceived to be a potential breakout star. Since many small-caps will often trade at lower prices, this screen was built to be a bit more accommodating. However, we drew the line at penny stocks by keeping the threshold at $1. (Not that there's anything wrong with penny stocks. But I've found the bid/ask on many to be relatively wide (percentage-wise) making them difficult to trade them.)

- **Average Dollar Trading Volume >= $500,000**
This is a different way to look at trading volume. Instead of looking at just the number of shares traded, this is looking at the number of dollars traded, i.e., the amount of money changing hands each day.

For example: If a stock was trading at $1, but the dollar volume was $500,000, that means 500,000 shares traded hands that day. If, however, I put in a minimum trading volume of 100,000 shares, then at $1, that would be only $100,000 worth of shares trading hands. While a minimum of $500,000 could potentially allow higher priced stocks with less volume through ($500,000 dollar volume divided by a $25 stock = 20,000 shares traded), the frequency of that happening is reduced considerably once you add in the other performance measures, not the least of which includes the Zacks Rank. Keep in mind that the $500,000 is simply a bare minimum. The share volume and dollar volume for the stocks that come through are typically much higher than that. Nonetheless, this establishes our minimum.

- **Estimated One Year EPS Growth >= 1.20 * the Industry Median, but Estimated One Year EPS Growth <= 50%**
Aggressive Growth stocks of course are all about the growth. Naturally, we're looking for outperforming growth rates. For this one, we want the stocks to be projecting growth rates at least 20% higher than the median for their respective Industry. But we are excluding stocks with actual growth rates greater than 50%. Why? This is a growth screen, isn't it? Yes it is. But we also want to keep the odds of success in our favor. And as I mentioned before, growth rates that are too high often don't pan out. In my testing, I have found that once the growth rate exceeds 50%, returns start to drop. On the occasions when they may tick up a bit, I normally see an accompanying increase in risk. Below this cut-off is the sweet spot and why it's in the screen.

- **P/E using F(1) Estimates <= Industry Median**
Like we've done in some of the previous screens, we're determining value by comparing the stock's valuation to that of its Industry. One thing to keep in mind is that oftentimes small-cap stocks or stocks with aggressive growth will trade at higher valuations than non aggressive growth stocks. Why? Because many traders are willing to pay a little more for these companies now, believing that they will likely be trading at even higher valuations later on if they wait. For many, this is true. Of course that doesn't last forever. But it can go on for a long time while the growth scenario is intact. This finds stocks with P/Es that are still trading at values under the median of their industry.

- **Price to Sales Ratio <= Industry Median**
Just like the P/E ratio, the Price to Sales industry comparison helps us find the stocks that are still reasonably priced (value-wise) and sometimes downright cheap.

- **Price to Sales Ratio = Bottom # 7**
We used the Price to Sales ratio one more time in this screen to narrow the list of stocks down to just the seven best. And we're

picking those lucky seven based on which of the Aggressive Growth stocks have the lowest P/S ratio.

Results

Over the last 10 years, using a one-week holding period, this strategy has generated an average annual return of 95.5% for a total compounded return of 83,453.4% (see Figure 8.1).

FIGURE 8.1 Small-Cap Growth (2000–2009, 1-week rebalance)

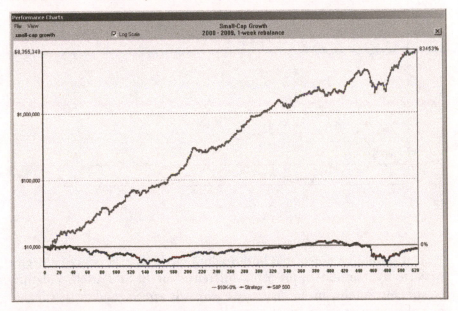

As with the other strategies we've outlined so far, the backtest results of this one also do not include commission costs or fees. A user on the other hand will indeed incur transaction costs, so his results will be lower.

Backtest results also do not account for trade impact. Too much money going in and out of a stock at one time can sometimes have an adverse effect on a person's order execution.

I point these things out so a trader can adopt realistic expectations when viewing a backtest report and deciding if a strategy is right for him.

One thing that's clear, however, looking at the trajectory of the returns, is that the strategy works and has a high probability of picking winning stocks.

I also tested this strategy using a two-week holding period for impressive results as well. The average compounded annual growth rate was 80.7% for an average total compounded return of 37,083.0% (see Figure 8.2.)

FIGURE 8.2 Small-Cap Growth (2000–2009, 2-week rebalance)

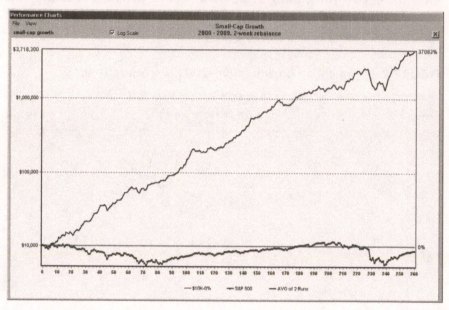

It should be noted that both trading methods experienced a degree of volatility, but none appreciably different than the S&P itself. Volatility is not uncommon in an Aggressive Growth screen, and in particular, one that focuses in on small-caps. But the returns can make it worthwhile.

Observations

Notice I used "only" a 20% excess growth rate over the industry's median, and I put a limit on the actual growth rate itself at 50% to pick these stocks. Not 100% or 500% or more. As I mentioned earlier when defining the different trading styles, overly excessive growth rates can oftentimes produce disappointing returns. In some cases, excessive growth rates are even worse than low growth rates.

To guard against shooting stars, which can quickly fizzle out on stocks priced for peak perfection (which is another way of saying a stock is priced on unrealistic expectations), keep searching for the top growth performers, but stay on planet Earth.

All-Cap Growth

Aggressive Growth isn't just for small-cap stocks. Let's take a look at this strategy and include all sized companies, with a few additional parameters as well, to get the most out of the expanded universe of stocks.

Parameters and Methodology

We're going to use the same base parameters as we did in the small-cap Aggressive Growth screen earlier, but with a few changes.

- **No Market-Cap Restriction**
  The first change to note is that there is no market-cap restriction. We removed the market value item altogether.

- **Zacks Rank #1**
  This item is the same as the small-cap screen. Even though, as I mentioned before, the Zacks Rank #1s have a larger percentage of small-cap stocks in that group, there's still plenty of mid-caps and large-caps in there, too. With the market-cap restriction removed, they will shine through in this screen.

- **Price >= $5**
  Raising the threshold back to $5 and higher.

- **Average Dollar Trading Volume >= $1,000,000**
  Increase to a minimum of $1 Million in average daily dollar volume traded.

- **Estimated One Year EPS Growth >= 1.20 * the Industry Median, but Estimated One Year EPS Growth <= 50%**
  Keep the same.

- **P/E using F(1) Estimates <= Industry Median**
  Keep the same.

- **PEG Ratio <= Industry Median**
  This is a new addition to the screen. And it's a great way of determining whether a company is considered undervalued or overvalued. It's especially useful for a growth screen when it's common for a stock to trade at a higher multiple; that is, P/E.

  Let's first start with a definition. The PEG ratio is simply the P/E ratio divided by the growth rate. A value of 1 or less is considered good (at par or undervalued), whereas a value of greater than 1, in general, is not as good (overvalued).

  Many believe this ratio tells a more complete story than just the P/E. For example: A company with a P/E ratio of 25 and a growth rate of 20 would have a PEG ratio of 1.25 (25/20 = 1.25). However, a company with a P/E ratio of 40 and a growth rate of 50 would have a PEG ratio of 0.8.

  Traditionally, investors would look at the stock with the lower P/E ratio and deem it a bargain (undervalued). But looking at it closer, you can see it doesn't have the growth rate to justify its P/E. The stock with the P/E of 40, though, is actually the better bargain since its PEG ratio is lower (0.8), implying it's undervalued with more potential value. Undervalued in relation to its projected growth rate.

  In other words, the lower the PEG, the better the value, because the investor would be paying less for each unit of earnings growth. The way we're using it in this screen, is by insisting that the PEG ratio be trading <= the median for its industry, in the same manner that we did for the P/E ratio and the P/S ratio.

- **Price to Sales Ratio <= Industry Median**
  Keep the same.

- **Price to Sales Ratio = Bottom #7**
  Keep the same.

Results

Over the last 10 years, using a one-week holding period, this strategy showed an average annual return of 51.6% for a total compounded return of 6,401.3% (see Figure 8.3).

FIGURE 8.3 All-Cap Growth (2000–2009, 1-week rebalance)

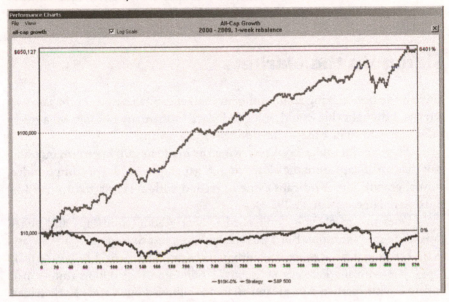

With a two-week holding period, the average compounded annual growth rate came in at 38.9% for an average total compounded return of 2,734.1% (see Figure 8.4).

FIGURE 8.4 All-Cap Growth (2000–2009, 2-week rebalance)

Both trading methods significantly outperformed the market during that period, with once again, no appreciable difference in risk.

Sizing Up the Markets

Since we've been talking about different market capitalizations in the last two screens, I thought this would be a good place to share my findings on a study I did in regard to just that—the different market-caps.

This came about as I was reviewing the market's 2009 performance and saw that small-caps were the clear winner, generating a 52.4% compounded annual growth rate. Mid-caps came in second with a 41.3% return. And in third were large-caps at 35.2%.

Does this mean you don't need to worry about mid-caps and large-caps, though? Not quite. But I put them all to a test to find out.

I created three screens: one with market-caps less than $1 billion (small-caps), one with market-caps between $1 billion and $5 billion (mid-caps), and one with market-caps greater than $5 billion (large-caps). Each screen also consisted of only stocks trading over $3 with an average daily trading volume of over 50,000 shares.

I then backtested these screens using a one-week holding period for each of the last eight years (2002–2009).

Note that in the following study, I show the S&P 500 only as a reference to see what the market was doing that year. The screens, however, and the different market-cap groups, did not exclusively consist of S&P 500 stocks, but rather a universe of over 8,600 stocks in our database.

Let's start from 2002 and work our way to the present:

- In **2002**, it was a lousy market with the S&P down −22.1%. And all capitalizations did poorly as well with large-caps down −20.3%, mid-caps down −19.4% and small-caps down −20.9%.

- **2003** was a different story with the S&P up 28.7%. Smalls performed spectacularly with an 84.7% return. Mid-caps were up 47.6%. Large-caps were up 39.2%.

- **2004** was a decent enough year for the market with the S&P up 10.9%. All the different caps did fine as well and finished up in roughly the same range: small-caps were up 19.8%, mid-caps were up 18.8%, and large-caps were up 17.6%.

- **2005** saw the edge go to the large-caps this time at 13.5%. Mids were up 8.3%. And smalls were up 4.3%, just under the market, which came in at 4.9%.

- In **2006**, large-caps were the winner again, albeit by a slim margin. Large-caps were up 20.3%. Small-caps advanced by 18.7%. And mid-caps increased by 17.4%. The S&P was up 15.8%.

- And then again, in **2007,** large-caps came in first at 11.0%. Mid-caps were up 2.9%. Small-caps actually showed a loss of −4.9%. (Both mids and smalls underperformed the market, which came in at 5.5%. And yes, it was surprising to see small-caps actually close down for the year.)

- As you know, **2008** was a total disaster all the way around. The S&P was down −37.0%. Large-caps dropped −40.1%. Small-caps were down −38.8%. Mid-caps were down −37.1%. There was no place to hide.

- **2009,** however, saw all caps snap back. The S&P was up 26.5%. Small-caps were up 52.4%. Mid-caps were up 41.3%. And large-caps were up 35.2%. (Even though small-caps were the clear winner, I doubt anybody would have been upset with a 41% performance in mid-caps and a 35% gain in large-caps.)

I've included a table showing how each of the market-cap groups did over the last eight years, highlighting which group was the top performer in each year (see Table 8.1).

TABLE 8.1 Market Capitalization Study

Year	Small-Caps	Mid-Caps	Large-Caps	S&P 500
2002	−20.9	−19.4	−20.3	−22.1
2003	84.7	47.6	39.2	28.7
2004	19.8	18.8	17.6	10.9
2005	4.3	8.3	13.5	4.9
2006	18.7	17.4	20.3	15.8
2007	−4.9	2.9	11.0	5.5
2008	−38.8	−37.1	−40.1	−37.0
2009	52.4	41.3	35.2	26.5
Average	14.4	10.0	9.6	4.2

S&P 500 shown as reference. Each capitalization study consisted of both S&P 500 and non-S&P 500 companies from a universe of over 8,600 stocks.

Over the last eight years, small-caps showed an average annual return of 14.4%. Mid-caps gained 10.0%. And large-caps were up 9.6%. But there were some interesting differences in several of those years, some quite sizeable as the groups rotated in and out of the top spot.

While the most significant outperformance was seen by small-caps; the mid-caps and large-caps also performed well, oftentimes with less volatility or drawdowns.

So what do all of these statistics mean, knowing that some market-caps are better than others in different years? It means that you should have a mix of everything in your portfolio. And by having exposure in all the caps, you can make sure you'll participate in the winningest group, no matter what.

Zacks Rank 5 or 4 to 1

This screen is a different take on an Aggressive Growth approach in that it's looking at aggressive earnings estimate revisions.

First, let's review some Zacks Rank facts:

- As you know, the Zacks #1 Ranked stocks (Strong Buys) have significantly outperformed the market by showing an average annual return of 27.27% over the last 22 years (since 1988). This compares to the S&P 500s return of only 8.86% per year.

- The Zacks #5 Ranked stocks (or Strong Sells) have significantly underperformed the market with an average annual return of just 1.7% a year.

- Only 5% of the stocks can get a Zacks #1 Rank. Likewise, only 5% of the stocks can get a Zacks #5 Rank. The Zacks #2 Ranks and Zacks #4 Ranks have a distribution of 15% each. So the #1s are in a very coveted spot and reserved for only the best stocks. And the #5s are reserved for the worst ones.

If a stock has a Zacks Rank of a #4 or #5 (Sell or Strong Sell), something huge would have to happen in order for it to leapfrog so many places to get to be a Zacks Rank #1. Part of that is aggressive upward earnings estimate revisions. And since earnings estimate revisions are one of the most powerful forces impacting stocks prices (where have I heard that before?), keying in on stocks with aggressive earnings estimate revisions (positive of course) is a powerful concept.

And that's what we're doing in this screen.

Parameters and Methodology

We're looking for companies that currently have a Zacks #1 Rank (Strong Buy) that were ranked a #5 or a #4 the previous week.

- **Zacks Rank = 1**
  Currently Ranked #1.
- **Zacks Rank (one week ago) >= 4**
  Was Ranked a #4 or #5 the previous week.

It should be noted that this screen does not produce a ton of stocks because seeing a stock go from a 5 or a 4 to a 1 is somewhat rare. But it'll usually produce a few stocks per week.

Results

A backtest of this strategy over the last 10 years using a one-week holding period showed an average annual return of 49.2% for a total compounded return of 5,466.4%. This compares to the S&P's −1.3% and −11.9%, respectively (see Figure 8.5).

FIGURE 8.5 Zacks Rank 5 or 4 to 1 (2000–2009, 1-week rebalance)

Even more impressive is the performance during the whole of the bear market of 2007 through mid-2009 (10/2007–3/2009) as the strategy produced a total compounded return of 132.8% vs. the S&Ps –42.7% during that same time (see Figure 8.6).

FIGURE 8.6 Zacks Rank 5 or 4 to 1 (10/2007–3/2009, 1-week rebalance)

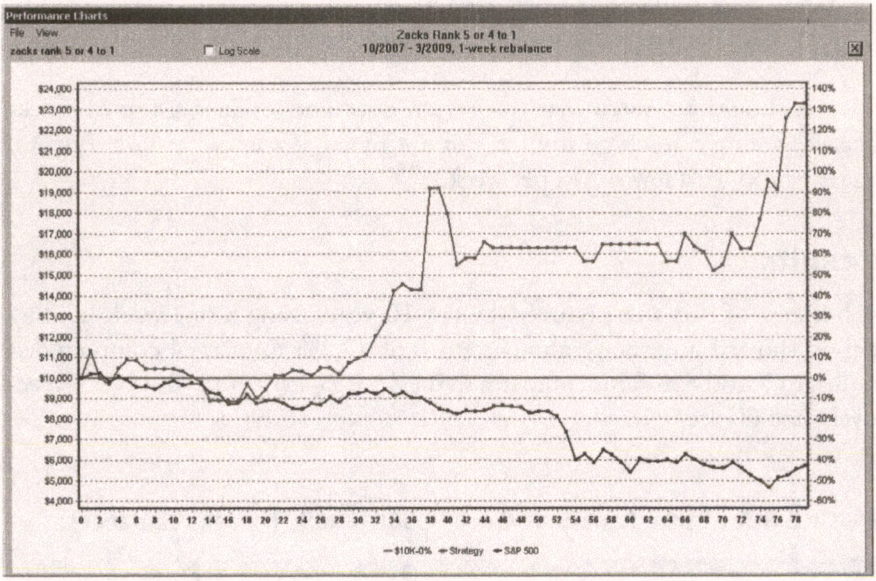

Once again, there will be periods when no stocks will qualify. You can see this on the chart where it flattens out (usually when the market is at its worst). But when there are stocks that do qualify, it's worth the wait.

First Profit

I find myself running this screen every earnings season. And I put this into the Aggressive Growth camp because of the herculean effort it takes to achieve that magical first profit.

> **This goes into the Aggressive Growth camp because of the herculean effort it takes to achieve that magical first profit.**

The concept behind this screen is to find companies that have just recently shown their first quarterly profit within the last year, or more specifically, companies that have not shown a profit for at least the previous four quarters, but have just produced their first profit in the most recently reported quarter.

Some of these companies will be relatively new and this recent profit may be the only profit in the company's history—so far. For others, they may have a long history of profitability, but have seen a contraction over the last year (for whatever reason) and have finally returned to profitability.

I like this concept because, if the trend has been one of improvement, there's a good chance that trend will continue. This is true whether you've *been* profitable or are *just getting* profitable.

But some (myself included) dislike buying companies that cannot show a profit. And there are many others who won't even consider a stock unless it's making money. Losing less than the previous quarter is, indeed, growth. And trimming the red each quarter is a big accomplishment, especially if the losses are less and less sequentially, quarter after quarter. But there's something entirely different about growth and being profitable. And those that are profitable are the stocks that will likely see the best new demand from new investors—people who are now, all of a sudden, willing to take notice of and pay attention to the stock.

Parameters and Methodology

Aside from the price, this screen really only keys in on two additional items. But they cover a lot of ground, which includes five quarters of past and present earnings.

- **EPS for the previous four Quarters <= 0**
  This means in each of the previous four quarters (except the most recently reported quarter) the company has reported earnings of less than or equal to zero, i.e., no profit.

- **EPS for the recently reported Quarter > 0**
  This time, the company reported earnings greater than zero, meaning they finally showed a profit.

- **I'm applying the preceding requirements to stocks trading at >= $5**
  As I've mentioned previously, my preference is to look at stocks trading over $5. However, if you're interested in cheaper priced

stocks, just remove this item. But note that you'll typically get a much larger list of stocks once the $5 minimum is removed.

The macroeconomic environment will also influence the number of qualifying stocks coming through as well. During periods of economic expansion, you'll likely see more stocks showing up. Although ironically, during long periods of expansion, there actually may be fewer stocks qualifying the beginning part of the screen since there will likely be fewer stocks "not showing a profit." And of course, during periods of economic contraction, there will likely be fewer stocks as well because, while there will be no shortage of stocks posting losses, there will likely be fewer digging themselves out until things get better. Of course, the individual company's own dynamics are always in play as well.

I believe using this screen as a stock finder rather than a trading strategy is the most appropriate way to use this one. Once the stocks come through, be sure to take a look at the earnings estimate revisions. Aggressive Growth stocks, whether they've just newly gotten in the black or not, should have an abundance of upward revisions. Their sales growth should be just as impressive if not more so.

This concept of first profit is simple but pretty powerful.

Summary

As you can see, screening for profitable growth stocks involves more than just searching for companies with the largest growth rates. In fact, as ironic as it sounds, companies with the highest growth rates typically end up not being the best growth stocks at all. But strong growth is indeed a hallmark of this trading style, and we looked at one of the optimum ranges that can produce a high probability of success.

We've also seen that certain valuation metrics can play a big role in an Aggressive Growth strategy as well. All things being equal, I'd rather be in an aggressive growth stock with attractive valuations rather than a growth stock that was considered overvalued.

In fact, good value is a common theme in almost all of my screens. And in Chapter 9, we'll look for stocks where value is the main component.

Winning Value Strategies

Next on deck is Value. Some may think value investing is boring. Or that you have to sacrifice returns for safety. Neither could be further from the truth. In fact, value investing has proven to be one of the most successful forms of investing over time. Value investing became famous from legendary investor Benjamin Graham and more recently Warren Buffett. Let's take a look at some winning Value style screens that work for both traders and investors.

There are five different value screens in this chapter, and a detailed performance study on the best valuation metrics and their results. Regardless of your trading style, there are some great tips to pick up in this section. And you'll probably look at value in a whole new way.

Value and Spark

As you've seen from several of the screens I have already highlighted, I'm a big fan of employing valuation metrics in virtually all of my styled approaches. And why not? The inclusion of these measures will typically reduce my risk and actually add to my returns. Plus, as I've said before, if I can buy a stock that I believe is at a quantifiable value, all the better. That, of course, will not prevent a "cheap" stock from ever going against me. But if a stock is going to be taken down, there's potentially more room for it to fall if there are excesses built into it than if it's intrinsically undervalued.

Let's dig deeper into these valuation metrics with our first value screen. But as I mentioned before, oftentimes, value stocks have been ignored or unloved for whatever reason. So the key for a successful Value style *trading* strategy (and by trading, I mean stocks you don't have to sit with for years to get your payoff but rather weeks instead) is to combine this value with a spark—a catalyst that will create investor demand.

Parameters

Let's begin with a list of the parameters and then we'll break them down one by one in the methodology section.

- **Zacks Rank <= 2**
- **P/E using F(1) Estimates <= Median Value for the S&P 500**
- **Price to Sales Ratio <= Median Value for the S&P 500**
- **Price to Book <= Median Value for the S&P 500**
- **Debt to Equity <= Median Value for the S&P 500**
- **Top # 7 Sectors based on the % Change F(1) Estimates (last 4 weeks)**
- **Top # 1 Stock in each Sector based on the % Change F(1) Estimates (last 4 weeks)**
- All of the aforementioned parameters are being applied to stocks with a **Price >= $5** and a **Dollar Volume >= $1 Million a day**

As you can see, there are four classical valuation items in this screen along with two other items to spot urgency.

Methodology

- **Zacks Rank <= 2**
  Zacks #1 and #2 Ranked stocks only (Strong Buys and Buys). One of the benefits of the Zacks Rank is that it's also a timeliness indicator. Utilizing the Zacks Rank of a #1 or #2 in a value strategy can help to identify when a stock is ready to respond.

- **P/E using F(1) Estimates <= Median Value for the S&P 500**
In previous screens, we compared many of our valuations to the median for their respective industries. In this one, we're comparing it to the median value for the market, i.e., the S&P 500—which as you know is a widely used benchmark or barometer for the overall U.S. equities market.

  This comparison allows us to screen for stocks that are considered undervalued to the market at any given point in time. In some years the average P/E might be higher than in other years and vice versa. But by demanding that these stocks have lower valuations than what the broader marketplace has determined to be fair value, there's a greater chance for upside if it happens to be trading below there.

- **Price to Sales Ratio <= Median Value for the S&P 500**
We're incorporating the same market comparison for the P/S ratio as we did with the P/E.

  Relative comparisons are also ideal when testing your strategies in the past. If the perception of what a fair P/S ratio is now, differs from what it was back then, the relative measure will always ensure that you'll find the stocks below that threshold (or above it if that's what you're looking for) regardless of where it is.

- **Price to Book <= Median Value for the S&P 500**
We have not used the Price to Book ratio (P/B) yet in any of our screens. But it's a perfect addition to a value screen as it helps to determine a company's intrinsic value.

  The Price to Book ratio is calculated as: Market Capitalization divided by Book Value.

  This can be done on a per share basis as well, i.e., current price / book value per share.

  Book Value is defined as total assets minus liabilities, preferred stock, and intangible assets. In short, this is how much the company is worth.

  Companies will typically sell for more than their Book Value in much the same way that a company will sell at a multiple of its earnings. As of September 2010, the median book value for the stocks in the S&P 500 was just above 2.0.

  In other words, the market (in general) has determined that a company selling at two times its book value is fair and normal.

  So a P/B ratio of 1 means the company is selling at less than what the company says it's inherently worth (according to its financial statements). Moreover, a P/B of 1 means it's selling at half of what the market's median is.

If the P/B is under 1, it means it's selling at less than its book value and even more at a discount to the market.

A P/B of 2 means it's selling at twice its book value (or roughly the current market median).

A P/B above 2, of course, means it's trading at even more than 2 times its book value and above the median for the market.

For this screen, we're comparing the company's P/B ratio to that of the market and screening for the companies that are trading at a discount.

• **Debt to Equity <= Median Value for the S&P 500**
The Debt to Equity ratio (or D/E as it's sometimes referred to) is a great item to use for gauging a company's financial health.

This item can be found under Ratio/Leverage in most screeners. The calculation for Debt to Equity is: Total Liabilities divided by Shareholders Equity.

The median debt to equity ratio for stocks in the S&P was 0.48 as of September 2010. A high number means the company has more debt to equity, whereas a lower number means it has less. Less is definitely better when it comes to debt. Of course, not all debt is bad. But the purpose for this screen is to find companies that are selling at a discount to the market. And in order for these stocks to truly be considered a bargain, we want to make sure that they look as healthy as possible to discerning investors. That means a lower debt load than what's normal for the market.

And that's how we're using it in this screen. Companies with a debt to equity ratio below the median for the market.

Note that, as with most ratios, each industry has its own "normal." So it's important to be aware of that when you decide to drill down further into a company's financials.

Now for the two "sparks" or catalysts:

1. Top # 7 Sectors based on the % Change F(1) Estimates (last 4 weeks)
We're narrowing down our selection list to the top (best) seven sectors with the highest upward earnings estimate revisions for the current fiscal year (F1) over the last four weeks. Why are we doing this? Because, as we've mentioned before, roughly half

of a stock's price movement can be directly attributed to the group that it's in. Since we're looking for the most overlooked and undervalued companies, but picking them out of a group that's now receiving the best upward earnings estimate revisions, that means there might be something beneficial happening on a systemic level, which in turn could help all of the stocks within that group. We've said it numerous times, but the most powerful thing to impact stock prices are earnings estimate revisions. And we're keying in on that very thing, in a top-down manner, with this one.

2. **Top # 1 Stock in each Sector based on the % Change F(1) Estimates (last 4 weeks)**
The preceding item just narrowed the list of stocks down to only those within the top seven sectors. This item now selects the top stock from each one of those top seven sectors based on that same item: the earnings estimate revisions for F(1) over the last four weeks. Rising earnings estimate revisions not only act as a spark for the group, but will also help distinguish which ones are being singled out for the most significant increased outlook. Of course, this screen isn't going to find the one stock in each group with the absolute highest earnings estimate upgrade without consideration for everything else. Instead, it's looking for the highest percentage earnings estimate revision out of all of the deeply discounted stocks that made it through our screen. This is an important point because the basis for a value stock is that somehow, the market got it wrong, that they have mispriced the stock for it to be selling at a discount to its peers like that and even to its own intrinsic value. But with sharp upgrades to not only the group that it's in, but to the stock itself, the analysts are clearly giving these stocks another look. And the belief is that the market will respond to this by bidding the stocks up to a fairer value (higher price) given all of the new information.

Results

From 2000 to 2007 (before the bear market of 2008 wreaked its havoc), this strategy, using a four-week holding period, generated an average annual return of 38.2% in comparison to the S&P's 1.2%. And it did so with literally less than half the risk (maximum drawdown) as the market (see Figure 9.1).

FIGURE 9.1   Value and Spark (2000–2007, 4-week rebalance)

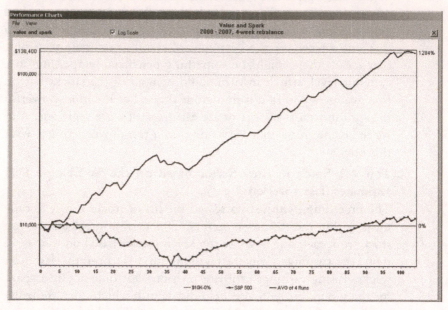

In Figure 9.2, we can see that 2008 wasn't as good, but it significantly beat the market with an average annual return (this time a loss) of –7.1% in

FIGURE 9.2   Value and Spark (2008-2009, 4-week rebalance)

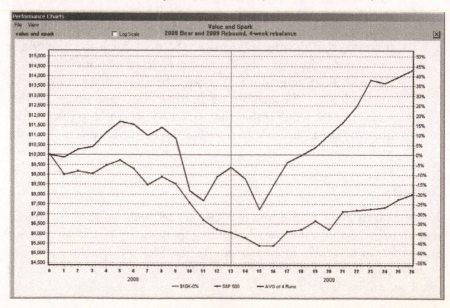

comparison to the market's −37.0% loss. But, in 2009, it continued its run of outperformance with an average annual return of 50.0% to the market's own impressive 26.5%. Between the worst of the bear market in 2008 and the subsequent rebound in 2009, the strategy was able to finish solidly in the black in spite of the market still being stuck underwater.

Overall, for the last 10 years, this strategy has shown an average annual compounded growth rate of 33.1% for a total compounded return of 1,737.8% (see Figure 9.3).

FIGURE 9.3 Value and Spark (2000–2009, 1-week rebalance)

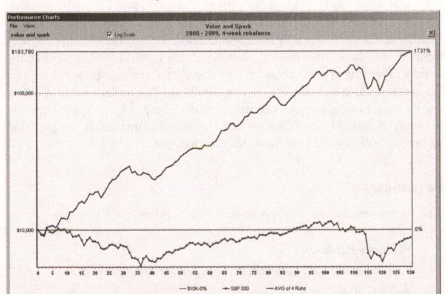

This value screen, while keying in on many classic valuation metrics, uses a different approach than other value screens out there. The key difference in this interpretation is that we're looking for not just discounted stocks but discounted stocks poised to move.

By making each stock qualify as a discount on no less than four strict valuation criteria *and* coupling it with two powerful price impact catalysts (three if you count the F(1) estimate revision to the sector and to the stock itself separately, along with the Zacks Rank) you get a list of stocks with virtually every reason to move higher.

R-Squared Growth

The title of this screen either scared people away or made them want to read more. If you're still reading, you're of course, one of the latter. Congratulations.

So let's get right to it. The name of the screen and its signature item is the R-Squared Growth Rate. And this is a measure of how close the actual earnings come to the earnings growth on a regression basis. In other words, how closely do the earnings conform to the regression line? (Don't worry, I'll expound on this in a bit.)

But what's all this talk about growth rates, you say? I thought we were looking for value? We are. And this screen hits hard on two valuation items. But there has to be a reason for an undervalued company to move higher, right? If not, these "undervalued" companies aren't really undervalued at all. If they're trading at a discount because there's no earnings growth to speak of, is that really a bargain? No. It may be cheap. But undervalued? Where's the value in buying a stock you may consider cheap if it never goes up? Or worse, goes down? None. That's where the growth comes in. In the previous screen, we had our catalysts. And this one does too.

Parameters

The parameters that go into this screen are as follows:

- **Zacks Rank <= 2**
- **R-Squared EPS Growth: In (range) between .50 and .66**
- **PEG Ratio <= 1**
- **P/E Using 12 Month EPS: In (range) 5 and 15**
- **% Change in Price over 4 Weeks > −5%**
- **Price >= $5**
- **Average 20-Day Volume >= 100,000**

Now let's take a look at what they mean.

Methodology

- **Zacks Rank <= 2**
  Zacks Rank #1s and #2s (Strong Buys and Buys).

- **R-Squared EPS Growth: In (range) between .50 and .66**
The range for an R-Squared value is between 0 and 1. (Or if you express it as a percentage, between 0% and 100%.) The higher the value, the closer the data points conform to the regression line. The lower the value, the worse it conforms to the regression line. For this, the data points we're talking about are EPS growth numbers.

A value of 1 means the data is a perfect fit—very hard to see. A value of 0 is the worst, meaning the data is scattered everywhere. In other words, if the data points are all over the place, it shows there's no rhyme or reason for how that data is coming in—extreme unreliability.

If, on the other hand, the data points are all plotting close to the regression line, that shows there's less deviation from the regression of the growth rate. And the less deviation there is, the more reliable (you would think) those numbers would be.

This item is used to get a sense of a stock's ability to produce trendline EPS results. Of course, there are no assurances that future data points won't veer off course. But knowing how closely matched the data points have been in the past is good to know.

What's interesting is that the distribution of the R-Squared values for the stocks in the universe is an inverted bell curve (or well curve) distribution (see Figure 9.4).

FIGURE 9.4　Bell Curve and Well Curve Illustration

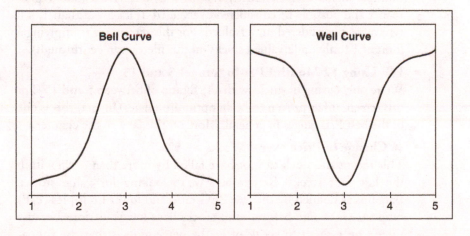

When you look at a normal distribution (bell curve), typically, the majority of the values will be in the middle of the ranges with smaller amounts on either side of the middle.

A well curve (abnormal distribution) has the majority of the data falling on either side with the smaller percentage of data in the middle.

For example: nearly 25% of the stocks had a value of .33 to .66. But roughly 38% of the stocks had lower values. And roughly 38% had higher values.

Usually, with a normal distribution, the majority of the data falls within the middle values with the smaller amounts of data falling on either side to form a symmetrical bell curve. This distribution was the exact opposite, with the majority of values falling on either side of the middle. So I decided to test it.

Before I did (and before I saw the distribution), I had at first thought that a value of 1 would produce the best results and 0 the worst. But in my testing, along with other items, these proved to be less reliable.

What I did find, however, was a range that produced the overwhelmingly best results. And that is: above the median with a 50% to 66% fit with the growth rate regression. And that's how we're applying it to this screen. (Okay, the geometry lesson is now over.)

- **PEG Ratio <= 1**
We've talked about the PEG ratio before, and we're bringing it out again for this one. Once again, it shows if the stock is trading at a multiple higher than its growth rate. If it is, it'll have a value higher than 1 and possibly be considered overvalued. If it's lower than 1, it'll typically be considered undervalued. For this screen, we're applying a limit of 1 (only undervalued stocks on this metric can get through).

- **P/E Using 12 Month EPS: In (range) 5 and 15**
We're only letting in stocks with a P/E ratio of between 5 and 15. For this screen, it has proven to be an optimum range. (In fact, this is one of the best P/E ranges in general. More on this later in the chapter.)

- **% Change in Price over 4 Weeks > −5%**
This means the stock cannot have fallen by more than −5% within the last four weeks. Remember, we're looking for value stocks. Bargains as defined by the low PEG ratio and lower multiples (P/E) ratio. As we've said before, some stocks have low valuations because there's no growth to speak of or the perception is that the fundamentals are only going to get worse—meaning they're not really discounted at all. If the stock is falling, maybe the market hasn't mispriced it. So by only looking at stocks that, at worst, are down less

than −5% (can be chalked up to noise), it shows that there doesn't seem to be anything wrong with it to pressure the price further. Note that this screen will find stocks that are up prior to getting in; flat prior to getting in; and down prior to getting in—just not down by more than −5%. What's interesting is that, if the stock is down by a few percent before we get in, and if we really think we're getting in on an undervalued gem (we do think that by running this screen), this lower "sale" price makes the entry that much more rewarding.

Results

Over the last 10 years, using a four-week rebalancing period, this strategy has produced an average compounded annual growth rate of 24.9% for a total compounded return of 829.7%, all while assuming less than a third of the risk/volatility of the market (see Figure 9.5).

FIGURE 9.5 R-Squared Growth (2000–2009, 4-week rebalance)

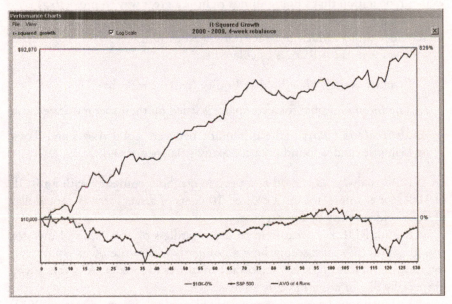

Even though there's no specific limitation placed on the number of stocks to come through, it'll typically generate, on average, of 3–5 stocks each period.

It should also be noted that this is another strategy that was actually able to finish in the positive during the devastating bear market of 2008 with an average compounded return of 14.2% vs. the S&P 500s −37%. Very impressive.

Plus, imagine your friends' faces when they ask you what your secret is and you tell them the R-Squared Growth Rate. After some blank stares and some head nodding (the kind when someone nods up and down but has no idea what you're talking about), they'll think you're a genius.

ROE for *Your* ROI

Another item I like to use when searching for value stocks is the Return on Equity (ROE). I like using this item in value screens because ROE is a good measure of management efficiency. In fact, it's a favorite screening criteria of many money managers and investors, including myself, because it tells you how successful a company is at using its shareholders' capital.

Moreover, companies with steadily increasing ROE are generally better managed with attention being paid to the details. Since a value stock is perceived as being incorrectly priced by the market, these companies need to try extra hard to show their true worth. And showing that your company is a well-run operation that's doing things right is a great way to prove that.

Once again, ROE shows how much profit a company is making on its shareholder equity (which includes reinvested earnings).

The formula for ROE is calculated as:

Income/Average Shareholders Equity (past 12 months)

The *Income* number for a company is listed on their Income Statement.

Shareholders Equity is the difference between Total Assets and Total Liabilities and is found on a company's Balance Sheet.

ROE is always expressed as a percentage. So a company with an ROE of 10%, for example, means it created 10 cents of assets for every one dollar of shareholder equity in a given year.

I think ROE is a great item to use regardless of what kind of investor you are. Why? Because seeing how a company makes use of its equity and the return it makes on it, are important measures to look at. And that's why I especially like to use it in value screens.

As I mentioned earlier, I particularly like to look for an increasing ROE. That is often a clue that management is doing something right and that their house is in order. It can also alert you to problems when it's falling, so beware.

Another great way to use the ROE is to compare it to its industry. Some industries require greater assets than others to run their business. For example, take the retail industry vs. the steel industry. Retail has a median

ROE of 11.8% (as of August 2010) whereas the steel industry has a median ROE of 5.8%. If you screened for only absolute numbers, you may miss some great stocks in some great groups.

Trying to find companies with the best ROE relative to their group (sector or industry, etc.) is one of the best ways of making an apples-to-apples comparison in an effort to find the top stocks. Then when you drill down, you can search for the optimum values and characteristics for your group.

One thing to look out for, however, is a company's debt level or leverage. Sometimes a company's ROE can be inflated by the use of debt to expand on operations. Excessive debt is never a good thing. So combining ROE with a leverage measurement like Debt to Equity can help keep overly leveraged companies off of your screens.

Cash Is King

In 2008, I read a news story about how Federal Reserve Chairman Ben Bernanke and Alan Greenspan were both saying that many companies had lots of cash on the books. They also said that businesses were in better shape now than they were during the last two economic contractions.

The article was quick to point out that they were excluding financial companies. But they also made it a point to say that many companies across the rest of the industries had socked away cash, reduced their debt, and cut inventories.

At the time, there were other articles published showing just how much money some companies had on hand by citing Microsoft's announced $40 billion stock buy-back plan. Nike was another one after announcing a $5 billion repurchase program. And so was Hewlett-Packard with their own $8 billion dollar buy-back program. (In fact, that was HPQ's third buy-back program in two years.)

That being said, I decided to put together a screen that looks for companies with solid cash positions. I did not do this in hopes that these companies would initiate repurchase programs of their own, even though that could be a benefit. I did this because companies with the strongest cash positions, coupled with low debt, reduced inventories, and the like, will be in the best position to weather a financial crisis as well as capitalize on the best of times.

Parameters and Methodology

Let's take a look at the Cash Is King screen by examining the parameters and how we're using them.

- **Cash and Marketable Securities > Previous Year**
  Having a strong cash position means companies will not have to depend on banks to finance their operations.

- **Debt to Total Capital < 5 Year Average Debt to Total Capital**
  Companies able to reduce their debt positions from their historical ratio is a sign of strength and a healthy balance sheet.

- **Cash Flow > Cash Flow from Last Year**
  This, too, is a sign of financial health.

- **Inventories < Last Year's Levels**
  Turnover of inventory (raw materials, unfinished goods, and finished goods) is how a company makes money. High levels of inventory for long periods of time is usually not a good sign.

- **Annual EPS Growth Rate > the Median for its Industry**
  This lets us focus on the top half of the companies in their peer group.

- **Projected One-Year EPS Growth Rate > 0 (i.e., better than last yr.)**
  At the time, companies expecting growth during the worst of the bear market were the ones I was favoring (along with all of the aforementioned items). But finding companies with growth, even though it seems obvious and quite commonplace in better times, is not a given, and it's something I'll regularly look for.

  By the way, as I have mentioned before, just because a company is projected to show growth does not necessarily mean they'll be rewarded in the market. Just like companies that are expected to show negative growth don't always go down. It's the earnings estimates, and more specifically, the earnings estimate revisions that truly drive the stock's price. But I'd prefer to find companies receiving upward earnings estimate revisions with growth than companies receiving upward earnings estimate revisions without it.

This was a screen I enjoyed running in the difficult times of 2008. And is now a screen I run regularly.

Price to Cash Flow

We mentioned Cash Flow in the previous screen. Another way to look at Cash Flow is through the Price to Cash Flow ratio (P/CF).

While the P/E ratio is probably the most common ratio in determining whether a company is undervalued or overvalued, the P/CF is another great ratio to do just that. Cash of course is vital to a company's financial health, especially nowadays, in order to finance operations, invest in the business, and so forth.

Part of what makes the P/CF item an effective way to check on the health of a company is that cash can't really be manipulated on the income statement like earnings can. This is one of the main reasons why some people like this measurement better than the P/E ratio; the net income of the cash flow portion rightly adds back in depreciation and amortization, since these are not cash expenditures. Whereas the net income that goes into the earnings portion of the P/E ratio does not add these in, thus artificially reducing the income and skewing the P/E ratio. This is why so many analysts prefer using the P/CF metric to judge a stock's value.

Just as the P/E ratio is calculated by dividing the price by its earnings per share, the P/CF ratio is calculated by dividing the price by its cash flow per share.

Also like the P/E ratio, the lower the number, in general, the better. But like so many other valuation metrics, be sure to compare the stock's P/CF to its industry, since different industries will have different numbers that are considered normal. For example: the median P/CF for gold mining companies (Aug. 2010) is about 17.4, but it's about 4.6 for telecom.

I'm not knocking the P/E ratio. It's an extremely valuable item when used correctly. But there are inefficiencies with virtually every valuation item. However, knowing each one's strengths and weaknesses can help you become a better trader and investor.

Statistical Analysis of P/CF, P/E, P/S, P/B, and PEG

Since this chapter is all about Value style screens, it seemed like the perfect place to expound on some of the statistical analysis I've done on the afore-mentioned valuation metrics, specifically: the Price to Earnings ratio (P/E), Price to Sales ratio (P/S), Price to Book ratio (P/B), Price to Cash Flow ratio (P/CF), and the PEG ratio (PEG).

I tend to do a lot of relative comparisons for finding value, knowing that different groups have different characteristics. Even the broader market's perception of what is normal can change in a meaningful way at different times, so making relative comparisons always keeps a person's screening techniques current and up-to-date (not to mention profitable).

But there's a time for using hard and fast values as well. And understanding what works and what doesn't and where the advantages reside can really help someone supercharge their trading.

The Test

In March 2010, I did a study on five of the most commonly used valuation items. (Don't feel bad if your favorite one isn't on the list. You can easily conduct a similar study on your own.) For the study, I did a 10-year test (2/2000–2/2010). I created a base screen that consisted of stocks trading >= $1, with an average 20-day share volume >= 100,000. I then added the item of interest to the screen and applied various value ranges. My findings follow.

But before we get into the results for the items themselves, let's take a look at our controls to better understand the performances that we'll be looking at.

Over the last 10 years, using a one-week holding period, the base screen produced an average compounded annual growth rate of 7.4%. Each stock in this portfolio was equally weighted. And so they are for the following studies.

Price to Cash Flow (P/CF)

Let's begin with the Price to Cash Flow (P/CF) since we just got done talking about that. The chart and list that follow displays the compounded growth rates for the different test ranges (see Figure 9.6).

FIGURE 9.6   Price to Cash Flow (P/CF) Study

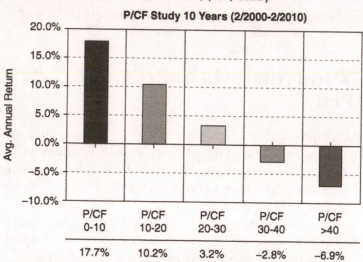

	P/CF 0-10	P/CF 10-20	P/CF 20-30	P/CF 30-40	P/CF >40
	17.7%	10.2%	3.2%	−2.8%	−6.9%

P/CF range >= 0 and <= 10: Average Annual Return: 17.7%
P/CF range > 10 and <= 20: Average Annual Return: 10.2%
P/CF range > 20 and <= 30: Average Annual Return: 3.2%
P/CF range > 30 and <= 40: Average Annual Return: −2.8%
P/CF range > 40:   Average Annual Return: −6.9%

The best performing range was 0–10 with a 17.7% annual return. The 10–20 range came in with 10.2%. Interestingly, there were about the same number of stocks in each of these two groups, although a tad more in the first one (average of 988 for group 1 and 867 for group 2).

So the statistical advantage resides in the first range (0–10), which also happens to be under the median P/CF value for the stocks in the S&P (10.37 as of August 2010). Staying in this range gives the trader his best odds for success in regard to this item.

I also did one more study and that was to apply the Zacks Rank #1 to the top performing set. (See the leftmost bar in the chart of Figure 9.7 for illustration.)

FIGURE 9.7 Price to Cash Flow (P/CF) Study and Zacks Rank #1

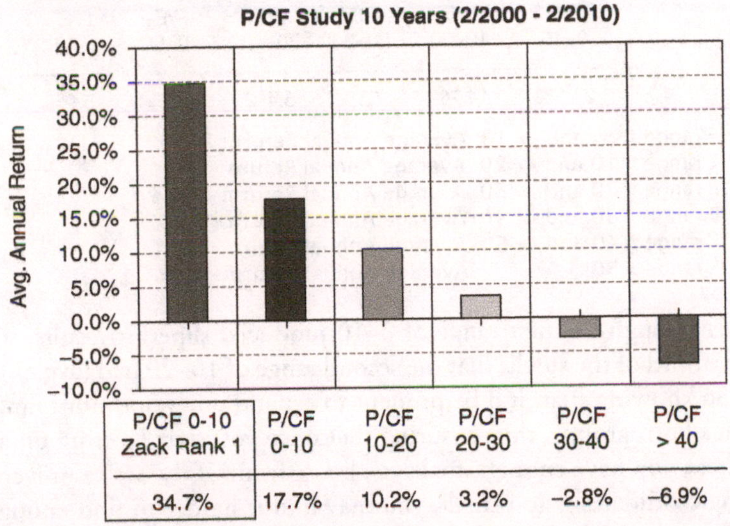
P/CF Study 10 Years (2/2000 - 2/2010)
Avg. Annual Return
40.0%
35.0%
30.0%
25.0%
20.0%
15.0%
10.0%
5.0%
0.0%
–5.0%
–10.0%
P/CF 0-10 Zack Rank 1
P/CF 0-10
P/CF 10-20
P/CF 20-30
P/CF 30-40
P/CF > 40
34.7%
17.7%
10.2%
3.2%
–2.8%
–6.9%

P/CF range 0–10 and Zacks Rank 1: Average Annual Return: 34.7%

Price to Earnings (P/E)

Next up is the Price to Earnings ratio (P/E). For this study, I used the P/E using the F(1) Estimates.

In the chart and list that follow, you'll see the compounded annual growth rates for the different P/E ranges (see Figure 9.8).

It's clear from this study that the lower P/E ratios did better than the higher ones with ranges 0–10 and 10–20 performing the best. By the time I got to the last few ranges in the study, the gains became almost nonexistent before finally tipping over into a loss.

FIGURE 9.8   Price to Earnings (P/E) Study

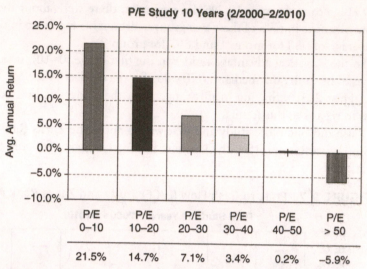

P/E range 0 >= and <= 10: Average Annual Return: 21.5%
P/E range > 10 and <= 20: Average Annual Return: 14.7%
P/E range > 20 and <= 30: Average Annual Return: 7.1%
P/E range > 30 and <= 40: Average Annual Return: 3.4%
P/E range > 40 and <= 50: Average Annual Return: 0.2%
P/E range > 50:   Average Annual Return: −5.9%

Even though the first range of 0–10 produced superior results, it had less than a third of the stocks that the second range of 10–20 had (avg. 305 vs. 1,095). So knowing that, it'd be prudent to expand one's optimum range to encompass both groups, thus ensuring that once you start layering on additional filters, you have enough stocks to choose from. If the active universe of beginning candidates is too small, you may find it harder to find enough of the stocks you're looking for.

By combining both ranges that would include P/Es of between 0 and 20, you now get an average annual return of 16.9% and a more meaningful list of stocks to pick from.

Does this mean that you should never buy a stock with a P/E above 20? Or above 50 because that showed a loss? Of course it doesn't. There are plenty of stocks that have done great above those levels and will do great above those levels. But in general, everything being equal, the advantage clearly lies with the lower numbers and more specifically, within those respective ranges.

Now let's see what that range of 0–20 looks like in comparison to the other ranges and also see how that optimum range performs with the Zacks Rank #1 added to it. (See Figure 9.9.)

FIGURE 9.9 Price to Earnings (P/E) Study and Zacks Rank #1

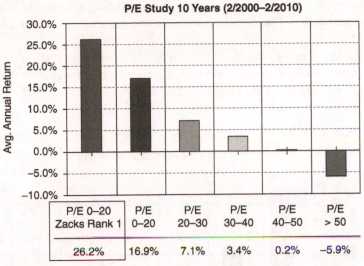

P/E Study 10 Years (2/2000–2/2010)

	P/E 0–20 Zacks Rank 1	P/E 0–20	P/E 20–30	P/E 30–40	P/E 40–50	P/E > 50
	26.2%	16.9%	7.1%	3.4%	0.2%	−5.9%

P/E range 0–20 and Zacks Rank 1: Average Annual Return: 26.2%

Price to Sales (P/S)

Let's do the Price to Sales ratio (P/S) next. See the compounded annual growth rates for the different P/S ranges in the chart and list that follows (see Figure 9.10).

FIGURE 9.10 Price to Sales (P/S) Study

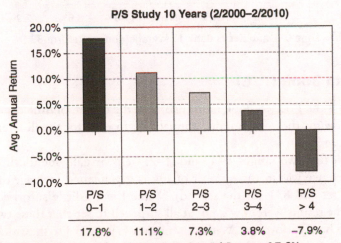

P/S Study 10 Years (2/2000–2/2010)

P/S 0–1	P/S 1–2	P/S 2–3	P/S 3–4	P/S > 4
17.8%	11.1%	7.3%	3.8%	−7.9%

P/S range >= 0 and <= 1: Average Annual Return: 17.8%
P/S range > 1 and <= 2: Average Annual Return: 11.1%
P/S range > 2 and <= 3: Average Annual Return: 7.3%
P/S range > 3 and <= 4: Average Annual Return: 3.8%
P/S range > 4:   Average Annual Return: −7.9%

From the preceding study, you can see that the best range was 0–1. The second range of 1–2 did fine enough, producing a return of 1.5 times the base group of 7.4%. But the first range was the clear winner at 2.4 times the control.

The last range in the study (> 4) is firmly in negative territory presenting the worst odds of success. What about the winning range plus the Zacks Rank #1? Even better. (See Figure 9.11.)

FIGURE 9.11 Price to Sales (P/S) Study and Zacks Rank #1

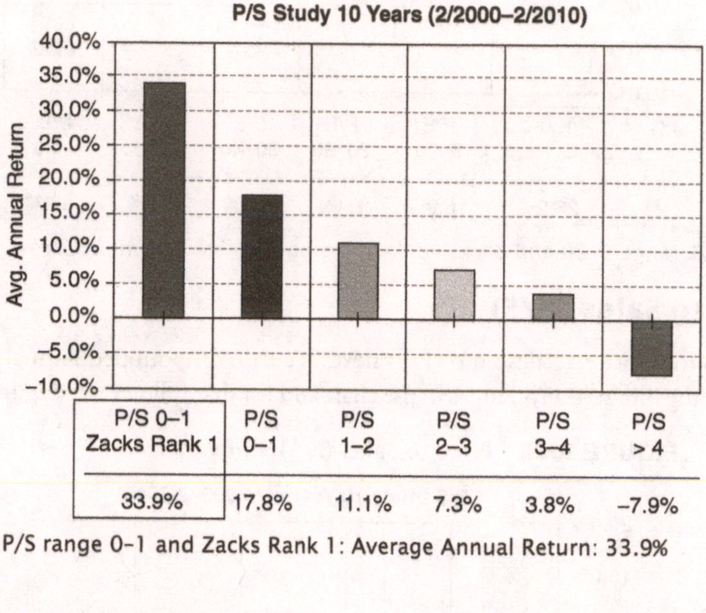

P/S Study 10 Years (2/2000–2/2010)

	P/S 0–1 Zacks Rank 1	P/S 0–1	P/S 1–2	P/S 2–3	P/S 3–4	P/S > 4
	33.9%	17.8%	11.1%	7.3%	3.8%	–7.9%

P/S range 0–1 and Zacks Rank 1: Average Annual Return: 33.9%

Price to Book (P/B)

Next up is the Price to Book ratio (P/B). See the corresponding chart and list that follow for the compounded annual growth rates for the different ranges (see Figure 9.12).

The first two ranges (0–1) and (1–2) were virtually identical. The only real difference was in the number of stocks it generated (average of 315 for the first set and 831 for the second). While I was a little surprised at how similar the results were, I was not at all surprised to see that these two ranges were the best performers. With the median P/B ratio for the stocks in the S&P 500 at just over 2 (2.12 as of Aug. 2010), staying under this mark makes sense.

Performance in each subsequent range seems to get cut in half as you go down the list before finally turning negative with a P/B ratio over 5.

FIGURE 9.12   Price to Book (P/B) Study

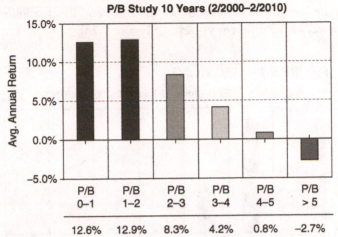

P/B Study 10 Years (2/2000–2/2010)

| | 12.6% | 12.9% | 8.3% | 4.2% | 0.8% | –2.7% |

P/B range >= 0 and <= 1: Average Annual Return: 12.6%
P/B range > 1 and <= 2:   Average Annual Return: 12.9%
P/B range > 2 and <= 3:   Average Annual Return: 8.3%
P/B range > 3 and <= 4:   Average Annual Return: 4.2%
P/B range > 4 and <= 5:   Average Annual Return: 0.8%
P/B range > 5:   Average Annual Return: –2.7%

Let's create one more study set by combining the top two ranges with the Zacks Rank #1 stocks added to it. (See Figure 9.13.)

FIGURE 9.13   Price to Book (PB) Study and Zacks Rank #1

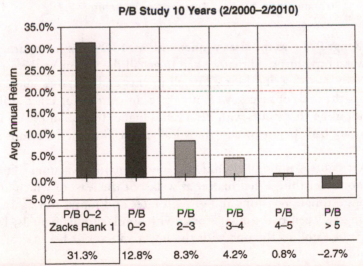

P/B Study 10 Years (2/2000–2/2010)

P/B 0–2 Zacks Rank 1	P/B 0–2	P/B 2–3	P/B 3–4	P/B 4–5	P/B > 5
31.3%	12.8%	8.3%	4.2%	0.8%	–2.7%

P/B range 0–2 and Zacks Rank 1: Average Annual Return: 31.3%

PEG Ratio (PEG)

Last but not least is the PEG ratio. See the chart and list that follows for the performances of the different values (see Figure 9.14).

FIGURE 9.14 PEG Study

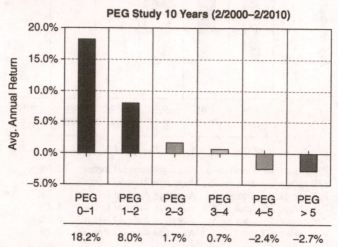

	PEG 0–1	PEG 1–2	PEG 2–3	PEG 3–4	PEG 4–5	PEG > 5
	18.2%	8.0%	1.7%	0.7%	−2.4%	−2.7%

PEG range >= 0 and <= 1: Average Annual Return: 18.2%
PEG range > 1 and <= 2: Average Annual Return: 8.0%
PEG range > 2 and <= 3: Average Annual Return: 1.7%
PEG range > 3 and <= 4: Average Annual Return: 0.7%
PEG range > 4 and <= 5: Average Annual Return: −2.4%
PEG range > 5:   Average Annual Return: −2.7%

Range 0–1 was the clear winner with an 18.2% annual return. I must say I was a little surprised that we had to get all the way up to the 4–5 range before we started seeing losses. For all intents and purposes, once you go above 2, the odds of success were no longer in your favor. Once again, that does not mean that stocks with PEG ratios higher than 2, or even 5 for that matter, are bad. It just means, statistically, you have the best odds staying under 1.

Of course, nobody should use any item in a vacuum. There are plenty of other things that matter as well, not the least of which are their earnings estimate revisions and growth rates and more. But again, when choosing between two similar stocks with similar fundamentals, I'll usually give the nod to the one with the lower valuations because of what I know here.

And like we did with the others, let's see what the results look like if we added the Zacks Rank #1 stocks to the top performing PEG range. (See Figure 9.15.)

FIGURE 9.15 PEG Study and Zacks Rank #1

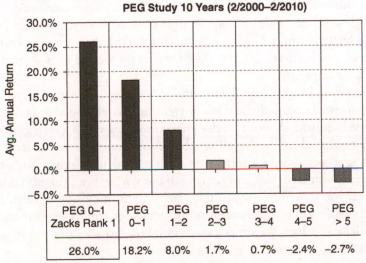

PEG range 0–1 and Zacks Rank 1: Average Annual Return: 26.0%

Combined Valuation Screen

So how would a screen do with all of these optimum values combined? Let's take a look. Over that same 10-year time span, I backtested this strategy using a one-week rebalancing period, a four-week rebalancing period, and a 12-week rebalancing period.

To summarize what's in the screen again, we have our base parameters:

- **Price >= $1**
- **Average 20-Day Volume >= 100,000**

The optimum values on key valuation metrics are:

- **Price to Cash Flow <= 10**
- **P/E using F(1) Estimates <= 20**
- **Price to Sales <= 1**
- **Price to Book <= 2**

- PEG <= 1
- Zacks Rank = 1

Using a one-week holding period, the strategy produced a 45.8% compounded annual growth rate with an average of 6–7 stocks held per period. Using a four-week holding period, it produced a 31.5% average compounded annual growth rate, with once again an average of 6–7 stocks in its portfolio. And finally, using a 12-week rebalancing period, the screen generated an average annual return of 20.7% while holding on average of 6–7 stocks at a time. Pretty impressive.

However, just because these items' value ranges have proven to be the best when tested singularly (and yes, pretty impressively together as the aforementioned statistics show), that does not mean they will necessarily produce *the best* results when they're all combined into one screen. In fact, we've already gone over many screens that have topped this—some with bigger gains, some with lesser risk and some with both. Moreover, this also does not mean that you'll want to use just these items to the exclusion of other items. Indeed, you'll most certainly want to include other criteria in your searches, not the least of which are other valuation items, growth rates, earnings estimate revisions, and more.

How's that? Imaging your favorite music groups all singing together on one song. Cool concept, right? But might not be that great in execution. What about all of your favorite furniture all crammed into one room? Or how about your favorite painters all painting on the same canvas? Can you imagine a Norman Rockwell family setting with Picasso faces on everyone and a Salvador Dali backdrop? My brain hurts just thinking about it.

My point is, don't think you have to or even should combine every single great idea or proven statistic together into one strategy. Certain items work better with other items. Use as many as you need to achieve the desired results you're after in your screen, which includes the number of stocks, the style of stocks it produces, the return on the screen, and the risk level to do it. And test everything out every step of the way. (We'll go over more on building and testing your strategies in Chapter 15.)

Use these and other items smartly in your screens and in your additional stock analysis. And just know that every stock you look at does not have to score perfectly on every item you can think of. If that was your standard, you'd never be able to buy a stock—ever. Use these statistics and others as guidelines and you'll be picking better stocks than you ever have before.

Summary

Value investing doesn't have to be the boring investment style that so many people think it is. And you definitely don't have to sacrifice performance to do it. As we mentioned before, one of the characteristics of value stocks is that, for whatever reason, they have been overlooked by the market or at least have been underpriced as evidenced by their valuations.

Of course, not every company with low valuations is undervalued. Many have low valuations and deservedly so. The best way to tell the difference is to look at the additional spark measures we covered, like earnings estimate revisions for example. It's also important to look at the company's relative valuation to its peers as well as its own historical valuation. And don't forget to look at a company's intrinsic value and balance sheet. But there's no need to pour over tons of financial statements. You can do all of this with a screener.

In the next chapter we'll be looking at Growth and Income strategies—in short, good companies that pay a solid dividend. One thing you'll notice is that a lot of dividend paying companies have great valuations as well. But these kinds of stocks command a style of their own. And that's what we'll discover in the next chapter.

Chapter 10

Winning Growth and Income Strategies

Now it's time for us to take a look at Growth and Income strategies. Like the Value style, some people wrongly think that this style is boring or that (aside from the dividend) there's no money in it. Nonsense! As we've seen with the Value style strategies, they can be quite exciting. And it's the same with dividend paying strategies—if you're doing them right.

In this chapter we'll highlight three dividend paying strategies. We'll also go over how some of the items we've used in the other styles can help us find the best income producing stocks as well. There's something in here for everybody. But the style is decidedly Growth and Income.

Growth and Income Winners

A Growth and Income investor is looking for just that—growth and income: income through the steady stream of dividend payments, but not at the exclusion of growth. Growth is a main component (hence the name). The combination of capital appreciation (stock moving higher) and the dividend payout make these great stocks to get into. And you don't have to want or need the income to find these stocks attractive. In fact, when you see the returns many can provide along with the lesser volatility and risk, these look like great stock candidates for any investor.

Parameters

The screen begins with the following parameters:

- **Zacks Rank <= 3**
- **Return on Equity >= Median for the S&P 500**
- **P/E using F(1) Estimate <= Median for the S&P 500**
- **Debt to Equity Ratio <= 1**
- **Beta <= 1**

Now for the dividend components:

- **Current Dividend Yield % >= Median for the S&P 500**
- **Current Dividend Yield % Top # 2 in each Sector**
- **Current Dividend Yield % Top # 7**
- And we're applying the above parameters to stocks with a **Price >= $5** and an **Average 20-Day Share Volume >= 100,000**

One of the first things you'll notice by looking at the list of parameters is that this is the first screen in which we've included stocks with a Zacks Rank of a 3 in addition to 1s and 2s. Let's take a look at why. And let's see how we're using all of the other items as well.

Methodology

- **Zacks Rank <= 3**
  In this screen we're including Zacks Rank 1s, 2s, and 3s. Many of the sought after dividend paying stocks will be large-cap companies. And as we've said earlier, there's a greater percentage of small-cap and mid-cap stocks in the Zacks #1 spot. There's also a good percentage of small- and mid-cap stocks in the #2 spot as well. While there's plenty of large-caps in both the #1 and #2 positions, you'll find a larger percentage of large-cap stocks in the #3 spot. Not because they aren't good companies, but because it's simply harder for a large-cap company to score high enough on the four Zacks Rank components

to move it up to that spot. The two hardest being "Agreement" (the percentage of analysts making earnings estimate revisions in the same direction), and "Magnitude" (the size of the estimate revisions). For large-cap companies, the law of size works against them. How so? Bigger companies will usually have more analysts covering them than smaller companies. And it's easier getting agreement on 3 analysts (2 out of 3 is 66%) as opposed to 15 analysts (you'd need 10 out of 15 analysts moving their estimates up in order to reach that same 66%). Same thing with magnitude. So we're opening our stock list up to Zacks Rank 1s, 2s, and 3s. But the 3s on this list would likely be considered top notch on anybody's list.

- **Return on Equity >= Median for the S&P 500**
  As noted before, ROE is a great way to see how efficiently a company is being run. We want to make sure these companies are doing a great job because we expect them to continue to be able to pay us our dividend. For this one, we want their ROE to be greater than the median ROE for the S&P.

- **P/E using F(1) Estimate <= Median for the S&P 500**
  This is an item that we've used regularly, albeit in different ways. But it's been a reliable way to find reasonably priced stocks. And that's one of the criteria for this screen. We're defining *reasonable* here as P/Es under the median for the market.

- **Debt to Equity Ratio <= 1**
  We're simply requiring that the debt to equity be less than 1. Some companies are capital intensive to run their businesses (and have a D/E of 2, for example), while others are less so (D/E of .5 or lower). So for this we're simply saying less debt than equity. Of course, we wouldn't expect a company paying an attractive dividend to have too high of a debt load. Nor would we want it to. Drawing the line at 1 is a good place to do so.

- **Beta <= 1**
  We're looking for lower beta stocks. Not excessively low, just less volatility than the market. A beta of 1 means it'll move as much or be as volatile as the market. A beta of 2 means it'll move twice as much or be twice as volatile as the market. That's great when it's moving up, but not so great when it's moving down. Less than 1 means it's less volatile. A value of .5 means it's half as volatile. For this screen, I simply want our stocks to be no more volatile than the market and ideally less.

In short, I do not want to be worrying so much about the stock's price while I'm waiting for my dividend. The market can be volatile enough. Don't need any extra volatility.

Now for the dividend components. They are:

- **Current Dividend Yield % >= Median for the S&P 500**
  First, we're looking for only those companies that have a Dividend Yield that's greater than the dividend yield for the market (S&P 500). That's not a huge threshold at the moment (only 1.46 as of Aug. 2010).
- **Current Dividend Yield % Top # 2 in each Sector**
  Next step is to narrow this list down to the top 2 dividend paying stocks in each of the 16 different sectors. That means we'll have narrowed down the list to the top 32 stocks.
- **Current Dividend Yield % Top # 7**
  Our last step is to select the top 7 stocks with the best dividends. That means it can pick up to as many as two stocks from the same sector. But no more. One of the reasons why we did this is we wanted to make sure we were diversified over at least a few, to a handful of sectors, since these will be longer-term holds. If, however, a sector is strong, I do not have a problem having two stocks representing it. But any more, considering there are *only* seven stocks, would be too many for me. The list it generates is quite diversified, and we want to make sure we take full advantage of it.

Results

Over the last 10 years, using a 12-week rebalancing period, this strategy generated an average annual compounded return of 20.6% for a total return of 565.6% (see Figure 10.1).

Even more impressive is that it was accomplished with an average of nearly 40% less risk/volatility than the S&P 500 during that time (average max drawdown of –25.9% vs. the S&P 500s –43.0%), even during the bear market of 2008.

FIGURE 10.1 Growth and Income Winners (2000–2009, 12-week rebalance)

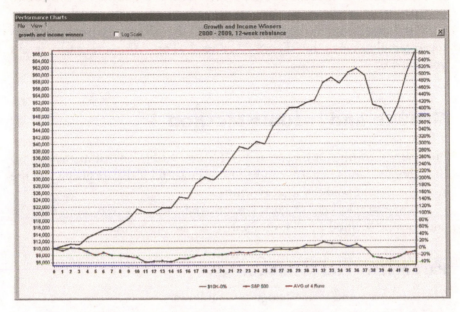

In fact, prior to that (2000–2007), the volatility/risk was more than 60% less than the S&P while still generating an average annual return of 24.6% vs. the market's 1.8% (see Figure 10.2).

FIGURE 10.2 Growth and Income Winners (2000–2007, 12-week rebalance)

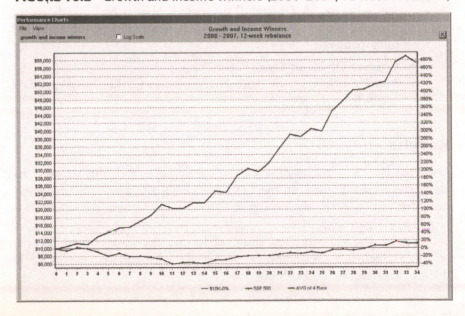

And just like in some of the other screens, you can modify this one to give you more stocks or less. The last item in the screen has us looking for the top 7 stocks with the best dividend yield (after all of the other criteria was met). Simply change the "Top # 7" to read "Top # (however many stocks you'd like)."

Growth and Income Method 1

Not every Growth and Income screen (or any screen for that matter) has to be elaborate. Simple screens can be just as powerful if they're giving you the stocks you want (and the strategy works).

For example, here's a great Growth and Income screen called Growth and Income Method 1 and it uses only three simple items.

Parameters and Methodology

The parameters and methodology are as follows:

- **Zacks Rank <= 2**
  Zacks Rank 1s or 2s, i.e., Strong Buys or Buys.
- **5 Year Historical Growth Rate >= 5%**
  This is the average annual growth rate over the last five years. Don't set the bar too high though. This is not an Aggressive Growth screen. The goal here is Growth and Income—good solid growth and good solid dividends.
- **Current Dividend Yield Top # 7**
  Top 7 stocks with the best dividends out of the list of qualified stocks from the preceding items.

Results

Over the last 10 years, using a 12-week holding period, this strategy has shown an average annual return of 29.6%. That's over a 1,250% total compounded return. Anybody looking for growth *and* income got it with this screen (see Figure 10.3).

As for the risk—it's not quite as low as the Growth and Income Winners screen, but it did show, on average, 23% less risk than the S&P 500 during that time, including 2008.

FIGURE 10.3 Growth and Income Method 1 (2000–2009, 12-week rebalance)

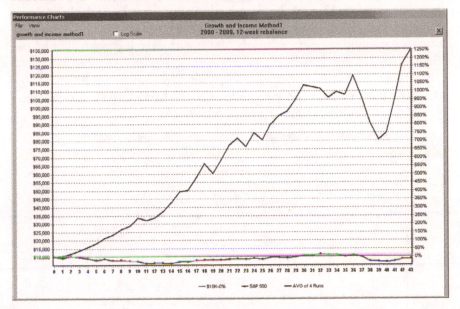

Modifying Your Strategies

Throughout this chapter and throughout this book, if you have found screens that you like and that have tested well, feel free to try and improve upon them or modify them to suit your liking. Do you want to try and reduce your risk level even further? Try adding in some additional valuation metrics. Are you interested in beefing up the growth part of the Growth and Income screen? Look into additional growth and profit items like sales growth, increasing margins, earnings estimate revisions, and more. Maybe you simply don't want to be in financials. A lot of finance companies and real estate investment trusts (REITs) pay dividends. Want to keep them off of your screen? Simply exclude them in your screening criteria.

In fact, I did just that as I hear that from a lot of people. That item would look something like this based on the screener you're using:

- **Sector <> Finance**
  The back to back "less than" and "greater than" signs create the operator "not equal". (I hear people call it a diamond sometimes.) Either way, that's the one to use for exclusion. And now all finance companies, past and present are excluded from this screen.

If you're curious how it did, here are the results: using the same 10-year time span and a 12-week holding period, this strategy (which excluded finance companies of all sorts) showed an average annual return of 24.5% for a total compounded return of nearly 800% with even less risk/volatility (see Figure 10.4).

FIGURE 10.4   Growth and Income Method 1—Excluding Finance Sector (2000–2009, 12-week rebalance)

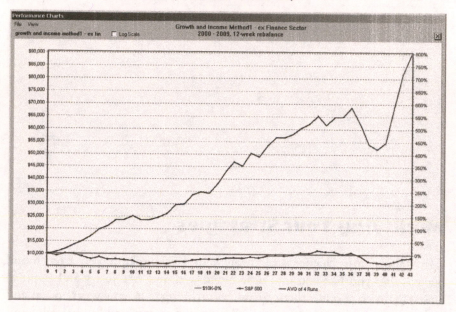

Make sure you test any and all changes to be sure you didn't kill your screen. This change helped. It lowered the risk while producing similar annual returns. But not every modification will. So test, test, and test before you invest.

Dividend Attraction

Here's another take on a Growth and Income screen with a specific focus on larger-cap stocks. And while large-cap, dividend paying stocks are already quite popular, here's why they could start to win an even larger audience.

With GDP growing more slowly in the United States (post financial crisis), expectations are for it to moderate below the more historical 3%+ growth rate we're used to.

One of the reasons for the projected slower growth rates is the across-the-board deleveraging we're seeing from businesses to individual households.

Some companies will find it harder to acquire credit/financing to expand their businesses (or start new ones). And many consumers will find it tougher to afford all of the goods and services they desire.

And while small-cap companies with innovative products and solutions will always have an audience, the larger, stable, and more solid companies will start to gain additional attention and become more sought after holdings.

Many larger companies are large because they have an established and loyal customer base with widespread usage of their products. In turn, they see steady and sustainable growth for their business. Financing is unlikely an issue for their operations. And they likely generate a great deal of cash.

But that's not all. As we've discussed, a lot of the big name companies will also pay their investors a nice dividend. And as different investment vehicles compete for investors' cash in this expected lower growth environment—the companies offering a little extra (dividends) could have an edge.

What's interesting is that a lot of companies have cut their dividends while others have stopped paying them altogether, making the search for good paying dividends that much harder. But they're out there if you're committed to finding them.

As I've mentioned before, smaller-cap growth companies will typically not pay a dividend, as they will pour all their money into growing their business. The larger companies with solid earnings, but without the aggressive growth rates that may have marked their earlier years, will often reward their investors by paying out a portion of their earnings in dividends.

And these are the companies we're looking for in this screen: strong stocks with good dividends and a solid track record.

Parameters and Methodology

The screen is made up of the following:

- **Zacks Rank <= 3**
  This will give us Zacks Rank 1s, 2s, and 3s—Strong Buys, Buys, and Holds respectively. No 4s or 5s—Strong Sells and Sells are excluded.

- **Market Value >= $2.5 Billion**
  With a market-cap requirement of $2.5 billion this will look at the larger mid-caps and all of the large-cap stocks.

- **5 Year Historical EPS Growth Rate > Median for the S&P 500**
  We're looking for a history of market beating growth.

- **Return on Equity > Median for the S&P 500**
  Efficient companies getting the best returns on shareholder equity.

- **Price to Cash Flow <= Median for the S&P 500**
  Just as the P/E ratio shows how many times a company is trading to its earnings (earnings multiple), this shows how many times it's trading to its cash (cash multiple). Like the P/E ratio, a lower number is better. For this, we're looking for companies with a P/CF multiple below the median for the market.

- **5 Year Historical Dividend Growth Rate > 0**
  We're looking for companies that have shown a history of maintaining their dividend or increasing it.

This screen will put a lot of great companies on your watch list. Of course, this will not preclude a company from deciding to cut their dividend in the future. But these additional measures should help us find some of the best dividend paying stocks with a history of success.

Comments

With many companies choosing to slash dividends or stop paying them altogether, many dividend investors are concerned about how they can guard against that happening to their stocks.

The short answer is you can't. (Sorry.)

The longer answer is: you can do everything you can to make sure your company is strong enough so that it's not put into a position where that has to happen. Here are three steps you can take now:

1. If a company's earnings are beginning to go down or their industry is going through a tough time, that is a warning sign. Of course, that does not mean your dividend is on the chopping block—yet. But when a company starts losing money, there's a greater chance that dividends could get cut than if they were humming along profitably.

   The growth items in your screen along with earnings estimate revisions and even just a favorable Zacks Rank should keep these companies off of your screens and out of your portfolio.

   Also, focusing in on the strongest industries helps as well. There's less of a chance for hardship in a top group.

2. Look at a company's cash flow. Is it rising or falling? Where is it in comparison to their historical cash flow? How about their debt? Are they taking on more debt? Why? How will that affect their earnings? Declining cash flows and increasing debt are not the things you want to see from a company expected to pay you money every quarter.

   You can look at the cash flow on an income statement or you can simply compare a company's current cash flow to its 5-year historical cash flow. If you see a meaningful decline, that's a warning sign. Also, take a look at the price to cash flow as well. As for debt, pay attention to their debt to equity levels, as well as shorter-term liquidity measures like the current ratio *(ratio to show how capable a company is to pay short-term obligations)* and interest coverage ratio *(another ratio to measure a company's ability to pay interest on its debt)*.

   And as mentioned above, take a look at the different valuation items like the P/CF ratio, the P/E ratio, and the P/B ratio and more.

3. Some will caution about looking for increased dividends or dividend yields as a sign of potential trouble. I don't necessarily share that belief. If a company is increasing its dividend to desperately attract funds, that's one thing. But you can usually spot their financial difficulties through all of the different valuations and metrics that we've already talked about.

   If, however, a company has increased its dividend over time and has continued to pay it, that is a good thing. The market usually cheers this as good news, not as a sign of future demise. And this shows management's confidence in the company. It's the cuts you have to worry about. But everything has to be taken into context.

   Take a look at a company's five-year dividend history. Also, take a look at their payout ratio *(this shows the percentage of earnings a company is paying out in dividends)*. Too high, and that could be a sign of trouble. But an increased dividend, from a sound company, with a strong balance sheet and income statement along with healthy growth prospects is not cause for alarm.

Growth and Income screens should be set up to identify strong and healthy companies. If these are companies you would invest in even without the dividend, you're on the right path.

There's no need to take a chance on a company with a humongous dividend that you feel shaky about. Strong companies don't need to give away the store. Something too high should be suspect.

But you can seek out the companies with the highest dividend if they meet all of your other criteria and are identified as sound, healthy companies. Begin your search for quality first. Then find the best yields from that list of top picks.

And if you find yourself in a company that cuts its dividend or stops it altogether, simply get out and find a new company that will be more than happy to pay you theirs.

Summary

There was a lot of great information in this chapter, not the least of which was how to identify companies in the best financial shape. This is something that every investor can use. And as we've illustrated, it's an important component in finding the best dividend paying stocks.

No need to wait for your retirement years to benefit from this ever-more popular asset class. Whether you're managing your hard-earned nest-egg or just starting to build one, Growth and Income investing can be fun. And as you've seen from the screens in this chapter, it can also be pretty rewarding.

11

Winning "All Style" Strategies (and Other Stuff That Works)

Let's take a look at some combination style strategies or "All Style" strategies as I like to call it. As you've seen from many of the different screens we've gone over already, incorporating different elements from each style is essential to finding the most profitable stocks consistently.

The Big Money Momentum strategy that we went over in Chapter 7 would not be as successful as it is now without a key valuation metric added. Likewise, that valuation metric alone would not be able to produce the types of returns it has generated without the strategic momentum elements in place.

We could go down the list, citing examples from the Aggressive Growth style, to the Value style, to the Growth and Income style. Even strategies that clearly belong in one category over another will share common characteristics with other styles.

By this time, many of you reading this book have already determined what kind of trader you are by the examples we've given. Whether you're using the strategies exactly as they're described or you're simply incorporating some of the ideas and building onto them, you likely have a better feel for which camp you fit into.

But our work is not finished yet. Let's take a look at a classic example of an "All Style" strategy and some new ways to screen for the most profitable stocks. Or as a friend of mine likes to call it, "stuff that works."

We highlight nine different screening strategies in this chapter, which include studies on broker rating upgrades, new analyst coverage, and even how to calculate price targets. But let's start with one of the most popular combinations, which is Growth and Value.

Finding Growth and Value Stocks the Right Way

Looking for growth and value is a winning combination, especially now, with an uncertain growth environment and changing valuations. And while there are still plenty of growth stocks and value stocks around, it's getting harder to find stocks that fit squarely into *both* categories.

Let's review: Growth investors focus on companies with great earnings growth. This makes sense since earnings drive prices. But nobody wants to overpay for good growth.

Value investors focus on low valuation metrics, like low P/Es for example. But many companies have low P/Es because they don't have any real growth to speak of. They lack earnings power. And people aren't willing to pay up for these stocks because there's nothing to pay up for.

But looking for both growth and value is a great combination and helps alleviate the pitfalls of having one but not the other.

There's a right way and wrong way to find both growth and value stocks. What I mean is this: Most people will start off looking for either one or the other, like looking for stocks with the biggest growth rates first, and then narrowing those stocks down to the ones with the smallest P/E ratios.

But if the biggest growth rate stocks all had high P/E ratios (let's say in excess of 20 or more, for example), are you really finding the best of the value stocks? No. You're only finding the growth stocks with the lowest valuations—even though they may be quite high.

Likewise, if you first screened for the lowest P/E ratios, and then narrowed that list down to the ones with the biggest growth rates; if the lowest

P/E stocks all had subpar growth rates, you'd only be selecting the best of the subpar growth stocks and not really getting both the growth and value you were looking for.

Some try to overcome this by plugging in classical metrics like P/Es under 20 and growth rates over 20. But you'll have a ton of stocks filling up that list, and you'd be digging through a bunch of average stocks, not the best of each category.

So how does one find these stocks the right way? I do it by using a uniform ranking on both categories. And that's the focus of this screen. It focuses on companies with the highest growth rates *and* the lowest P/E ratios, all at the same time.

Parameters and Methodology

The screen starts off with the following parameters:

- **Companies with 5 Year Historical Growth Rates in the top 20 percentile of all companies.**
  Using a uniform rank of 1–99 (99 being the best growth rates), I screened for stocks ranked 80 or better, meaning better than 80% of all the other companies out there in terms of growth rates.

- **Companies that also happened to have the lowest P/E ratios— lower than 80% of all other companies.**
  Again, using a uniform rank of 1–99 (this time 99 having the lowest P/Es), I screened for stocks ranked 80 or better, meaning companies with P/Es lower than 80% of all the other companies out there.

Explaining the Rankings Methods

How do uniform, histogram, and ordinal rankings work? Read on to find out.

Uniform Rank
In short, a uniform rank will place approximately equal numbers of companies in each fractile. If there are several fractiles of companies with the same value for the variable selected, they will be assigned a rank in the middle of the range they would otherwise fill.

What? If I had a set of data with different values, I could create a number of categories (let's call them buckets) to put them in. From there, I'd group the data into approximately equal sized data sets and put them into different buckets. Once that's done, I could determine which groups had the higher values (vs. the other data sets) and which ones had the lower values, comparatively speaking. It allows the user to make a quick determination of which data points are in the top or bottom percentile of any given set of values.

One can also use a histogram ranking method or even an ordinal ranking method. Each one can be more appropriate, based on what the user is trying to accomplish. For our purposes, the uniform rank is best.

Histogram Rank

If you're interested: A histogram rank will create equal-length intervals based on high and low values within each group. This shows the distribution of values on a selected item. However, if there's a wide range of values with a number of outliers, this ranking method will have small numbers of companies in the top or bottom ranks and a large number of companies in each of the middle ranks. (Because of the wide range of values and potential for outliers, we're not using this method.)

Ordinal Rank

An ordinal rank simply ranks the data by their values based on the number or data in the group. (With so many stocks and values, the ordinal method would create an unwieldy list and is not suited for this task. Ordinal ranks are best for smaller sets of data and values.)

I round out the screen with the following items:

- **Zacks Rank <= 2**
  Strong Buy and Buys as ranked by Zacks.
- It's all applied to stocks with a **Price >= $5,** with an **Average 20-Day Trading Volume >= 100,000 shares or more.**

So with this screen, we're not starting with one and then looking for the other. The order of the aforementioned parameters is irrelevant. If I switched it around, I'd get the same stocks, because essentially I'm demanding that the companies have to have *both* growth rates *and* valuations in the 80th percentile, i.e., better than 80% of all the other stocks out there. Only the stocks in the 80th percentile on each item make it through.

In other words, the screen will not give you the absolute highest growth rates or absolute lowest P/E ratios, unless it also happens to score the best on the other metric as well. For example, a stock with a growth rate of 100% in the 96th percentile will not come through if the P/E is 75 and in the 15th percentile. Only stocks that are in the top percentiles on *both* items are selected.

The accompanying example shows what a screened list would look like with the uniform ranks in the report. The higher the ranks, the better they scored. And while each score may be slightly different, they are all in the 80th percentile on both growth (best growth rates) and value (lowest P/Es) (see Figure 11.1).

FIGURE 11.1 Growth and Value (Uniform Ranking) Screenshot

Company	Ticker	5 Yr. Hist. EPS Rank 1-99 (higher # = best EPS)	5 Yr Hist EPS Gr	P/E Rank (1-99) 1-99 (higher # = lowest P/E)	P/E using 12 mo EPS	Current Price	Avg Daily Vol 20 days	Zacks Rank
NONFOOD RETAIL WHOLESALE								
Cash Am Intl	CSH	84	20.57%	82	9.94	$35.10	173,776	2
DRUGS								
Astrazeneca Plc	AZN	80	17.19%	87	8.52	$51.22	819,069	2
Hi Tech Pharma	HITK	88	27.34%	87	8.43	$20.58	127,492	1
MEDICAL CARE								
Healthspring In	HS	88	26.95%	86	8.86	$26.77	797,635	2
Geneva Health	GTIV	91	33.16%	87	8.64	$22.11	298,066	1
TELECOMMUNICATIONS								
Hexe Corp	HRS	84	20.54%	81	10.06	$44.78	753,406	2
TELECOMMUNICATIONS SERVICES								
Partner Comm	PTNR	92	34.88%	84	9.38	$16.29	188,971	2
INSURANCE								

By the way, one of the reasons why I assigned the lower P/Es a higher ranking value (aside from it making sense) is that I could then add up which stocks had the highest total score to determine the best ones on those combined metrics.

Every time you run the screen, you'll get a list of market-beating growth rates with the lowest P/Es. What a great combination.

And of course, you can apply this ranking technique to virtually any item.

Sales and Margins

While everybody understands sales, margins might bring up a few question marks. So let's start at the beginning.

First and foremost, sales are *the* most important thing to a company. Everything else stems from that. Without sales, there really wouldn't be anything else to analyze. Sales growth numbers show you how that company is growing.

However, just because sales are increasing doesn't always mean that profits are increasing too. Sales at the expense of profits does not work. So paying attention to profit margins is another important thing to look at.

Sales at the expense of profits does not work.

Margin is simply a ratio and the calculation is: Net Income divided by Sales.

So if a company's margin is 15% for instance, that means the company's net income is 15 cents for every $1 of sales it makes. But if a company's expenses are growing faster than their sales, this will reduce their margins. In general, a company with increasing margins is becoming more profitable and is better managed, i.e., their costs are under control.

In addition to a company's sales, look at their earnings too, of course. But take a look at their profit margins as well. Are they going up or down? In other words, are they making more on each dollar of sales or less? This is important stuff to know.

In fact, I've seen plenty of examples of companies posting great numbers but getting smacked down because of decreasing margins. This, indeed, can make the difference between investors buying a company's earnings announcement or selling it.

Parameters and Methodology

The parameters for this strategy are:

- **12 Month Trailing Sales Growth (Current Quarter / 1 Quarter Ago) >= Relevant Industry Average**
  Looking for the top companies in their industries.
- **Current Net Margin >= 5 Year Average Net Margin**
  Steady to increasing profit margins are what we're after.
- **Current Net Margin >= Net Margin from 1 Quarter Ago**
  If a company's profit margin fell last quarter, there's a chance it might fall yet again. So we're excluding those companies whose margins fell in the previous quarter.

- **Zacks Rank <= 2**

  You see me use the Zacks Rank a lot. And that's because the Zacks Rank works. It's one of the best, if not the best rating system out there. As I've mentioned, one of the main components to the Zacks Rank is earnings estimate revisions. The whole idea being that companies receiving upward earnings estimate revisions have a tendency of receiving even more upward earnings estimate revisions. This helps paint a solid picture moving forward. And this ties perfectly into a sales and margins screen because earnings are directly related to margins. Based on what the margin is, this will determine what you're left with as profit. So the Zacks Rank is an ideal addition to hopefully finding companies that will see an increase in margins.

Take note: Some aggressive growth companies may see tightening margins at times. As a company expands its business and increases its operations, that can come at a cost sometimes. This is will often be overlooked, however, if the growth rate makes up for this. This can be expected for some companies in the earlier part of their growth cycle. Doesn't mean it has to happen. But this is often forgiven for these aggressive growers.

Aside from aggressive expansion, however, decreasing margins are not a good sign, and you'd be well served to look at a company's margins after each and every earnings report. Seeing what's happening to a company's margins can be an early warning signal for good times ahead or trouble on the horizon.

Relative Price Strength

This is an interesting screen. It doesn't quite belong in the price momentum category, because it focuses on relative price movement. In reality, that could mean stocks that happen to be going down less than the market. (Not the exact definition of momentum.) This, of course, also means beating the market on the way up, too.

This is one of those items that has great application but doesn't really fit in a category of its own. Although I've found myself using the relative price strength items in every style of screen at one time or another.

In this screen, we're looking for stocks that are outperforming the market. And if they're performing better, it's likely because there's a good reason for them to be doing so. If not, they probably wouldn't be.

But once again, this is about *relative* price strength. I point this out because there are periods when virtually everything is going down. So screening for absolute positive price changes will oftentimes come up with zero results in these periods, just when you need them the most.

On the other hand, when the market is doing nothing but going up, you want to get into the pacesetters and outperformers, not the laggards or underperformers that are going up only because the rising tide is raising all the ships.

If your stocks are consistently going up less than the market, or going down more, you're leaving money on the table by sticking with those relative price strength losers.

But looking for the relative price strength winners will always put the outperformers on your list in both good times and bad.

Parameters and Methodology

This screen combines the relative price change winners with a little bit of growth and a little bit of value as well. The screen starts off with:

- **Relative % Price Change—12 Weeks > 0**
- **Relative % Price Change—4 Weeks > 0**
- **Relative % Price Change—1 Week > 0**
  We're looking for stocks that are outperforming the S&P 500 over the last 12 weeks, 4 weeks, and 1 week.

By the way, this differs from the Big Money screen, not just on the time periods, but also in its instruction. The Big Money screen seeks the best price performers in absolute terms. This screen, at this stage, is only looking for stocks that have outperformed the S&P—stocks that have outperformed on a relative basis. Then we'll add our fundamentals to this list of stocks.

The fundamentals that are added to this screen are:

- **Zacks Rank = 1**
  We're pulling out the big gun by including only the Zacks Rank 1s.
- **% Change in Current Year (F1) Estimates over last 4 Weeks > 0**
  To keep the positive fundamental outlook and to support the relative price performance, I'm requiring each stock to have received upward earnings estimate revisions over the last four weeks.
- **Price to Sales <= 1**
  Can't leave my favorite valuation metric off.

- **Price to Sales Bottom # 10**
  To keep the list to a manageable size, we'll call on the Price to Sales item once again and limit it to the 10 stocks with the lowest P/S ratio.
- All of the parameters were applied to stocks trading at a **Price >= $5** with an **Average 20-Day Volume of >= 100,000**.

Results

Over the last 10 years (2000–2009), using a one-week holding period, this strategy has produced an average annual return of 37.5% for a total compounded return of 2,352.0% (see Figure 11.2).

FIGURE 11.2   Relative Price Strength (2000–2009, 1-week rebalance)

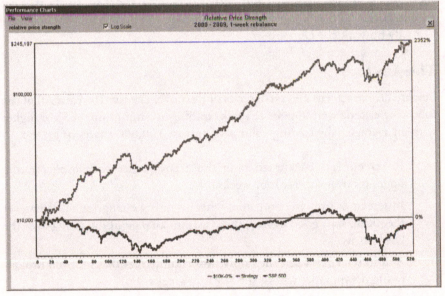

I also like that it has shown less risk (lower maximum drawdown) than the market, coming in at *only* –39.7% at its worst, to the S&P 500s –54.7%. That's more than –27% less risk and volatility than the market.

While this Relative Price Strength strategy is not going to unseat our top price momentum strategies any time soon, it's a great screen to see what new stocks are coming through. And any stock showing up on this list is worth an additional look.

Broker Rating Upgrades

Let's take a look at some more "stuff that works." Here's one we all know and love. In fact, I'm sure we've all had the pleasure of waking up one morning and seeing that a broker has upgraded one of our stocks. Usually that stock is in for a good day, and likely several days or more after that.

Unfortunately, we've probably all had the experience of waking up and seeing one of our stocks downgraded, too. Usually that stock is in for a rough day, and probably more days to follow.

While nobody can perfectly predict an upgrade or guard against a downgrade, it's important to know how the market reacts to these things, so you can stay in your upgraded winners (or buy if you're on the fence) and consider getting out if a downgrade comes your way.

Tests have proven that stocks with broker rating upgrades outperform those that don't get upgraded and outperform, even more so, stocks that get downgraded.

By how much? Let's see.

The Test

I created three screens and ran a series of tests over the last 10 years. All of the following criteria were applied to stocks trading at a minimum of $5 or higher with an average daily trading volume of at least 100,000 shares or greater.

> In screen 1: I backtested only those companies with broker rating upgrades over the last four weeks.

> In screen 2: I tested companies with no rating change at all. Whatever the rating was, good or bad, there was no change in the rating over the last four weeks.

> And in screen 3: I screened only those companies that received broker-rating downgrades within the last four weeks.

I then backtested each screen using a one-week rebalancing period, which checked the rating change status every week.

Results

The tests pretty much confirmed what I had already suspected—but the magnitude was a lot larger than I thought. In Figure 11.3, you can see how each of the three screen tests stacked up.

FIGURE 11.3 Broker Rating Upgrades vs. Broker Rating Downgrades (2000–2009)

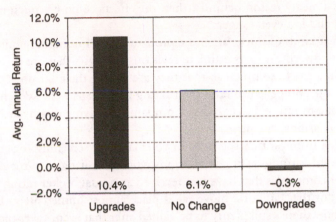

The broker rating upgrades over the last 10 years showed an average annual return of 10.4%. The ones with no rating change at all showed an average annual return of 6.1%. And the stocks with broker rating downgrades actually showed a loss of −0.3%.

So the upgrades beat the ones with no rating change by nearly twice as much. And they outperformed those with downgrades even more. In fact, that was the difference between making money and losing money.

As I've said before, I'm not that concerned about the absolute broker rating per se, and whether it's good or bad. But I am interested in the broker rating change. It's the change in the broker rating that is most important. And as these statistics show, broker rating changes indeed can and do influence stock prices, if only at least for the short-term.

It's the change in the broker rating that is important.

The next time one of your stocks is upgraded or downgraded, remember this study and how the odds stack up—whether they're for you or against you.

Of course, every downgrade is not going to result in a loss. But the statistics clearly show there is a likelihood of at least some short-term pain.

Likewise, every upgrade is not going to result in a gain, but the odds are most definitely in your favor that there will be some short-term upside. If there's a meaty reason behind either, the effects could be much more pronounced and last even longer.

What kinds of stocks are more prone to broker rating upgrades? Stocks receiving upward earnings estimate revisions. Analysts that are getting more bullish on a stock, so much so that they are raising their earnings estimates, will be more compelled to raise their rating outlook as well. Which ones are more prone to rating downgrades? Companies receiving downward earnings estimate revisions, of course.

Aside from putting the odds in your favor by screening for companies with upward earnings estimate revisions, you can cut right to the chase and screen for companies that have just received an actual broker rating upgrade. Yes, a lot of that euphoric move takes place almost immediately. But these studies show there's still plenty to be gained after that event takes place in the days and weeks afterward.

By the way, just like we did with the valuation studies in Chapter 9 using the P/E, P/S, PB, P/CF, and PEG ratio, I also ran a test to see how the Broker Rating Upgrades would do when adding the Zacks Rank #1 to it. Not surprising, the returns more than doubled, going from an annual 10.4% to an annual 22.7% (see Figure 11.4.)

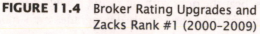

FIGURE 11.4 Broker Rating Upgrades and Zacks Rank #1 (2000–2009)

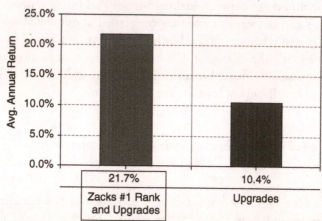

With an average of 43 stocks passing this screen each period, you'll likely want to narrow that list down to a more manageable size. So experiment by adding in some of your favorite criteria from your favorite style to it. As it is now, the screen isn't a Momentum screen or an Aggressive Growth screen. It's not Value or Growth and Income. It's just an excellent idea that works. But you can build upon it however you choose to reflect your style preferences.

New Analyst Coverage

While we're talking about broker rating upgrades, another interesting dynamic is seeing a stock receive new analyst coverage.

One of the things that generates analyst coverage is investor interest. And as new coverage is initiated, it becomes more visible, which in turn, means potentially more demand (read higher prices). This is often the case because analysts almost always initiate coverage with a positive recommendation. (Why write a research report on a company that's not widely followed only to say it stinks?)

And when it comes to companies with little to no analyst coverage, that one new recommendation can sometimes give portfolio managers the validation they need to build a position. (And the more money they can invest, the more they can potentially influence prices.)

The best way to use this information is to look for companies with analyst coverage that has increased over the last four weeks. Look at the number of analyst recommendations now in comparison to the number of analyst recommendations four weeks ago. An increase in coverage is bullish whereas a decrease in coverage is bearish.

It's typically more bullish if the increase went from none to one or if the coverage was minimal to begin with. (Going from 25 to 26 isn't going to have the same impact because that 26th analyst isn't discovering anything "new.") But increased coverage is better than decreased coverage—assuming the coverage is positive, of course.

Parameters

Here's a screen that looks at stocks that had two or less analysts covering them within the last four weeks, but now have three or more, meaning new coverage was just recently added.

- **Number of Broker Ratings four weeks ago <=2**
  No more than two analysts were covering the stock four weeks ago.
- **Number of Broker Ratings now >= 3**
  There are at least three analysts covering the stock now.

- **Average Broker Rating <= 2**
  Once again, I'm not that concerned about the rating itself. But since analyst recommendations tend to be bullishly biased, I'd prefer to not have them be bearish.

And for good measure . . .

- **% Change in Q(1) Estimates >= 0**
  Upward revisions for the current quarter.

- **% Change in F(1) Estimates >= 0**
  Upward revisions for the current year. Companies that receive upward estimate revisions have a tendency of receiving even more upward estimate revisions. This, in combination with the stock's increased visibility due to new coverage, can be quite powerful.

- I'm applying all of the preceding parameters to stocks with **Prices >= $5** and an **Average 20-Day Volume >= 50,000 shares**.

Once again, the screen I set up had it going from two analysts covering it to three. However, you can set this screen up for fewer analysts or more. You can go from one to two or five to six or whatever you choose. You might be surprised at how many you find each week.

Run this screen in tandem with the broker rating upgrade screen. This new coverage is often bullish. And the prices typically respond accordingly. Plus, a new bullish broker rating can serve as an upgrade to the average broker rating if it improves it.

Top Stocks, Top Industries

Let's look at another item that can put the odds in your favor for stock picking success: sticking with stocks in the best industries.

We've all heard the old adage; half of a stock's price movement can be attributed to the group that it's in. In fact, I've said it at least once or twice already in this book. And I've also used it in some of the screens. Now let's take a look at some statistics to see just how profitable it is to be in the best industries.

The first step is to determine how you're going to rank the industries. In other words, what item will you use to determine if an industry is good or bad? You'll need an item that has indisputably proven itself to be an excellent indicator of stock price movement. So for this, I'm going to use the Zacks Rank. More specifically, the Zacks Industry Rank.

With the best Zacks Rank stocks beating the market in 20 of the last 22 years, it's a highly predicative item. And since an industry is nothing more than a group of stocks in a similar business, this is a perfect way to rank the industry.

How is the Zacks Industry Rank created? It's simply the average Zacks Rank for all of the stocks in the industry. So an industry with an average Zacks Rank (Zacks Industry Rank) of 1.6 is better than an industry with an average Zacks Rank of 1.9. (By the way, the Zacks Rank can also be applied to sectors, too. What's this called? The Zacks Sector Rank, of course.)

The test was quite simple: I put our expanded industries (also known as X industries—all 261 of them) into two groups: the top half (better half, i.e., the industries with the best average Zacks Rank) and the bottom half (the industries with the worst average Zacks Rank).

It was no contest. Over the last 10 years, rebalancing the screens each week, the top half beat the bottom half by a factor of nearly 4 to 1 (266.9% vs. 73.7%) (see Figure 11.5). The line on top is the performance of the best industries. The one below it is the performance for the worst industries.

FIGURE 11.5 Top 50% Zacks Ranked Industries vs. Bottom 50% Zacks Ranked Industries (2000–2009, 1-week rebalance)

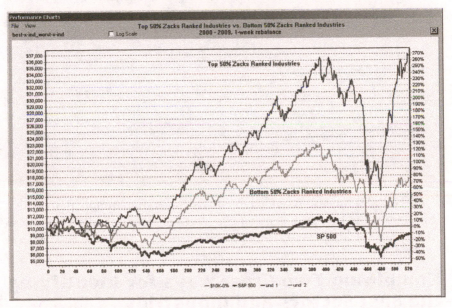

Keep in mind that even the worst industries had some Zacks Rank 1s in it. And even the best industries had some Zacks Rank 5s in it. That goes to show the power of simply being in the best group.

What would happen if I applied only the Zacks Rank #1s to just the top Zacks Ranked Industries? Even better. The next chart shows a comparison of the Top 50% of Zacks Ranked Industries with all of the Ranks included vs. the Top 50% of Industries with only the Zacks Rank #1 stocks included. Both did great. But it's clear that selecting the best stocks in the best groups can increase your returns even more. This study showed that the Top 50% of Industries with only the Zacks Rank #1s selected added to the already impressive returns by a factor of over 3.5 times (963.4% total return vs. 266.9% total return) (see Figure 11.6).

FIGURE 11.6   Top 50% Zacks Ranked Industries (all Zacks Ranks vs. only Zacks Rank #1s) (2000–2009, 1-week rebalance)

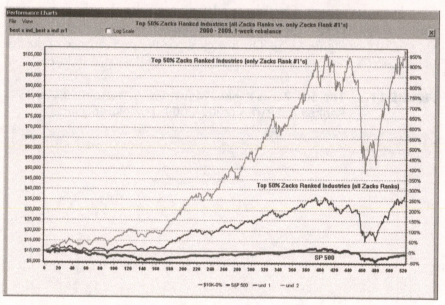

This idea can also be added to any style of screen. Simply put, picking stocks from the best groups presents a clear advantage. And even more so when you're picking the top stocks within them.

Combining Two Great Ways for Identifying the Best Sectors and Industries

Here's another great way to rank the Sectors and Industries. It's a combination of two of my favorite group analysis screens.

Using the Zacks Rank (for stocks, sectors, and industries) has clearly proven to be a winning approach. You'll remember, however, that I also like to screen for the top sectors based on the percentage of stocks trading within 10% of their 52-week high (see Chapter 7 for reference).

Both are great approaches and I'll often combine the two to create a unique list of the top groups. Here's how to do it.

1. Rank the Sectors based on the average Zacks Rank.
2. Rank the Sectors based on the percentage of stocks trading within 10% of their 52-week highs.

Once again, these are my two favorite ways to rate the sectors. Groups with the best Zacks Ranks outperform those with worse Zacks Ranks. And groups with a higher percentage of stocks trading at or near their 52-week highs, shows something positive is happening to the entire group.

First, I numerically rank the sectors with the best Zacks Rank. Then I do the same for the sectors with the highest percentage of new highs. I'll then add the scores together from each method to get a composite. And then lastly, I'll re-sort the total score from lowest to highest to give me the best Sectors.

This way I'm getting the best Zacks Ranked groups (those with the highest upward earnings estimate revisions) as well as the groups with the best responsiveness as evidenced by their price performance and their position within their 52-week high price range.

I have found this to be a great combination for identifying the best groups and something you might want to give a try.

Earnings Yield

This screening technique is not only a great way to determine a stock's attractiveness (read undervalued or overvalued), but it's also a great way to determine the overall market's attractiveness as well.

A stock's earnings yield measures just that, the anticipated yield (or return) an investment in a stock could give you based on the earnings and the price paid for the stock.

The calculation is the inverse of the P/E ratio. So a stock trading at a price of $35 with earnings of $3 has a P/E ratio of 11.67. This means it's selling at 11.67 times earnings. Another way of looking at it is that you're paying $11.67 for $1 of earnings.

The earnings yield is calculated as earnings/price. Using the same example, a stock with $3 of earnings trading at a price of $35 ($3/$35) has an earnings yield of 0.0857 or 8.57%. The earnings yield, also known as the E/P ratio, is expressed as a percentage. So a yield of 8.57% would also mean 8.57 cents of earnings for $1 of investment.

The earnings yield, of course, can change as the prices and earnings change. The same is true for the P/E ratio as well. However, the most common way people will use this ratio is to compare it to other stocks and to compare the yields to the 10 Year T-Bill. Conventional wisdom has it that, if the yield on the stock market (S&P 500, for example) is lower than the yield on the 10 Year T-Bill, then stocks might be considered overvalued.

If the yield on the S&P 500 is greater than the 10 Year T-Bill, stocks would be considered undervalued. The theory behind this is that bonds and stocks are competing for investors' dollars. And to attract investment interest in stocks, a higher yield needs to be paid to the stock investor for the extra risk being assumed compared to the virtual risk-free investment offered in U.S.-backed Treasuries.

If earnings go up, the yield goes up. If earnings go down, so does the yield. Prices also affect the yield, but they move inversely. If prices go up, the yield goes down. And if prices go down, the yield goes up.

In June of 2007, the yield on the 10 Year T-Bill was 4.95%. However, the earnings yield on the S&P 500 was 4.19%. Not much of a risk premium on a risk-based investment.

Remember, if the earnings yield on stocks is below the T-Bill rate, stocks are considered overvalued. (I should point out that within months, the market began to falter.)

I also happened to write about this in March of 2009. At that time, the earnings yield on the S&P 500 using the 12-month projected earnings estimate was 9.51%, compared to the 10 Year Treasury of 2.89%.

With yields well above the 10 Year, conventional wisdom said that stocks were undervalued. Of course, they could have continued to get more undervalued. But the market was quickly bid up, resulting in one of the largest rallies we've ever seen. And the earnings yield spotted this value when almost no one did.

So where is it now? As of early September 2010, the earnings yield for the S&P is 8.08%, compared to the 10 Year Treasury yield of 2.61%.

So the market isn't as much of a bargain as it was back in March of 2009, but it's still way better than the 10 Year and suggests that stocks are still the more attractive investment. (By the time you read this in this book, it'll be well past September of 2010, so we'll know which way the market has gone from here.)

Either way, the earnings yield is a great way to compare the potential returns on the stock market and other competing investments. The pros do it. And you can, too.

Calculating Price Targets

Have you ever looked at an analyst's price target and wondered where they came up with that number? I hate to say it, but I've looked at enough price targets to conclude that I shouldn't be looking at price targets.

I've seen some so far out there that I couldn't imagine how a company could even get near it. And at other times, so low (and seemingly unattended to) that the price is already well above it, meaning you would have gotten out just as the biggest part of the stock's move was beginning.

True, price targets aren't meant to be set-in-stone promises, and they shouldn't be used in a vacuum either. But it'd be great if they could make a bit more sense and be a little more realistic.

So here's a way to create your own price targets.

Many people use P/E ratios to determine a company's perceived under- or overvaluation. But you can also use the P/E ratio to determine upside and downside price targets as well.

The two most common P/E ratios used are the:

- P/Es using the Trailing 12 Months (or 4 quarters) of Earnings
- P/Es using the F1 (or Current Fiscal Year) Estimates

First, the P/E ratio is simply price divided by earnings. For example, if a stock's price is $30 and its earnings are $1.25, then its P/E would be 24. ($30 price or "P"/$1.25 earnings or "E" = 24 P/E ratio). If that stock's earnings rose to $2.00, the P/E would now be 15 ($30 price/$2.00 earnings = 15 P/E).

And the most logical conclusion would be to see the stock's price rise until its most recent multiple (or P/E ratio) of 24 was hit again. Why is this so logical? Because people had just been willing to pay 24 times a company's earnings and they probably still are (or thereabouts) if there's reason to believe the company's earnings will continue to improve.

So $2.00 (earnings) × 24 (the previous multiple or P/E ratio) = $48 (price). So the price target I'd have for that stock would now be $48. (And you could do the same thing on the downside, too.)

What you'll find most of the time is that a stock's P/E ratio using EPS actuals is higher than its P/E ratio using its forward estimates. That's because of the uncertainty regarding projected earnings vs. the certainty of actual earnings.

As the company continues to report (and meets its projections), the forward P/E ratio typically increases, which means the stock price increases as the earnings projections are coming to fruition.

And as more optimism grows over future earnings growth, you may see the P/E ratio grow even more, getting even higher than its previous multiple.

The calculation to figure out your stock's price target is:

Price × [(current P/E)/(forward P/E)] = future price (or price target)

In other words, let's say a stock's price was $50 and its current P/E was 20. Let's also say its forward P/E was 15.

That's $50 × (20/15) = $66.50 price target.

Another way of saying this is: 15 goes into 20 = 1.33 times. So $50 multiplied by 1.33 equals your price target of $66.50.

Once again, this makes sense, because if investors are willing to pay 20 times earnings now, assuming the company's earnings forecast looks good, why wouldn't they be willing to pay at least that in the future?

Finding stocks trading under their calculated price targets is easy with a stock screener. Let's see how to set one up.

Parameters and Methodology

The screen I'm running finds stocks with price targets of at least 10% more than their current price.

- **Price Target >= 1.1 * the Current Price**

  Current Price × (current PE / forward P/E) >= 1.1 × Current Price

  That means we're looking for stocks whose price target is at least 10% higher than its current price.

And for good measure:

- **P/E Ratio < the Median for its Industry**
  Stocks with P/Es that are less than the median P/E for their Industry, should have more room for P/E growth.

     In fact, these two dynamics work great together. Not only are we expecting to see the forward P/E climb to a multiple that people have already expressed comfort in paying for actual earnings, but if the Industry is doing well and the stock's P/E is under the median, we can also hope to see the P/E expand even further (multiple expansion). If people are willing to pay X times earnings for companies in a particular Industry, there's no reason to believe that they wouldn't be willing to pay a little more than what they were used to for that stock now, especially if the company's outlook is even stronger.

This screen produces plenty of great stocks to consider trading that are well under their price targets. And this screening item can be added to any of the screening styles.

Note that the Price Target screening item should not be used as a stand-alone screen for picking stocks. The fundamentals are an integral part of the stock selection process. If the fundamentals are expected to deteriorate going forward, there's no reason for a company's future P/E to grow to the old P/E. Just the opposite, it should decline because investors will expect to pay less for lower earnings.

But by adding this item to any of your favorite screens or simply just adding this to a screen's report, you can get a better idea of the stock's future price expectations and targets.

Summary

In the preceding chapters, we covered each of the four main trading styles with lots of great screens and plenty of winning trading strategies. In this chapter, we showed how to incorporate the best of two or more strategies into one. As you can see, the combinations are virtually endless. But all you have to do is decide which styles and stock picking characteristics are right for you and incorporate them accordingly.

Things like broker rating upgrades or new analyst coverage are not the sole property of any particular style, of course. Nor are things like how to calculate price targets or earnings yield. Those would simply be categorized under "stuff that works." And that's a toolbox anyone can dig into.

The beauty of it all is that there is not just one way that works. There are hundreds of ways that work. Likely thousands. And methods that haven't even been discovered yet. But once you've identified which style or styles are right for you and it has been proven to work, you'll be on your way to becoming a better trader and achieving your trading goals.

In the next chapter, we take a look at Technical Analysis. This too, can be applied to any and all styles. We'll start off by looking at what kind of information a stock's price and volume readings are really saying about the stock itself and what others in the marketplace appear to be saying about the stock as well.

Chapter 12

Applying Technical Analysis

N ow let's turn our attention to Technical Analysis. While Fundamental Analysis (FA) looks at the value and outlook for a stock, Technical Analysis (TA) essentially shows the demand for a stock and how it perceives those fundamental valuations. This chapter goes into that and more as we detail several price and volume screens along with moving averages as well.

I should note that some fundamental guys pooh-pooh TA while some technical guys do the same for FA. But nowadays, most people give both techniques the respect they deserve.

I have a long history of using fundamental analysis to pick winning stocks. But my experience using TA goes back just as far. That being said, I prefer to look at TA more as a confirming indicator, if FA is used first. In other words, once my fundamental criteria are met, I can then look at the charts. But if TA is used first, it can act as a spotting indicator. In other words, a method to put stocks with certain technical analysis characteristics on my radar screen so I can then layer my fundamental analysis on top.

You can also do both at the same time and those are the screens we're going to start off with.

Increasing Price and Volume

What's better than increasing stock prices? Increasing volume to go with it!

Rising prices and increasing volume of a stock can be a sign that new buyers are coming in and some short sellers may be giving up. But rising prices and decreasing volume suggests a lack of new buyers and waning underlying pressure.

Just as a ball on top of a hose needs more and more water pressure to push it higher; the same is true to an extent in the markets. Once you let up on that water pressure, the ball will fall back down. And when buying demand eases up, so will the market.

I also like seeing those volume bars at the bottom of a price chart moving up as the price does because it's a great way to spot institutional buying. Regular everyday investors do not have the power to move the market or to make a noticeable blip on a volume's bar chart. But big institutional traders do. And nothing can move a market more than seeing these guys pile in. Especially since it can often take them weeks, if not longer, to build a position. This volume increase shows that the market might be getting ready to respond in a big way.

When you hear someone say the market was up or down in big volume, that's more than just an interesting fact. To the technically savvy, that can act as a clue to investor sentiment.

Parameters and Methodology

Let's construct a basic screen to find just those kinds of companies.

- **Price >= $5**
  I still prefer to look at stocks over $5. This is a not a requirement for this screen. But it happens to be my personal preference.
- **Average 20-Day Volume >= 100,000**
  Want to see volume starting from a respectable level. If there's no volume to begin with, any increase will get picked up, but will be virtually meaningless. I believe 50,000 to 100,000 is a fine daily level to start from.
- **Recent Week's Price > Price from 1 Week Ago**
- **Price from 1 Week Ago > Price from 2 Weeks Ago**
  The preceding price items look for two weeks of price increases.
- **Weekly Volume > Weekly Volume from 1 Week Ago**
- **Weekly Volume from 1 Week Ago > Weekly Volume from 2 Weeks Ago**
  The volume items above look for two weeks of volume increases. This combination of both price and volume increases helps me see true demand that seems to be building over time. There may be an occasional light day here and there, but in total, I want to see it growing week by week.

Note that while the daily average volume is 100,000, that means the weekly average volume will be 500,000 or more. Each successive week should see an even larger total in volume.

By the way, "only" one-week volume spikes will not make it through. The two-week minimum keeps these occurrences off this screen. This is important for me because sometimes, one-week volume spurts can be meaningless. (Not always, as we'll see in another section, but sometimes.) And worse, humongous one-week price spikes (often it's really only just one day but enough to move the needle on the weekly bar) can often coincide with end-runs or turning points. The second week's price *and* volume gives this screen its value and reduces the chances of unimportant price and volume events getting through, not to mention potentially detrimental volume spikes showing up on this screen. If a stock can string together a second week of increasing price and volume, now I'm ready to pay attention.

What kind of volume increases are we looking for? Not excessive. We simply want to see an increase over a couple of weeks. Noticeable, but not irregular; 10, 20, 50, even a couple hundred percent. The key is two weeks in a row or more.

This basic screen will generate a varying number of stocks based on how the overall market is performing. When there are a lot of stocks coming through, I'll often expand the screen to encompass one more week of price gains and one more week of volume increases. If forced to choose between the additional week of increased price or increased volume, I'll take the volume. My experience has found that extra week to be quite meaningful for spotting the potential bigger gainers down the pike.

TA and FA Winners

Let's put this into practice now with a fully fleshed-out strategy that combines both fundamental analysis with technical analysis. This strategy could just as easily have gone into the "All Style" group, but the TA portion is an instrumental piece to this and would not work nearly as well without it.

Parameters and Methodology

- **Zacks Rank <= 2**
  Strong Buys and Buys from Zacks. Why wouldn't I?
- **Price to Sales < Median for its X Industry**
  My favorite value item.
- **Estimated One Year EPS Growth > Median for its X Industry**
  Let's give it a reason to move.

- **Price × Volume >= $500,000**
  Bare minimum.
- **Recent Week's Volume > Volume from 1 Week Ago**
  Nice.
- **Volume from 1 Week Ago > Volume from 2 Weeks Ago**
  Accumulation.
- **Volume from 2 Week's Ago > Volume from 3 Weeks Ago**
  There's that magical third week. Is that institutional buying?
- **% Change in Price 24 Weeks Top # 30**
- **% Change in Price 12 Weeks Top # 20**
- **% Change in Price 4 Weeks Top # 7**
  I pulled out some of the Big Money Price action at the end. This was an easy way of getting my price momentum inputted, but gave it a little leeway for a missed week here or there. Even the best stocks will pull back from time to time and we wanted to be accommodating enough to keep solid performers from dropping off prematurely.

Results

Over the last 10 years, using a one-week rebalancing period, this strategy produced a compounded annual growth rate of 62.9% vs. the S&P's –1.3% (see Figure 12.1).

FIGURE 12.1 TA and FA Winners (2000–2009, 1-week rebalance)

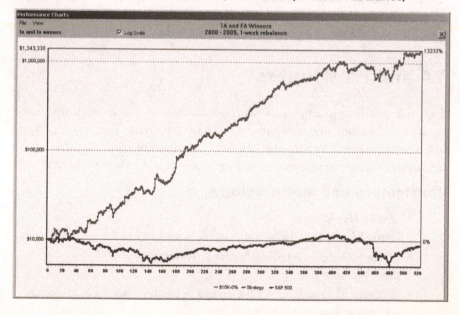

Once again, high-flying strategies like this are not without their risk and volatility. The maximum drawdown for this strategy using a one-week holding period was –40.9%. When you add in transaction costs, that could both lower the return and increase the user's drawdown.

The strategy also works well with a four-week holding period generating an average annual return of 42.9%. Although, the average maximum drawdown was a bit higher at –45.7% and was seen during the bear market of 2008. (See Figure 12.2.)

FIGURE 12.2 TA and FA Winners (2000–2009, 4-week rebalance)

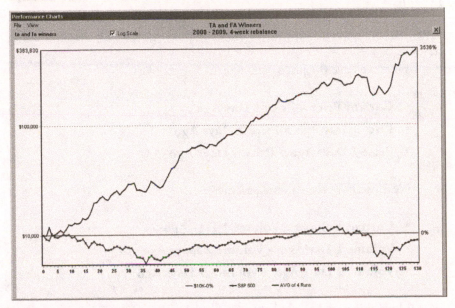

In a testament to the importance of the volume portion of this screen, I tested it without the required three weeks of volume increases. The screen held up (which is also a testament to the other criteria), but without it, the returns were reduced by as much as 20.5 points on the one-week and 8.1 points on the four-week. It's a still a pretty good screen without the increased volume. But it's even better with it!

3 Days Up, Price and Volume

Here's another version of the Price and Volume screen (looking at daily price and volume action rather than weekly) that I use quite regularly when I'm looking for stocks that are getting hot and gathering momentum.

This screen looks for stocks that have shown three days worth of increasing prices accompanied by three days worth of increasing volume. I have found that stocks meeting these criteria have a tendency to keep on moving in that same direction. For instance, if a stock is falling on increasing volume, it could be a sign that people are getting out and that new shorts (bets that a stock will go down) are being put on.

Likewise, if a stock is moving higher on increased volume, it can be a sign that new buyers are coming in (and maybe with more conviction) and some short sellers may be giving up (buying back their bets for lower prices).

The parameters for this are easy. And the price and volume pattern that this screen looks for is used to spot a potentially strengthening market.

First, we have the price parameters:

- **Current Price > Price 1 Day Ago**
- **Price 1 Day Ago > Price 2 Days Ago**
- **Price 2 Days Ago > Price 3 Days Ago**

Next, we have the volume parameters:

- **Current Volume > Volume 1 Day Ago**
- **Volume 1 Day Ago > Volume 2 Days Ago**
- **Volume 2 Days Ago > Volume 3 Days Ago**

I love this one. Largely because, instead of focusing on just the biggest gainers (which often are one-day events that have been missed), this spots price momentum *and* accumulation. Very bullish signs!

Also, I mentioned in the previous section that I like looking for at least two weeks of increasing price and volume because sometimes, one-week volume spikes can be meaningless. All of that is true. However, when I see a clear pattern of sequentially increasing price and volume, often that pattern of responsiveness distinguishes it from the other innocuous price and volume changes and makes it worth looking into.

I use the 3 Days Up, Price and Volume quite a bit. But I also use a few other iterations of this as well for completely different reasons.

I'm going to outline three additional variations of this strategy. One is for finding stocks that could be about to fall. Another is for finding stocks that should continue to fall. And the last one is for finding stocks that could be about ready to turn up.

Let's begin by looking for stocks about to fall.

3 Days Up in Price, 3 Days Down in Volume

Using three days again of both price and volume, this screen looks for stocks running out of gas.

Prices are going up but volume is dropping in each successive day. The market is running out of buyers. Or those that are buying are either too few or don't have enough conviction (not enough money behind it).

Just like the ball on top of a hose example we've discussed, if the water pressure from the hose lessens, that ball is going to fall. In this case, the volume is the water pressure and the stock price is the ball.

If volume is dropping while prices are moving up, it can often be a foreshadowing that prices could soon be falling.

Once again, this price and volume pattern is for spotting a potentially weakening market.

The screen starts off with the same rising price parameters:

- **Current Price > Price 1 Day Ago**
- **Price 1 Day Ago > Price 2 Days Ago**
- **Price 2 Days Ago > Price 3 Days Ago**

But next, it looks for decreasing volume:

- **Current Volume < Volume 1 Day Ago**
- **Volume 1 Day Ago < Volume 2 Days Ago**
- **Volume 2 Days Ago < Volume 3 Days Ago**

Pay attention to your stock if you see this happening to one that you're in.

3 Days Down in Price, 3 Days Up in Volume

This one is for spotting stocks heading lower that look like they mean business.

As I wrote earlier, if a stock is falling on increasing volume, it could be a sign that people are getting out and that new shorts (bets that a stock will go down) are being put on.

And that has been my experience.

This price and volume pattern is for spotting a potentially bearish market. The price parameters are first again, but this time we're looking for falling prices:

- **Current Price < Price 1 Day Ago**
- **Price 1 Day Ago < Price 2 Days Ago**
- **Price 2 Days Ago < Price 3 Days Ago**

The volume parameters on the other hand are rising.

- **Current Volume > Volume 1 Day Ago**
- **Volume 1 Day Ago > Volume 2 Days Ago**
- **Volume 2 Days Ago > Volume 3 Days Ago**

Stocks dropping on increased volume look set to continue in that same direction. Consider getting out if you find yourself in a stock like this.

3 Days Down in Price, 3 Days Down in Volume

Finally, I'll use this one to try and spot companies where the selling pressure (even if only temporarily) has run its course.

If prices are falling and volume is drying up, buyers are on the sidelines. But the sellers are gone, too. This can be a clue that it might be safe to go in the water. Once the selling has abated, these new buyers can come in.

The price and volume pattern on this one is used for spotting a potential end to a down move and an indicator that stocks are ready to move up.

The price parameters still show it falling:

- **Current Price < Price 1 Day Ago**
- **Price 1 Day Ago < Price 2 Days Ago**
- **Price 2 Days Ago < Price 3 Days Ago**

But the volume parameters are falling too.

- **Current Volume < Volume 1 Day Ago**
- **Volume 1 Day Ago < Volume 2 Days Ago**
- **Volume 2 Days Ago < Volume 3 Days Ago**

If the market has run out of sellers, it might just be time for the buyers to take their chance and get in. This screen helps spot those stocks.

This kind of TA (simple price and volume patterns) can be easily set up in a capable screener. And these screens, as simple as they may seem, can give you an early warning sign of a stock's future price direction, especially when combined with the appropriate long or short fundamentals.

Moving Averages

You can't have a discussion on TA without talking about moving averages. Fortunately, you don't have to be a technician to use them. They're pretty plain and simple and very straightforward. In the broadest sense, moving averages help define a trend. Pick a time frame and apply a moving average, and you can determine the trend or price bias over that period.

There are short-term moving averages, medium-term moving averages, and long-term moving averages. Let's look at the most popular ones and see what they mean. Short-term moving averages help gauge the short-term direction of the market, whereas longer-term moving averages take a bigger picture view.

Long-Term Moving Average (200-Day)

The 200-day moving average would be a long-term moving average.

In general, if a stock breaks the 200-day moving average on its way down, that's generally thought to be bearish, and the long-term trend could be turning lower. Tons of stocks did this in 2008 (see Figure 12.3).

FIGURE 12.3 200-Day Moving Average

The 200-day moving average can also act as support. If a stock comes down, but stops at the major moving average and then starts moving higher from there, it can act as a firm underpinning of support for the stock. Kind of like a moving trendline (see Figure 12.4).

FIGURE 12.4 200-Day Moving Average as Support

And just like breaking the 200-day moving average on the way down can oftentimes signal a downtrend, an upside breakout through the 200-day moving average can oftentimes signal the beginning of a new uptrend for a stock (see Figure 12.5).

FIGURE 12.5 200-Day Moving Average Upside Breakout

It was interesting listening to the news in mid-2009 because even non-financial news stations, when they gave their stock market update, would cite the 200-day moving average and speculate whether the market would get through it or not.

It was nice to see the general media outlets digging deeper and trying to inform their audience. But occasionally, I couldn't help but wonder how many times some of those newscasters had ever used those words before.

But they were right to talk about the 200-day moving average, because it's considered one of the most important moving averages for determining a long-term trend (or trend change).

Medium-Term Moving Average (50-Day)

The 50-day moving average can be quite useful as well. It's more of an intermediate snapshot of the price trend and is more sensitive than the longer-term 200-day moving average.

A rising moving average with the price trading above it is bullish (see Figure 12.6), whereas a descending moving average with the price trading below it is bearish (see Figure 12.7).

FIGURE 12.6 Rising 50-Day Moving Average Is Bullish

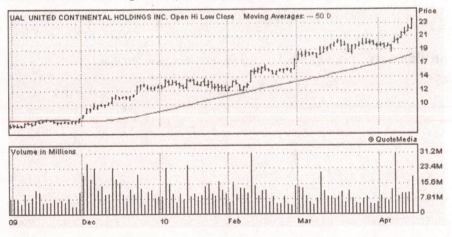

FIGURE 12.7 Descending 50-Day Moving Average Is Bearish

Short-Term Moving Averages (10-Day and 20-Day)

Even shorter-term signals can be seen with the 10-day and 20-day moving averages. A stock trading above the 10-day or 20-day moving average is bullish, especially when the moving average is moving up (see Figure 12.8).

FIGURE 12.8 Price Above 10-Day Moving Average/Bullish

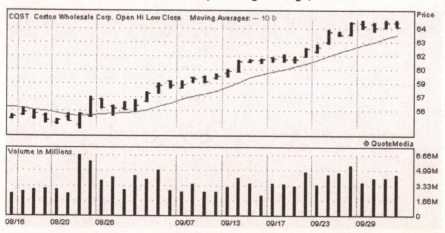

And a stock trading below the 10-day or 20-day moving average is bearish, especially when the moving average is going down (see Figure 12.9).

FIGURE 12.9   Price Below 20-Day Moving Average/Bearish

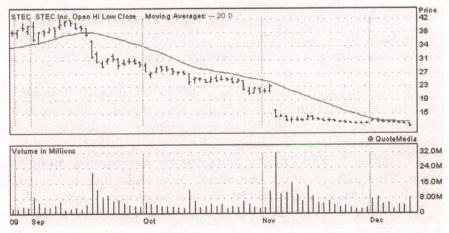

Moving average crossovers can also be valuable. When the quicker moving average (10-day, for example) is above the slower moving average (20-day), this is thought to be short-term bullish. Likewise, when the shorter-term moving average is trading below the longer-term moving average, this is thought to be short-term bearish (see Figure 12.10).

FIGURE 12.10   10-Day and 20-Day Moving Average Crossover/Bearish

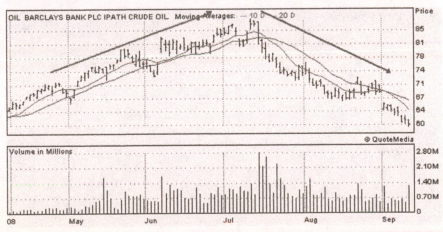

These four moving averages are just some of the different kinds of moving averages out there. And these would be considered simple moving averages. It's simply taking the average price, over however long of a period that was specified (10 days, for example), and plots a continuous line on a chart, which changes each day as the price changes.

There are also exponential moving averages, moving average envelopes, weighted moving averages, and more. But when it comes right down to it, the moving average is an indicator to identify trends and trend changes in a stock's price.

If you were bullish and looking for a stock to buy, especially if you were interested in holding onto it for a while, then screening for stocks above their 200-day moving average would put plenty of excellent candidates onto your watch list (although probably too many).

By adding the 50-day moving average to your screen, you'd narrow the list down further by requiring the stocks to be above both the longer-term (200-day), and the medium-term (50-day) moving average.

Of course stocks can be above both of those and still be below the shorter-term moving averages as well. By adding both the 10-day and the 20-day moving averages to your screen, you would narrow the list down even more, generating a list of stocks that would be considered bullish on all three time periods (long-term, medium-term, and short-term) (see Figure 12.11).

FIGURE 12.11   Above the 10, 20, 50, and 200-Day Moving Averages/Bullish

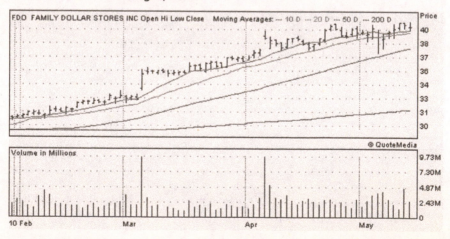

Each screener is different, but in general, the logic is pretty straightforward. If you're looking for stocks with prices above the 10-day, 20-day, 50-day, and 200-day moving average, the parameters would look something like this:

- **Current Price > 10-Day Moving Average**
- **Current Price > 20-Day Moving Average**
- **Current Price > 50-Day Moving Average**
- **Current Price > 200-Day Moving Average**

If you're looking for bearish stocks, just have the price be under the moving average by using the less than (<) operator.

By the way, just because you now have a list of stocks that are above all of those moving averages, that doesn't mean you should just buy any one of them on the list. Since you'll get quite a few, start adding in your favorite style characteristics to better find the stocks that not only meet those moving average criteria but also meet the other important fundamental criteria as well.

Get Specific (Screening for Moving Average Crossovers and More)

You can also get more specific on exactly what you want.

We talked about moving average crossovers. If that's what you'd like to find, you can tell the screener to find it. Just be specific. Think about it; just because a stock is above the 10-day and the 20-day moving average doesn't necessarily mean the 10-day moving average itself is above the 20-day moving average. They could be reversed.

To ensure the 10-day is above the 20-day, the parameter would look something like this:

- **Current Price > 10-Day Moving average**
- **10-Day Moving Average > 20-Day Moving Average**

Now you can be sure that each stock that comes through your screen has a bullish 10- and 20-day moving average crossover.

Note: I didn't need to go so far as to say that the current price had to be above the 20-day moving average even though I wanted it to be. Why? Because I had already specified that it had to be above the 10-day moving average. And I also specified that the 10-day moving average had to be over the 20-day moving average. Since the price was above the 10-day, and the 10-day was above the 20-day, the price would naturally have to be above the 20-day moving average as well.

I point this out for one simple reason: don't worry about being a bit redundant in your screens if it helps you clarify what your logic is and what you're trying to do. If you have an extra line in there because it completes the thought process or rules you're plugging in, so be it. Your stocks won't come out any better or worse if your screen is constructed more or less elegantly.

You can even find stocks that just crossed over a specific moving average that day or find crossovers that just crossed over that day as well.

For example: let's say we want to find a stock that just crossed over its 50-day moving average. It's easy to do. Here's what that screen would look like:

- **Current Price > 50-Day Moving Average**
- **Price 1 Day Ago < 50-Day Moving Average**

This will produce stocks that literally just crossed up and over their 50-day moving average that day (see Figure 12.12).

FIGURE 12.12   Newly Crossed 50-Day Moving Average

What about a bullish short-term moving average crossover? Just set your parameters to look for those stocks. The following example shows the 10-day moving average having just crossed above the 20-day moving average:

- **10-Day Moving Average > 20-Day Moving Average**
- **10-Day Moving Average (1 Day Ago) < 20-Day Moving Average (1 Day Ago)**
- **Current Price > 10-Day Moving Average**

All of these stocks will have had a bullish 10-day and 20-day moving average crossover that day (see Figure 12.13).

FIGURE 12.13   New 10-Day and 20-Day Bullish Crossover

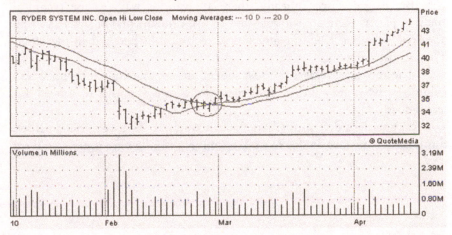

You can even specify that a stock's price isn't above a moving average by more than a certain amount. For example: let's say you're looking for stocks that are trading above the 200-day moving average but no more than 5% above it. This is set up in the following parameters:

- **Current Price > 200-Day Moving Average**
- **Current Price < 1.05 * 200-Day Moving Average**

Now add in your favorite fundamentals and you're all set.

Moving averages alone don't tell the whole story. Just because a stock is above or below a specific moving average, you should still make sure it meets all of your other fundamental criteria as well.

Use technicals, like moving averages, to spot potential price events to then be validated or invalidated with the fundamentals. Or use them as confirming indicators or nonconfirming indicators of your prior fundamental findings.

Either way, screening for moving average set-ups is easy. And combining them with your favorite fundamental criteria makes it even better. It doesn't matter whether you're looking for stocks in confirmed uptrends or confirmed downtrends, stocks going sideways or stocks at critical turning points, you can put them all at your fingertips in your stock screens.

Summary

Are we done already? Not to worry. There's more technical analysis in Chapter 13. There, we'll dissect a stock's chart pattern.

But as we've seen already, there are various ways to use technical analysis, just as there are various ways to use fundamental analysis. And no one style, whether it be fundamental or technical, is better than the other. They're just different.

The moving averages we just looked at are one way. The price and volume patterns are another. And these are classic examples of proven TA techniques.

So now let's dive into Chart Pattern Analysis. As I mentioned earlier, this is one of my favorite forms of TA, and in the following pages, you'll see why.

13

Identifying Chart Patterns

Another form of technical analysis (TA) focuses on the identification of Chart Patterns on a stock's price chart. Whether you are a fundamental trader or technical trader (or both), the question of all questions (aside from knowing *what* to buy or sell) is *when* to buy or sell.

Fundamentals, of course, are ultimately the key in determining the price or value of a stock. And statistics have shown that companies receiving upward earnings estimate revisions outperform the market, while companies receiving downward earnings estimate revisions underperform the market.

But technical analysis, like price and volume patterns and moving averages (which we just discussed) and chart pattern identification (which we're going to look at now), can give you insight about when the market is ready to react to those fundamentals.

Very often, the price action on a chart can form meaningful patterns. These chart patterns reflect the collective buying and selling sentiment of the market and can, in turn, be used in trying to forecast future price direction and the timing surrounding it.

Keep in mind that nothing is foolproof. But a strong fundamental outlook combined with a good technical viewpoint creates a very potent combination for the trader and investor.

Different chart patterns can be classified as either continuation patterns or reversal patterns:

Continuation Patterns generally will *continue* in the direction of the trend. For example: if a stock is in an uptrend and then pauses or enters into a period of consolidation (i.e., trading is temporarily confined to a well-defined pattern or range), the expectation is that the market will ultimately breakout to the upside and continue the direction of the trend.

If the trend was down prior to the consolidation, the expectation would be for the stock to breakout to the downside and continue the direction of the downtrend.

Reversal Patterns have a tendency of *reversing* the trend. These consolidation patterns can signal a reversal in both uptrends as well as downtrends.

But whether continuation patterns or reversal patterns, research has proven that some chart patterns have high forecasting probabilities. Let's take a look at some of the most predictive chart patterns and see what they mean and how to trade them.

> **Research has proven that some chart patterns have high forecasting probabilities.**

These patterns include:

- Symmetrical Triangles
- Ascending Triangles and Descending Triangles
- Wedges
- Flags and Pennants
- Rectangles
- Head and Shoulders

What do these chart patterns all have in common? They were all patterns in some of the biggest market moves.

Let's take a look at the characteristics for each one of these patterns.

Symmetrical Triangles

Symmetrical Triangles are continuation patterns that generally mark a pause in the preceding trend. It's identified as having two converging trendlines that take the shape of a sideways triangle. (See Figure 13.1).

FIGURE 13.1 Symmetrical Triangles

Symmetrical Triangle
in an Uptrend (Bullish)

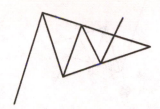

Symmetrical Triangle
in a Downtrend (Bearish)

This pattern can mean the market has simply gotten ahead of itself and it needs to consolidate or it truly is in a period of indecision and is looking for direction. Attempts to push higher are met by selling and attempts to push lower are met with buying. Each new lower high and higher low becomes shallower than the last. Volume will usually diminish during this period as well.

Eventually, the symmetrical triangle resolves itself and often with an explosive breakout in the direction of the preceding trend.

Uptrends/Bullish

The majority of the time, a symmetrical triangle in an uptrend will breakout to the upside. A high volume breakout is more reliable than a low volume breakout.

Downtrends / Bearish

Symmetrical triangles in downtrends will typically breakout to the downside. However, an increase in volume is not required for a successful breakout. In fact, a significant increase in volume might be considered suspect. Although, volume should start to increase as the downside move continues.

Identifying and Drawing the Pattern

Triangles are usually quite easy to see on a chart. Especially when the lines have already been drawn in. To identify a symmetrical triangle pattern on your own, remember that it has to have at least four points: two points at the top to draw the downward slanting trendline and two points at the bottom to draw the upward slanting trendline. Connecting the high point and the subsequent lower high forms the top part of the triangle. Connecting the low and the subsequent higher low forms the bottom part of the triangle.

Symmetrical triangles in uptrends are bullish, while symmetrical triangles in downtrends are bearish. (See Figure 13.2.)

FIGURE 13.2 Symmetrical Triangles / Uptrends and Downtrends

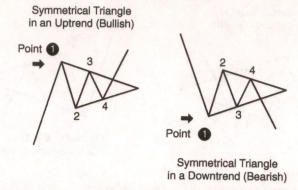

Symmetrical Triangle
in an Uptrend (Bullish)

Symmetrical Triangle
in a Downtrend (Bearish)

For a bullish symmetrical triangle pattern, the first point (the point farthest left, i.e., the earliest point) is at the top. For a bearish pattern, the first point is at the bottom. A triangle can have more than four points. The accompanying image (see Figure 13.3) has six points.

FIGURE 13.3 Symmetrical Triangle with Six Points

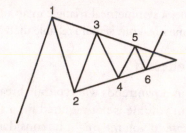

Measured Moves (Minimum Profit Targets)

To determine your projected minimum profit target, measure the distance between points 1 and 2. This is the widest part of the triangle and is often referred to as the base (see Figure 13.4). For example: if the top of the base (point 1) was $56 and the bottom of the base (point 2) was $50, the base would be $6. This is your measured move.

To project your minimum profit target, identify at what price the stock broke through the triangle. For this example, let's say $54. Then add $6 to the breakout price of $54 and you have your minimum projected profit target of $60. (See Figure 13.4 again.)

FIGURE 13.4 Symmetrical Triangle / Measured Move

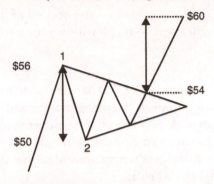

Failures and Stop-Out Points

There are different failure points based on how you enter the trade.

If you enter the trade after a breakout, you should use a move below the apex point as your failure point and exit the trade (see Figure 13.5).

FIGURE 13.5 Symmetrical Triangle / Failure

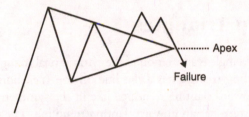

If you get in before a breakout occurs in anticipation of one, a move below the last point of the triangle (e.g., point 4 in a four pointed triangle or point 6 in a six pointed triangle, etc.) should be your failure point, and you should consider exiting the trade. (See Figure 13.6.)

FIGURE 13.6 Symmetrical Triangles / Early Entry Failure

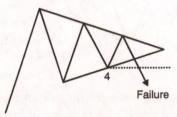

For the more experienced chart pattern trader, you might choose to stay in a little longer if you believe the pattern is being re-drawn into a new pattern such as a larger triangle, or a bullish flag, or even a wedge. This can makes sense if your early entry was near the bottom of the pattern and staying in a little longer still keeps your risk within your level of tolerance.

Summary

The word *symmetrical* in describing the triangle is used loosely and is more of a way of distinguishing it from an ascending triangle and descending triangle. The symmetrical triangle doesn't have to be symmetrical per se, but as stated earlier, it does have to have two converging trendlines: the top line slanting downward and the bottom line slanting upward so that they eventually come together to form a right sided triangle.

Since this pattern is a continuation pattern, it's most profitable to trade this in the direction of the preceding trend.

You can get in after a breakout has occurred or you can choose to get in early in anticipation of a breakout taking place. Either way, pay attention to the volume and your failure points and the symmetrical triangle will become a trusted pattern in your trading.

Ascending Triangles

The Ascending Triangle is a variation of the symmetrical triangle. The difference is that the ascending triangle has a flat line on top (i.e., horizontal trendline) instead of a downward slanting trendline like in the symmetrical triangle. The bottom of the pattern has an upward slanting trendline. The two lines eventually come together to form a flat-topped, right-sided triangle. (See Figure 13.7.)

FIGURE 13.7 Ascending Triangle

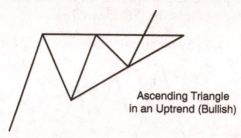

Ascending Triangle
in an Uptrend (Bullish)

The ascending triangle is a continuation pattern. It's generally considered bullish and is most reliable when found in an uptrend.

In ascending triangles, the market becomes overbought and needs to consolidate. As prices try to advance, they are turned back by selling.

Buying then re-enters the market, and prices soon reach their old highs. Resistance is met again and they are turned back once more. Resistance occurs at approximately the same high price each time (horizontal trendline), while new buying on the pullbacks serves to lift the support levels higher (upward slanting trendline).

This bullish price action most often leads to an upside breakout in the direction of the preceding trend, as the old highs are taken out and prices are propelled even higher as new buying comes in. Volume usually diminishes during the formation of the pattern, but explodes on the breakout.

Uptrends / Bullish

As in the case of the symmetrical triangle, ascending triangles in uptrends are bullish and the breakout is generally accompanied by a marked increase in volume. Low volume breakouts should be watched carefully because they are more prone to failure. Ascending triangles in downtrends are less reliable and are, therefore, not a part of the most predictive chart patterns set-ups.

Identifying and Drawing the Pattern

Ascending triangles are also quite easy to see on a chart. To identify an ascending triangle pattern on your own, remember that it has to have at least four points: two points at the top to draw the horizontal trendline and two points at the bottom to draw the upward slanting trendline. Connecting the two, approximately equal high points, forms the top (flat) part of the triangle. Connecting the low and the subsequent higher low forms the bottom part of the triangle.

Ascending triangles in uptrends are bullish.

For a bullish ascending triangle pattern, the first point (the point farthest left, i.e., the earliest point) is at the top. (See Figure 13.8.)

FIGURE 13.8 Ascending Triangle in Uptrend / Identification

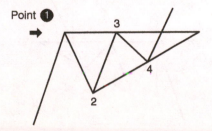

And just like symmetrical triangles, an ascending triangle can also have more than four points. The accompanying image has six. (See Figure 13.9.)

FIGURE 13.9 Ascending Triangle with Six Points

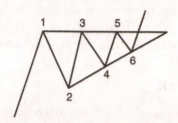

Measured Moves (Minimum Profit Targets)

To determine your projected minimum profit target, measure the distance between points 1 and 2. This is the widest part of the triangle and is often referred to as the base.

For example: if the top of the base (point 1) was $70, and the bottom of the base (point 2) was $63, the base would be $7. This is your measured move.

To project your minimum profit target, identify at what price the stock broke through the ascending triangle. This is easy to predict even if it hasn't yet broken out because the breakout point is essentially the high of the pattern, that is, the flat trendline at the top.

So if the breakout price is $70, then add $7 to that price and you get your minimum projected price target of $77. (See Figure 13.10.)

FIGURE 13.10 Ascending Triangle / Measured Move

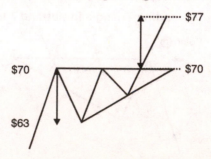

Failures and Stop-Out Points

There are different failure points based on how you enter the trade.

If you enter the trade after a breakout, you should use a move below the apex point as your failure point and exit the trade (see Figure 13.11). A secondary failure point could be placed at the last point (or point 4), also shown in Figure 13.11 (see the gray dotted line showing this scenario). This additional failure point is usually only used if the breakout and subsequent trading have not extended beyond the length of the pattern (i.e., apex) and the risk levels are still within your tolerance. (Figure 13.11 depicts an ascending triangle in an uptrend for illustration.)

FIGURE 13.11   Ascending Triangle / Failure

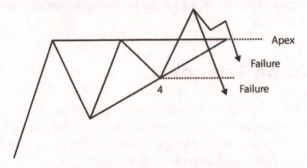

If you get in before a breakout occurs in anticipation of one, a move below the last point of the triangle (point 4 in this example) should be your failure point, and you should consider exiting the trade. For the more experienced trader, you might choose to stay in a little longer if you believe the pattern is being re-drawn into a new pattern, such as a larger ascending triangle or a rectangle. If this is the case, use the bottom of the base (point 2) as the failure point and exit below there (see the dotted line in Figure 13.12

FIGURE 13.12   Ascending Triangle / Early Entry Failure

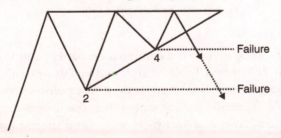

that shows this scenario). This can makes sense if your early entry was near the bottom of the pattern and staying in a little longer still keeps your risk within your level of tolerance. (Figure 13.12 depicts an ascending triangle in an uptrend for illustration.)

Summary

Since this pattern is a continuation pattern, it's most profitable to trade this in the direction of the preceding trend. And remember that it's most reliable when found in uptrends. In fact, the ascending triangle has an astounding success rate, breaking out to the upside 70% of the time.

You can get in after a breakout has occurred or you can choose to get in early in anticipation of a breakout taking place. This high probability pattern is a great bullish indicator.

Descending Triangles

The Descending Triangle is basically the reverse of an ascending triangle. The flat line (horizontal trendline) is on the bottom and a descending trendline defines the top part of the pattern. The two lines come together to form a flat-bottomed, right-sided triangle. (See Figure 13.13.)

FIGURE 13.13 Descending Triangle

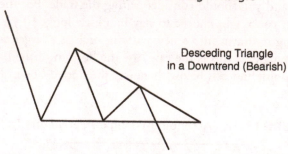

Desceding Triangle
in a Downtrend (Bearish)

The descending triangle is a continuation pattern and is generally considered bearish. It is most reliable when found in a downtrend.

In the descending triangle, prices drop to a point where they are considered oversold. Tentative buying comes in at the lows and prices perk up. The higher prices however attract more selling and the old lows (horizontal trendline) are re-tested. Buying once again lifts prices, although it results in a lower high (downward slanting trendline). New selling comes in and pushes it back down.

This bearish price action typically leads to a downside breakout to new lows, continuing the direction of the downward trend. Volume decreases during the formation of the pattern but should noticeably increase on the breakout.

Downtrends / Bearish

Descending triangles in downtrends are bearish and the breakout usually sees an increase in volume. A low volume breakout should be carefully watched. Descending triangles in uptrends are less reliable and are therefore not a part of the most predictive chart pattern set-ups.

Identifying and Drawing the Pattern

Descending triangles are easy to spot. To identify a descending triangle on your own, remember that it has to have at least four points: two points at the bottom to draw the horizontal trendline (you'll draw a line connecting the recurring lows) and two points at the top to draw the downward slanting trend line (a line connecting the lower highs).

Descending triangles in downtrends are bearish.

In bearish descending triangles, the first point (the point farthest left, i.e., the earliest point) should be at the bottom. (See Figure 13.14.)

FIGURE 13.14 Descending Triangle in Downtrend / Identification

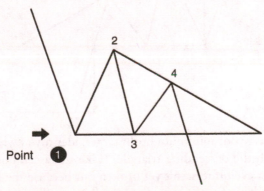

Like the other triangles covered so far, the descending triangle can have more than four points. (See Figure 13.15, which has six points.)

FIGURE 13.15   Descending Triangle with 6 Points

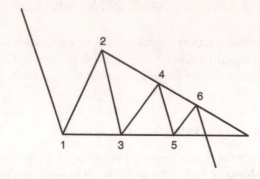

Measured Moves (Minimum Profit Targets)

To determine your projected minimum profit target, measure the distance between points 1 and 2. This is the widest part of the triangle and is often referred to as the base.

For example: if the bottom of the base (point 1) was $50 and the top of the base (point 2) was $60, the base would be $10. This is your measured move. (See Figure 13.16.)

FIGURE 13.16   Descending Triangle / Measured Move

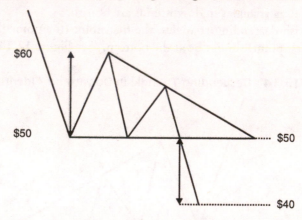

To project your minimum profit target, identify at what price the stock broke through the descending triangle. (Like the ascending triangle, this is easy to predict even if it hasn't yet broken out because the breakout point is essentially the low of the pattern (i.e., the flat trendline at the bottom). So if the breakout price is $50, then subtract $10 from that price and you get your minimum projected price target of $40. (Refer back to Figure 13.16.)

Failures and Stop-Out Points

Since the descending triangle in a downtrend is bearish, a breakout to the upside would constitute a failure.

If you enter the trade after a breakout, you should use a move above the apex point as your failure point and exit the trade. (See Figure 13.17.) A secondary failure point could be placed at the last point (or point 4) in this example. See the gray dotted line showing this scenario. This additional failure point is usually only used if the breakout and subsequent trading has not extended beyond the length of the pattern (i.e., apex) and the risk levels are still within your tolerance. (Figure 13.17 depicts a descending triangle in a downtrend for illustration.)

FIGURE 13.17   Descending Triangle / Failure

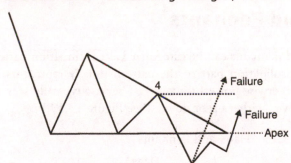

If you get in before a breakout occurs in anticipation of one taking place, a move above the last point of the triangle (point 4) (see Figure 13.18), should be your failure point, and you should consider exiting the trade. For the more experienced trader, you might choose to stay in a little longer if you believe the pattern is being re-drawn into a new pattern, such as a larger descending triangle or a rectangle. If this is the case, use the top of the base

FIGURE 13.18   Descending Triangle / Early Entry Failure

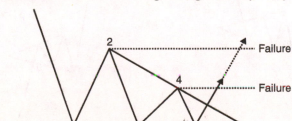

(point 2) as the failure point and exit above that (see the top-most dotted line in Figure 13.18 that shows this scenario). This can makes sense if your early entry was near the top of the pattern and staying in a little longer still keeps your risk within your level of tolerance. (Figure 13.18 depicts a descending triangle in a downtrend for illustration.)

Summary

The descending triangle is a continuation pattern that is most reliable when found in downtrends. This makes it a high probability bearish chart pattern.

Whether you choose to trade it early or wait for a confirming breakout; act as a short seller or use it to exit longs, the descending triangle can help you accurately spot stocks that look to be headed lower.

Flags and Pennants

Both flags and pennants can be categorized as continuation patterns.

The consolidation part of the pattern usually represents only a brief pause in an otherwise powerful market. They are typically seen right after a big, quick move – either up or down. (See Figure 13.19.)

FIGURE 13.19   Flags and Pennants

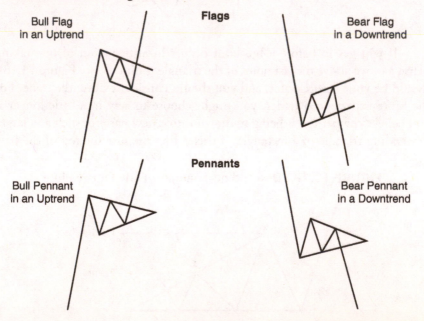

The market then usually takes off again in the same direction. Research has shown that flags and pennants are some of the most reliable chart patterns to trade. And they can be found in some of the most explosive price moves.

Flags: Uptrends / Bullish

Flag patterns in uptrends are bullish. They are typically referred to as simply bull flags. Bull flags are characterized first by a sharp upward price move. This can be one big day or multiple days of progressive price action. The steepness of the move can sometimes look almost like a straight line up (like a flagpole). The consolidation that follows is identified by a short series of lower tops and lower bottoms that slant against the trend. The trendlines that can be drawn on the top of the pattern and the bottom of the pattern run parallel to one another (like a downward sloping rectangle). Volume typically diminishes during this time-out, but then explodes higher as it breaks out.

Flags: Downtrends / Bearish

Flags in downtrends are bearish. Bear flags look like the inverse of bull flags. Bear flags are characterized by a sharp downward price move, followed by a short series of higher lows and higher highs. The trendlines that can be drawn also run parallel to one another. But this time, it looks like an upward sloping rectangle. Volume will also typically diminish during this period, but will expand on the downside breakout.

Pennants: Uptrends / Bullish

Pennants in uptrends are bullish. Pennants look very much like small symmetrical triangles. But the characteristic, nearly straight up, pole-like move that precedes the pennant part, makes its identification unmistakable. The pause after the sharp move higher is defined by two converging trendlines that form a small right sided triangle. Just like in the flagging patterns, volume should dry up during the pennant part and then explode higher on the breakout.

Pennants: Downtrends / Bearish

Pennants in downtrends are bearish. Bear pennants look like upside down bull pennants. In the bear pennant, there's a big move to the downside, followed by a short consolidation pattern that looks like a small triangle. The market then breaks out to the downside in the same dramatic way that set the pattern up in the first place. Volume drops off during the pennant part, but then quickly picks up on the breakout.

Identifying and Drawing the Patterns

Flags and pennants are some of the easiest patterns to spot on a chart. And just like all the other patterns described so far, you need a minimum of four points to draw a flag or pennant: two points at the top of the pattern and two points at the bottom. Remember, the defining lines of a flag run parallel to each other. The flag part should also slant against the trend. The defining lines of a pennant converge to form a small triangle that points to the right.

Flags in uptrends are bullish, while flags in downtrends are bearish.

In both bullish and bearish flags, the first point should be the point farthest left, that is, the earliest point. In uptrends, the first point of the flag should be at the top of the pattern. In downtrends, the first point of the flag should be at the bottom. (See Figure 13.20.)

FIGURE 13.20 Flags / Identification

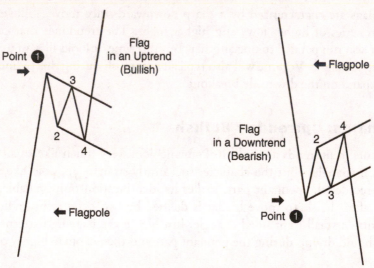

The same is true for bullish and bearish pennants. In bull pennants, the first point should be the point farthest left and at the top. In bear pennants, the first point should be the point farthest left and at the bottom. (See Figure 13.21.)

FIGURE 13.21   Pennants / Identification

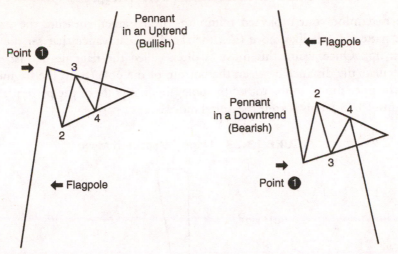

Pennant
in an Uptrend
(Bullish)

Point ❶

3

2

4

← Flagpole

← Flagpole

Pennant
in a Downtrend
(Bearish)

2

4

3

Point ❶

Flags and pennants can also have more than four points. The bull flag and bear pennant illustrations in Figure 13.22 show them with six points each. However, because these types of consolidation patterns typically form over short periods of time, it's less likely to find patterns with more than six points.

FIGURE 13.22   Flags and Pennants with Six Points

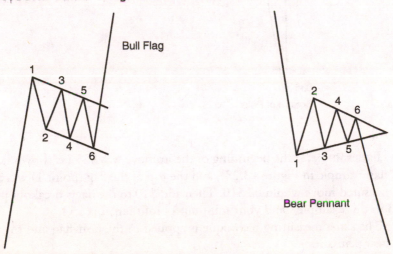

Bull Flag

1
3
5
2
4
6

Bear Pennant

2
4
6
1
3
5

Measured Moves (Minimum Profit Targets)

To determine your projected minimum profit target, measure the size of the pattern's pole-like move (i.e., the sharp price advance that set the pattern up). Once again, this move is often called the flagpole or just pole. Calculate the distance between the bottom of the pole (from the beginning of the price move) to the top of the pole (the first point of the pattern). (See Figure 13.23.) This is your measured move.

FIGURE 13.23 Flags / Measured Move

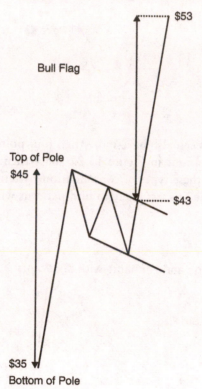

For example, if the beginning of the upmove was $35 (as shown in the bull flag example in Figure 13.23), and the top of the flag (point 1) was $45, the measured move would be $10. Then add $10 to the flag's breakout point ($43 in this example), and your minimum profit target is $53.

The same measuring technique is applied to the bear flag and the bull and bear pennant.

Bear Pennant

In the bear pennant example in Figure 13.24, calculate the size of the flagpole, i.e., the distance between the beginning of the price move (beginning of the pole-like move) to the first point of the pattern (end of the pole-like move).

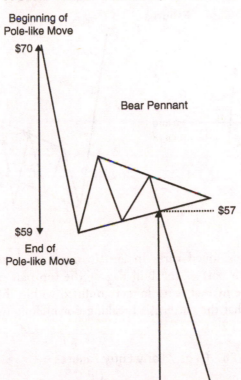

FIGURE 13.24 Pennants / Measured Move

Beginning of
Pole-like Move

$70

Bear Pennant

$59

$57

End of
Pole-like Move

$46

For instance: if the beginning of the sharp down move was $70 and the bottom of the pennant (point 1) was $59, the measured move would be $11. Subtract $11 from the breakout price ($57 in this example), and your minimum profit target is $46.

Failures and Stop-Out Points

Bull flags and bear flags follow the same basic rules when it comes to failure points.

If you enter the trade after a breakout, you should use a move through the second point as your failure and exit the trade. If the flag is a small pattern that doesn't slant too steeply against the trend, you might consider using the fourth point (or the sixth point for instance in a 6-point flag) as your failure point. But do this only if it stays within your tolerance for risk. (Keep in mind, the first tip-off that a flag breakout might not succeed is the fact that the market is making its way back into the pattern as opposed to the customary explosive move out of it.) (See Figure 13.25.)

FIGURE 13.25 Flags / Failures

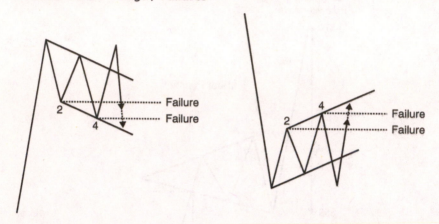

If you get positioned early in anticipation of a breakout, a move through the bottom part of the bull flag or the top part of the bear flag (enough so that the market is no longer confined within the parallel trend lines) is your cue that the pattern is breaking down along with its implications. (See Figure 13.26.)

FIGURE 13.26 Flags / Early Entry Failures

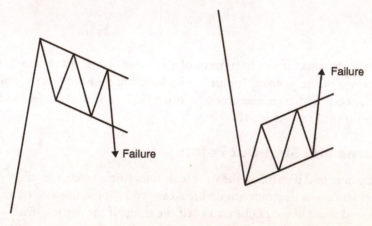

Bull pennant and bear pennant failures are virtually identical to symmetrical triangle failures. This makes sense because a pennant is really nothing more than a small triangle. (The preceding pole-like move that distinguishes the pennant from an ordinary triangle does not change what constitutes a failed consolidation pattern.)

If you enter the trade after a breakout, you should use a move below the apex point as your failure point and exit the trade. The image at the right of Figure 13.27 depicts a bull pennant breakout and then failure. The failure point is the same for a bear pennant as well. A move through the apex is your failure point and you should exit the trade. (See Figure 13.27.)

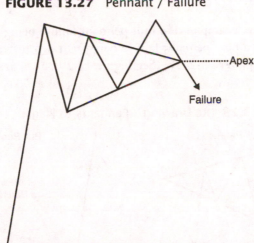

FIGURE 13.27 Pennant / Failure

If you get in before a breakout occurs in anticipation of one happening, a move through the last point of the pennant (e.g., point 4 in a four-pointed pennant or point 6 in a six-pointed pennant, etc.) should be your failure point and you should consider exiting the trade. (Figure 13.28 depicts both a bull pennant and bear pennant for illustration.)

For the more experienced trader, you might choose to stay in a little longer if you believe the pattern is being re-drawn into a new pattern, such as a larger pennant/triangle or flag or even a wedge. This makes sense if your early entry was close to the failure point and staying in a little longer still keeps your risk within your level of tolerance.

FIGURE 13.28 Pennants / Early Entry Failures

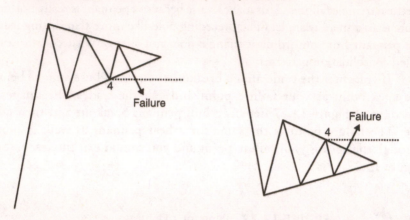

Included are examples of a bull pennant failure being re-drawn into a bull flag, and of a bear pennant failure being redrawn into a bear flag. Can you see the new pattern in gray? (See Figure 13.29.)

FIGURE 13.29 Re-Drawing / Pennants to Flags

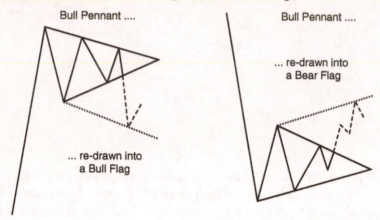

Summary

The flag and pennant patterns are continuation patterns and are most reliable when traded in the direction of the trend. In general, the breakout of the flag or pennant and the move that follows should be approximately the same size as the sharp move (flagpole) that preceded it.

These patterns are often traded before they breakout for many reasons. Of course, their high probability of success is one of them. But also, since flags and pennants are typically small, short-term patterns, it doesn't take long to see if the trade will be a winner or not. And since the patterns are typically small, there's usually only a relatively small distance between an early positioning and a potential failure point.

So whether you decide to get in early in anticipation of a breakout or if you prefer to wait for the confirming breakout before you do, history has shown that these patterns have produced some spectacular price action. Now you know how to incorporate these dynamic patterns into your own trading.

Rectangles

Rectangles are continuation patterns. They are consolidation areas that are usually resolved in the direction of the trend. The horizontal trendlines, of course, run parallel in a rectangle. Buyers and sellers seem equally matched at this point. The same highs are constantly tested, as are the same lows within this trading range. And while volume doesn't seem to suffer like it does in other patterns, volume should noticeably increase on the breakout. (See Figure 13.30.)

FIGURE 13.30 Rectangles

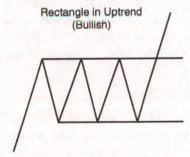

Rectangle in Uptrend
(Bullish)

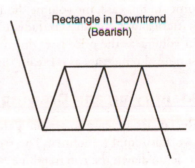

Rectangle in Downtrend
(Bearish)

The rectangle has a good success rate as a continuation pattern. But it should be noted too, that after it's broken out, it has a higher tendency to pullback (make a retracement) to the original breakout area. After a successful test, it'll then continue in the direction of the breakout and resume the trend. (Figure 13.31 shows an example of a breakout in an uptrend, then retracement, and then the resumption of the breakout/trend.)

FIGURE 13.31   Rectangle / Retracement and Resumption

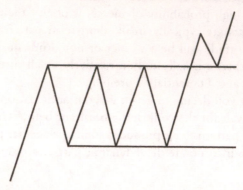

Uptrends / Bullish

The majority of the time, a rectangle in an uptrend will breakout to the upside. A good way to confirm the bullish bias is to see if the volume increases as it trades up to the top of the pattern and decreases as it falls to the bottom of the pattern. The increase in volume on the upside shows more buying interest. Volume will also pickup on the upside breakout as well.

Downtrends / Bearish

Rectangles in downtrends will breakout to the downside the majority of the time. In this case, the volume should increase as it trades to the bottom of the pattern and diminish as it trades to the top of the pattern. Again, the increase in volume as the price goes down helps confirm the downside bias. Volume should also increase as it breaks through the bottom of the rectangle as well.

Identifying and Drawing the Pattern

Rectangles are easy to see on a chart. These trading ranges are confined by two horizontal trendlines. The rectangle has to have at least four points in order to drawn the two trendlines: two equal high points to draw a line across to form the top trendline and two equal low points to draw in the bottom trendline. While a rectangle needs to have at least four points, it will often have six and can have even more. In fact, it's more common for a rectangle to have more than four points rather than only four points. (Figure 13.32 illustrates a rectangle with four and with six points.)

Rectangles in uptrends are bullish, whereas rectangles in downtrends are bearish.

FIGURE 13.32 Rectangles with Six Points

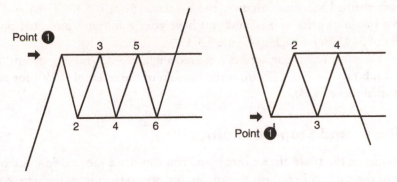

For a bullish rectangle, the first point (the point farthest left, i.e., the earliest point) is at the top. For a bearish rectangle, the first point is at the bottom.

Measured Moves (Minimum Profit Targets)

To determine your projected minimum profit target, measure the distance between points 1 and 2. This is the widest part of the triangle and is often referred to as the base. For example: if the top of the base (point 1) was $37 and the bottom of the base (point 2) was $30, the base would be $7. This is your measured move. (See Figure 13.33, which uses a rectangle in an uptrend for illustration.)

To project your minimum profit target, identify at what price the stock broke through (or should break through) the rectangle. (Determining

FIGURE 13.33 Rectangle / Measured Move

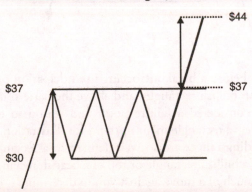

the projected breakout price is easy since the horizontal trendline areas are already defined.) In this instance, the breakout price is $37. Then add $7 to the breakout price of $37 and you have your minimum projected profit target of $44. (Refer back to Figure 13.33.)

The same technique applies for a rectangle in a downtrend, except that you'll subtract the base ($7) from the bottom of the rectangle ($30) for your measured move ($23).

Failures and Stop-Out Points

If you enter the trade after a breakout, you can use a move below the bottom of the pattern in bullish rectangles and above the top of the pattern in bearish rectangles as your failure point and exit the trade. However, if the size of the rectangle puts a move like that outside of your risk tolerance, you can use another technique to arrive at a stop-out point. That technique is to watch the volume on a pullback. If the retracement move back inside of the rectangle is made on increasing volume, that can be a sign that the breakout is failing or has failed. Decide how much room you're willing to give it and exit the trade. (Figure 13.34 depicts a rectangle in an uptrend for illustration.)

FIGURE 13.34 Rectangle / Failure

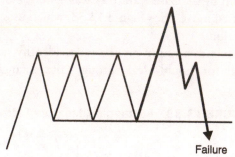

Failure

If you get in before a breakout occurs in anticipation of one, a move below the pattern in bullish rectangles and above the pattern in bearish rectangles, should be considered a failure point and reason to exit the trade. (Figure 13.35 depicts a rectangle in an uptrend for illustration.)

Since the trading ranges are so well defined in a rectangle, getting in near the bottom of a bullish rectangle or top of a bearish rectangle means you won't need to see much of a move against you to determine it to be a failure.

FIGURE 13.35 Rectangle / Early Entry Failure

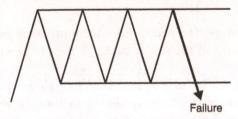

Failure

Summary

The rectangle is most reliable when traded as a continuation pattern. But pay attention to the volume as it can reveal the market's upside or downside bias, i.e., an increase in volume as it trades up in the pattern is bullish, and an increase in volume as it trades down in the pattern is bearish. Overall, volume doesn't really diminish that much within the pattern itself as it does with other patterns, but again, volume should increase as it breaks out.

Depending on how big the rectangle's size (base) is you can trade the range within the rectangle: buy at the bottom of the rectangle and sell at the top of the rectangle. Of course, you should allow enough time to pass to make sure an established range is in place. For less experienced traders, however, you might want to avoid countertrend trading, such as buying the lows in a bearish pattern and selling the highs in a bullish pattern, as you might get caught the wrong way when an in-trend breakout occurs. (Figure 13.36 illustrates range trading in a bullish rectangle in an uptrend.)

FIGURE 13.36 Rectangle / Range Trading

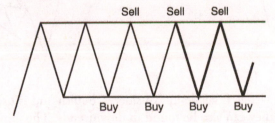

The rectangle is a great pattern to trade. It has a high probability of success, and the clearly defined support and resistance lines make early entries or breakout entries easy to do. And if you miss the breakout, you can always get in after a successful retracement and position yourself before it resumes the trend.

Wedges

The Wedge pattern can be classified as both a continuation pattern and a reversal pattern. The slant of the wedge makes it easy to identify which is which.

The wedge looks similar to a symmetrical triangle in that they both have converging trendlines that come together at an apex. However, wedges are distinguished by a noticeable slant, either to the upside or to the downside. The wedge can look similar to a pennant or a flag as well, because wedge patterns are often preceded by a pole-like move like that of a pennant or flag. (See Figure 13.37.)

FIGURE 13.37 Wedges

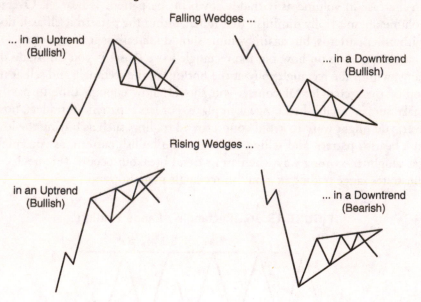

A falling wedge is generally considered bullish and is usually found in uptrends. But they can also be found in downtrends. The implication, however, is still generally bullish. This pattern is marked by a series of lower tops and lower bottoms.

A rising wedge is generally considered bearish and is usually found in downtrends. They can be found in uptrends, too, but would still generally be regarded as bearish. Rising wedges put in a series of higher tops and higher bottoms.

Falling Wedge: Uptrends / Bullish

Falling wedges in uptrends are bullish continuation patterns. As with the bull flag, the bullish wedge in an uptrend slants downward and against the trend. Volume dries up during the formation of the patterns but then increases as it breaks out to the upside. While the wedge has similar characteristics to that of the pennant and the flag, the duration of the wedge (i.e., the size of the pattern or the amount of time it takes before a resolve or breakout happens) is longer.

Falling Wedge: Downtrends / Bullish

Falling wedges in downtrends are bullish. This pattern can be characterized as a reversal pattern. This wedge slants in the direction of the trend, but is in fact, bullish, serving as a reversal to the downtrend. Volume will diminish during the formation of the wedge but increase as it breaks out to the upside.

Rising Wedge: Uptrends / Bearish

Rising wedges in uptrends are bearish reversal patterns. The rising wedge slants upward in the direction of the trend, but is a bearish pattern that serves to reverse the uptrend downwards. Volume should drop off as this pattern is being formed and increase as it breaks through the bottom of the wedge.

Rising Wedge: Downtrends / Bearish

Rising wedges are bearish continuation patterns. Just like in a bear flag, the bearish wedge slants up and against the downtrend. Volume will typically diminish during the formation of the wedge and increase on the downside breakout of the pattern.

Identifying and Drawing the Pattern

Wedges are easy patterns to identify and draw on a chart. You need a minimum of four points to draw a wedge: two points at the top of the pattern to draw the upper trendline and two points at the bottom to draw the lower trendline. The upper and lower trendlines will converge (come together) to form an apex. In short, the wedge looks like a slanted right triangle with one trend line a little longer than the other. While having four points is the minimum number of points needed to draw a wedge, it's not uncommon to have five or six points or more. Figure 13.38 shows wedge patterns with various numbers of points. Regardless of the number of points, however, the implications remain the same. Falling wedges are generally bullish and rising wedges are generally bearish. Proper identification shows that the first point should be the point farthest left, i.e., the earliest point. In uptrends, the first point of the wedge should be at the top of the pattern. In downtrends, the first point should be at the bottom (see Figure 13.38).

FIGURE 13.38　Wedges / Identification

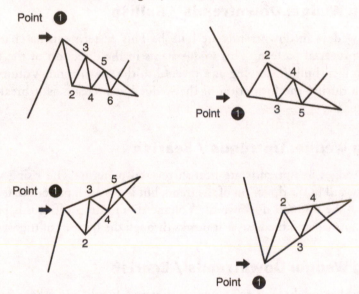

Measured Moves (Minimum Profit Targets)

To determine your minimum projected profit target, measure the distance between points 1 and 2. This is the widest part of the wedge and is often referred to as the base.

　　For example: If the top of the base (point 1) was $52 and the bottom of the base (point 2) was $47, the base would be $5. This is your measured move (in green) (see Figure 13.39).

　　To project your minimum profit target, identify at what price the stock broke through (or should break through) the wedge. If the breakout point is $49 (as in the preceding bullish falling wedge example), simply add the base ($5) to it to get your minimum projected profit target of $54.

FIGURE 13.39 Wedge / Measured Move

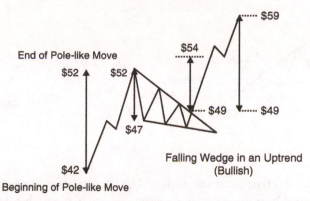

Whether it be a falling wedge or a rising wedge; bullish pattern or bearish, the measuring technique is the same.

A secondary measuring technique involves measuring the pole-like move if one preceded it. This is done in the same manner as described in the section on flags and pennants. Determine the size of the pole-like move (i.e., the sharp price advance that set the pattern up) and calculate the distance between the bottom of the pole (beginning of the price move) to the top of the pole (first point of the pattern). This is your measured move. Add that to the wedge's breakout point for your secondary or extended minimum projected profit target.

Failures and Stop-Out Points

If you enter the trade after a breakout, you can use a move through the last point as your failure and exit the trade. (In Figure 13.40, in the falling wedge example to the bottom left, it's point 4. In the falling wedge example to the bottom right, it's point 5.) You can also decide to use a move through the apex of the wedge pattern as your failure and exit there. However, if the size of the wedge is too big or the slant of the slope is too steep, waiting for an apex violation might put the risk level outside of your level of tolerance. If that's the case, use the last point instead. In the falling wedge examples (again in Figure 13.40), the last point and the apex are in close proximity to each other, so using an apex violation gives the trade a bit more room without much additional risk. But it's a good idea to determine your risk before you place a trade so you'll always know what to do and how much you could lose if the pattern fails. (See Figure 13.40.)

FIGURE 13.40 Falling Wedges / Failures

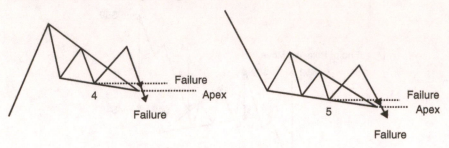

The same is true for rising wedges. Use the last point as your failure and exit the trade. Only use an apex violation/failure if it's within your level of risk tolerance (see Figure 13.41).

FIGURE 13.41 Rising Wedges / Failures

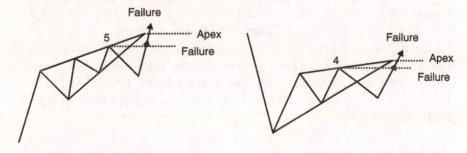

Pay attention to volume changes as well. If the pattern is failing on increased volume, it's likely that even more price action in that direction is coming. Even if you can tolerate a further out stop-out point (i.e., an apex failure), you might choose to exit the trade earlier on this sign.

If you get in before a breakout occurs, use a move through the wrong side of the pattern as your failure and exit the trade. Note that the last point isn't used as a failure for an early entry; because the wedge slants either up or down against the trend, it can move past the last point and still trade within the pattern itself. So a move through the wrong side of the pattern (meaningful enough so the wedge is no longer intact), should be your failure point and exit the trade.

Be aware that if the size of the wedge pattern is big enough or the slant of the slope is steep enough, it can trade within the confines of the pattern and against your position. So you might choose to exit the trade before a pattern failure takes place if the trade is against you and you run the risk of exceeding your level of risk tolerance. But pay attention to the volume because it can give clues to its bullishness or bearishness. If volume starts increasing as it's going up, it could be a sign of its bullish tendencies. And if the volume is increasing while it's going down, it could be a sign of its bearish tendencies. These clues can help you keep your losses smaller by potentially exiting earlier. (Figure 13.42 depicts early entry failures.)

FIGURE 13.42 Wedges / Early Entry Failures

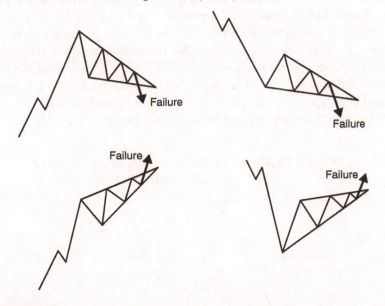

Summary

Wedge patterns can be both continuation patterns and reversal patterns. Although, they are most common as continuation patterns.

The wedge can be a powerful pattern and has an excellent success rate in forecasting breakouts. The pattern can be even more powerful and profitable when preceded by a pole-like move, like that of a flag or pennant. Volume typically decreases during the formation of the wedge but increases on its breakout.

Whether you use the wedge as a signal for a continuing trend or a reversal; or whether you get in early in anticipation of a breakout or if you wait for a confirming breakout before you do, these classic wedge patterns can provide great insight and give your trading an edge.

Head and Shoulders

The Head and Shoulders pattern is one of the most widely recognized reversal patterns and one of the most reliable bearish signals when found in uptrends. It can also be used as a bearish continuation pattern as well when found in downtrends.

The head and shoulders pattern usually forms at the top of an uptrend, signaling the end of its run. The reason why it's called a head and shoulders is because the first high (left shoulder) and third or last high (right shoulder) are both lower than the second or middle high (head), making the pattern look vaguely like a silhouette of a person's head and shoulders. A trendline can be drawn connecting the lows after the first two peaks and extending it out to the right. This trendline is called the neckline. While the head and shoulders pattern won't win any art awards for interpretation of the human form, it should definitely be lauded for its excellent track record at signaling the end of an uptrend. Volume should diminish on each successive high, further signaling that a top is likely being formed (see Figure 13.43).

FIGURE 13.43   Head and Shoulders in an Uptrend / (Reversal Pattern—Bearish)

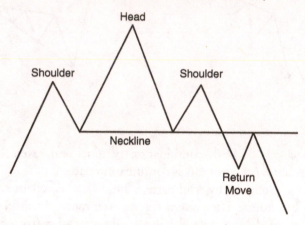

Uptrends / Bearish (Reversal)

The head and shoulders pattern typically indicates that the market is starting to lose steam. Sellers come in at the first highs (left shoulder) and push the market lower, marking the beginning of the neckline. Buyers soon return to the market and ultimately push through to new highs (head) although, on weaker volume. These new highs are quickly turned back and the downside is tested again, establishing the neckline. Tentative buying re-emerges and the market rallies once more (right shoulder), but it fails to take out the previous high. Volume is also the weakest on this attempt.

Buying dries up and the market tests the downside yet again. New selling comes in at the lows and pushes the market through the neckline. Volume should increase on the downside breakout. After its initial breakout, a return move is typically seen on lighter volume. The return move comes up to test the underside of the neckline (previous support). This old support is now considered resistance and sends the market back down on increased volume to make newer lows.

Downtrends / Bearish (Continuation)

The head and shoulders pattern can also be found in downtrends. When found in downtrends, the pattern is likely to continue the direction of the downward trend. (See Figure 13.44.)

FIGURE 13.44 Head and Shoulders in a Downtrend / (Continuation Pattern—Bearish)

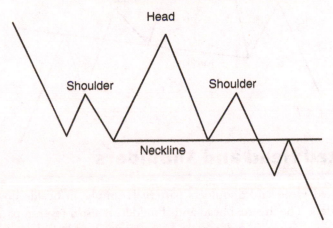

Identifying and Drawing the Pattern

The head and shoulders pattern is usually quite easy to see, especially when it's at the top of an uptrend. The three tops, with the middle one (head) higher than the ones to the left and right of it (shoulders) make it easily recognizable. The neckline is also easy to draw in. Simply draw a line connecting the low after the left shoulder to the low after the head and extend it out to the right. The move down after the left shoulder has been put in might pause at the extended neckline once reached, but should soon break through it to the downside on increasing volume.

Note: The shoulders do not have to be the same height as each other. They simply should be lower than the head. Moreover, the neckline does not have to be horizontal. It can be slanted upward (and often is) or even downward. (Although when slanted downward, a breaking of the horizontal plain from the beginning of the neckline on increased volume is usually the signal that the downside breakout is underway.) Lastly, the head and shoulders pattern can also form what's called a "complex" head and shoulders. This is when the head portion actually looks like it has two highs or heads. The term *complex head and shoulders* can also be used to reference a pattern with two left or two right shoulders. The image shows a complex head and shoulders in a downtrend with two heads and an upward slanting neckline. (See Figure 13.45).

FIGURE 13.45   Complex Head and Shoulders

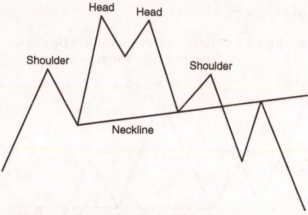

Inverted Head and Shoulders

The Inverted Head and Shoulders pattern is simply an upside down head and shoulders. The inverted head and shoulders is also a reversal pattern and is bullish when found in a downtrend. It can also be a bullish continuation pattern as well, when found in an uptrend.

The inverted head and shoulders pattern usually forms at the bottom of a downtrend and is a signal that the downside might be coming to an end. The dynamics are the same, just reversed. The head is lower than the shoulders on either side of it and a trend line (neckline) can be drawn connecting the reactionary highs after the first (left) shoulder and head have been put in. Volume should diminish with each new low attempt and increase on the upside breakout of the neckline. A "return move" back down to test the neckline is typical. The neckline, which was the previous resistance level, now acts as support and sends the market back up on increased volume to make newer highs. (See Figure 13.46.)

FIGURE 13.46 Inverted Head and Shoulders in a
Downtrend / (Reversal Pattern—Bullish)

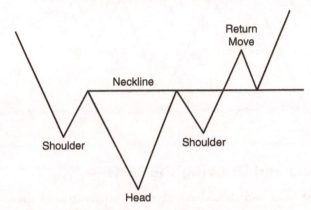

Downtrends / Bullish (Reversal)

Once the first low (left shoulder) is put in, buying comes into the market and lifts prices higher. This high marks the beginning of the neckline. Sellers come back in and push the market to new lows (the head). The low of the head should be made on lighter volume than that of the left shoulder. A rally from the head sends prices back up to the same vicinity as before, establishing the neckline. What's noteworthy is the volume aspect on the upmoves. Volume on this rally will likely be greater than the rally from the left shoulder. The market is then sent lower once again (right shoulder), although on the weakest volume yet. New buying enters the market and sends prices back to the highs. The volume on this rally should be bigger than the previous upside attempts. And an upside breakout through the neckline should be accompanied by an even bigger increase in volume.

Uptrends / Bullish (Continuation)

The inverted head and shoulders pattern can also be found in uptrends. When found in uptrends, the pattern is likely to continue the direction of the upward trend. (See Figure 13.47.)

FIGURE 13.47   Inverted Head and Shoulders in an Uptrend / (Continuation Pattern—Bullish)

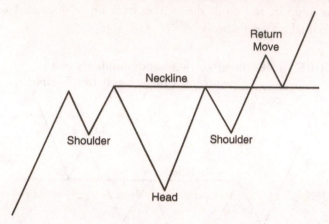

Identifying and Drawing the Pattern

The inverted head and shoulders pattern is just as easy to spot as the head and shoulders pattern, especially when the inverted head and shoulders is at the bottom of a downtrend. The three bottoms, with the middle one (head) being lower than the two lows on either side of it (left and right shoulders), makes for easy identification. Drawing the neckline is also easy; simply connect the reactionary highs from the left shoulder and head with a trendline across the top and extend it to the right. A breakout is seen when the move up from the right shoulder breaks through the top of the neckline on a big increase volume.

Remember, the lows of the inverted shoulders do not have to be even, although they should both be shallower (higher) than the inverted head. Also, the neckline does not have to be horizontal. It can be slanted downward (as is often the case) and even upward. When the neckline is slanted upward, it's not uncommon to consider the upside breakout as having begun once it breaks through the horizontal plane of the start of the neckline on increased volume. The inverted head and shoulders pattern can also form a complex inverted head and shoulders by having either two inverted heads or two inverted left or right shoulders. (Figure 13.48 shows a complex head and shoulders in a downtrend with two inverted heads, two inverted left shoulders and an upward slanting neckline.)

FIGURE 13.48 Complex Inverted Head and Shoulders

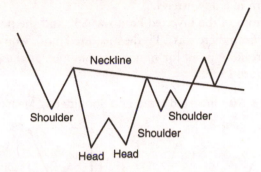

Measured Moves (Minimum Profit Targets)

To determine your projected minimum profit target, measure the distance between the top of the head and the point of the neckline that's perpendicular to it (i.e., straight down from the top of the head). This is the measured move. (See Figure 13.49.)

FIGURE 13.49 Head and Shoulders / Measured Move

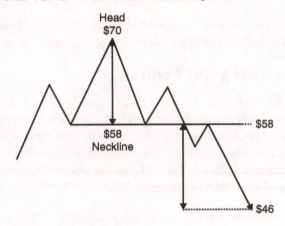

For example, if the top of the head is $70 and the point of the neckline straight down from there is $58, your measured move would be $12. To project your minimum profit target, identify at what price the stock broke through (or should break through) the neckline and subtract the $12 from the breakout point of $58 in this example and you've got your minimum profit target of $46. (Figure 13.49 illustrates a bearish head and shoulders reversal in an uptrend.)

The same measuring technique would be used for an inverted head and shoulders pattern in a downtrend.

If the bottom of the inverted head was $30 and the point of the neckline straight up from there was $35, the measured move would be $5. Simply add $5 to the breakout point for your minimum measured move profit target of $38. (See Figure 13.50.)

FIGURE 13.50   Inverted Head and Shoulders / Measured Move

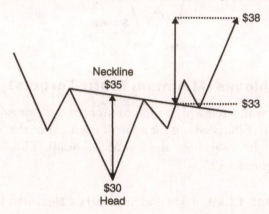

Both of the techniques just described can be identically applied to the head and shoulders or inverted head and shoulders continuation patterns as well.

Failures and Stop-Out Points

If you enter the head and shoulders or inverted head and shoulders after a breakout (breakout through the neckline), it should not meaningfully move back through the neckline again. The return move (if there is one), will typically come back to the broken neckline, but it will not trade through it. If it does, use this as a failure point and exit the trade. (Figure 13.51 shows a bearish head and shoulders breakout and failure.)

FIGURE 13.51   Head and Shoulders / Failure

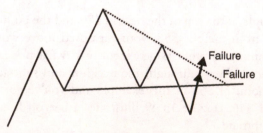

You can also draw a trendline from the head to the right shoulder and use that as an additional failure point. (See the dotted line.) If a return move makes a small breach of the neckline and you're looking for additional failure confirmation, this can provide it. A return move through these failure points, especially on increased volume, should be your cue to exit the trade. (Figure 13.52 shows a bullish inverted head and shoulders breakout and failure.)

FIGURE 13.52 Inverted Head and Shoulders / Failure

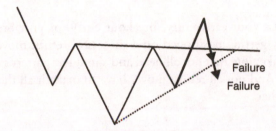

If you enter the trade before a breakout occurs (i.e., after the right shoulder has been formed and the market is making its way back to the neckline), in anticipation of a breakout taking place—draw a trendline from the head to the right shoulder (as just described) and use that as a potential failure point and exit the trade. (Figure 13.53 shows a bearish head and shoulders failure.)

FIGURE 13.53 Head and Shoulders / Early Entry Failure

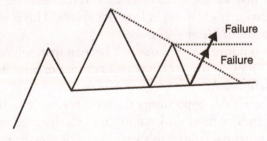

You can also draw a horizontal line from the right shoulder and extend it out to the right. A move through the plane of the right shoulder can also act as a failure point and additional confirmation that the trade is failing/has failed. Moreover, the likelihood of a failure is also increased if these failure moves are made on increased volume. (Figure 13.54 shows a bullish inverted head and shoulders failure.)

FIGURE 13.54   Inverted Head and Shoulders / Early Entry Failure

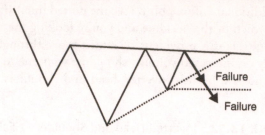

If you miss your early entry, breakout entry, or post breakout entry, you can still try getting positioned on a successful return move back to the neckline. But take note that not all head and shoulders patterns have to make a return move. And not all return moves have to make it all the way back to the neckline either.

Trading the Head and Shoulders Failure

As stated at the beginning of this chapter, the head and shoulders pattern found at the top of an uptrend is one of the most widely recognized reversal patterns and one of the most reliable bearish signals when found in uptrends. But the failed head and shoulders found at the top of an uptrend can also be one of the most powerful bullish chart patterns as well.

Of course the word "failure" simply refers to the fact that the bearish reversal expectations of the head and shoulders in an uptrend have failed to fully materialize. Instead, the market has decided it's not done moving higher and is actually getting ready to explode to the upside. This is one of the most powerful chart patterns I have ever traded.

Sometimes a downside breakout will be seen first, followed by a quick recovery. Other times the market never gets a chance to breakdown and starts its trek higher right away.

We can identify this opportunity the same way we spot the failure. Just like we drew a trendline from the head to the right shoulder to be used as an indication for a potential failure, this trendline will now be used as our first signal that an upside move could be in the offing. Volume plays an important role here. An increase in volume should follow the prices higher. The experienced trader might consider taking a position at this point. Confirmation, however, is seen once prices break through the high of the right shoulder. (Draw a horizontal line from the top of the right shoulder and extend it out to the right.) A significant increase in volume on a breakout of this plane should be seen. If a bullish position hasn't been taken yet, this is the place to do so. The ensuing move is typically fast and dramatic with an explosive increase in volume. (See Figure 13.55, which illustrates this.)

FIGURE 13.55 Head and Shoulders in an Uptrend "Failure" / (Bullish)

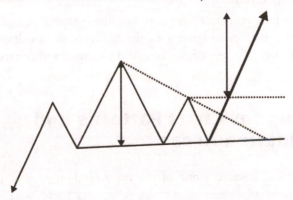

You can also do the same with an inverted head and shoulders pattern in a downtrend—just reversed. Draw a trendline from the head to the right shoulder and draw a horizontal line from the bottom of the right shoulder and extend it out to the right. These trendline breakouts will be your signals for trading the inverted head and shoulders failure. Let me add, however, I have found the head and shoulders failure at the top of an uptrend to be more reliable than the inverted head and shoulders failure at the bottom of a downtrend.

Note that legitimate head and shoulders "failure" trades (i.e., continuation trades) are rare. Take care in distinguishing it from an ordinary reversal failure. Lastly, once you've positioned yourself to take advantage of the failure trade, continue to monitor the volume and consider using a pullback through the right shoulder's plane as the first potential stop-out point followed by the neckline.

Summary

The head and shoulders patterns (regular and inverted) are most commonly traded as reversal patterns and are most reliable when traded as such. They can also, at times, act as continuation patterns as well. Where these patterns form and the type of trend they are found in (uptrend or downtrend) will reveal if they are bullish or bearish.

The failed head and shoulders can also be a reliable and explosive continuation pattern. But this failure trade is much rarer because the vast majority of the time the head and shoulders patterns act as reversals.

Volume plays an important part in the patterns identification and correct implication. Paying attention to the volume will increase your success rate in trading these patterns.

The next time you see a head and shoulders pattern, regardless of where it's found in the trend or whether it's right side up or upside down (inverted), get excited because it's one of the best and potentially profitable chart patterns to trade.

Screening for Chart Patterns and Consolidation Areas

Now that we just covered some of the most predictive chart patterns and identified how to spot them on a chart, what they mean, and how to trade them, let's take a look at how to screen for them.

Let's say you wanted to find a symmetrical triangle pattern in an uptrend. First let's define an uptrend.

Uptrend Parameters

There are many ways you could set this up. But one of the easiest ways is to simply plug in the moving averages.

First the short-term moving averages:

- **Current Price > 10-Day Moving Average**
- **Current Price > 20-Day Moving Average**
- **10-Day Moving Average > 20-Day Moving Average**

Then the longer-term ones:

- **Current Price > 50-Day Moving Average**
- **Current Price > 200-Day Moving Average**
- **50-Day Moving Average > 200-Day Moving Average**

These parameters alone are enough to put plenty of stocks with obvious symmetrical triangles on your radar screen. But you can take it a step further by adding in the price elements of the pattern itself.

Chart Pattern Parameters

All you have to do is define the size of the pattern by the length of time it took to develop (e.g., one-month pattern, two-month long pattern, three-months long, etc.). Then put in the logic. Remember, a triangle pattern has at least four points: two highs (first one higher than the second one), and two lows (first one lower than the second one).

It could look something like this for a three-month long pattern:

- **Moving High over last 90 days > Moving High over last 60 days**
  Specifically, what it'll do is find stocks whose high price between 90–60 days ago is greater than the high price from 60–30 days ago. This means the first high (point 1 of the triangle pattern) will be higher than the second high (point 3) of the pattern. This creates the top part of the pattern and would be where the descending trendline would be drawn.

- **Moving Low over last 90 Days < Moving Low over last 30 days**
  This will find stocks whose low price within the last 90–60 days ago is lower than the low price from 30 days ago. This means that the first low (point 2) of the pattern will be lower than the second low (point 4) of the pattern. This would be the bottom of the pattern and where the ascending trendline would be drawn. (See Figure 13.56 for an example of a symmetrical triangle again and the point placements.)

FIGURE 13.56 Symmetrical Triangle in an Uptrend / Point Placements (Bullish)

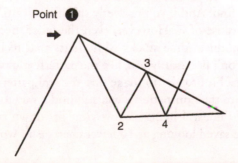

And to make sure your first high point isn't lower than a higher high just a few days before that, I'll often add this other expression in:

- **Moving High over last 150 Days < Moving High over last 90 days**
  This means that the high price within the last 150–90 days will be lower than the high price within 90–60 days ago. I'm trying to eliminate finding patterns that formed after a much higher high was seen prior to my first high point being selected. In short, I'm trying to preclude patterns that formed after a meaningful drop in price. By specifying that the two months prior to my high point time-range is lower, that increases my chances that the recent 90–60 day's high prices I'm spotting are nearer the top of its recent range, which is what I'm looking for with this example.

This simple screen will find stocks that are in uptrends and that meet the characteristics of a 90-day set-up for a symmetrical triangle pattern. To search for smaller patterns over a shorter time span, simply shorten the dates. To look for larger patterns, open the date ranges up.

Additional Comments

I have found that by drawing a picture of the pattern on a piece of paper and then writing the logic down (along with the date ranges of where each point should fall into) makes it easier to construct on a computer.

The wording of the parameters may be different on different screeners. Each screener's syntax can vary. The only thing necessary to set the above screen up is a screener that has historical daily data. That's needed in order to generate a moving average. And it's also needed to specify what date ranges your highs and lows need to fit into. If you have that, you should be able to set this up with no problem.

Note that it's not necessary to get overly detailed when setting these chart pattern screens up. Why? Because the more exacting you get, the fewer pattern-stocks it'll find. And if you're overly specific, a legitimate pattern may get passed over because of it. However, even the most specific chart pattern criteria will still produce some stocks with charts that technically meet the requirement but won't necessarily *look* like the pattern you were screening for. So it's better to be a bit broader to make sure the real patterns you're looking for get through since the non-patterns will still find a way to pop up anyway.

Plus, even if the extra items narrow your list down from 45 stocks to 35 stocks, the time saved looking at 10 fewer charts isn't worth the chance of missing a good one.

The Pattern That Called the Market Top *and* Bottom in 2007 and 2009

Let's wrap up our discussion on chart patterns by looking at which pattern called the market top (before virtually anybody else did) and then which pattern was there at the bottom (when most people were turning away).

Head and shoulders patterns are notorious for reversing uptrends and signaling the start of a new downtrend. This was never more evident than in 2007.

Months before the stock market began its collapse at the end of 2007, there was a classic bearish head and shoulders pattern looming ominously at the top of the market? See if you can spot it? (Figure 13.57 first shows an illustration of a head and shoulders pattern.)

FIGURE 13.57 Illustration of Head and Shoulders Pattern

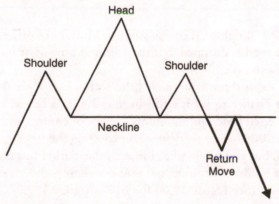

Next is a chart of the Dow Jones without the head and shoulders drawn on it (see Figure 13.58).

FIGURE 13.58 Dow Jones Market Top in 2007

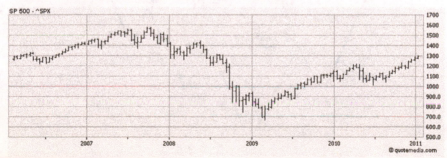

And lastly is the Dow chart with the head and shoulders outlined (see Figure 13.59).

FIGURE 13.59   Head and Shoulders Pattern That Called the Market Top in 2007

You can see it, right? Of course you do. Millions of others saw it too—even before the market dropped, but they didn't know what it meant. And if you didn't, now you do.

So what about those who missed the warning sign on the way down? They had their chance to try it again in mid 2009. What was that pattern? The bullish inverted head and shoulders pattern of course.

Earlier in 2009, when everyone was expecting the stock market to go to zero (not really, but you know what I mean), the market was quietly forming one of the most bullish bottoming patterns out there—the inverted head and shoulders pattern. (See Figure 13.60 for an illustration.)

FIGURE 13.60   Illustration of Inverted Head and Shoulders Pattern

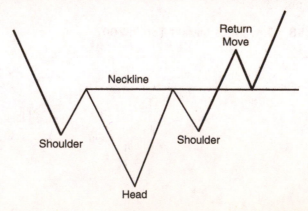

Figure 13.61 shows the chart, sans any overlays.

FIGURE 13.61 Dow Jones Market Bottom in 2009

And then the chart with the inverted head and shoulders on top (see Figure 13.62).

FIGURE 13.62 Inverted Head and Shoulders Pattern That Called the Market Bottom in 2009

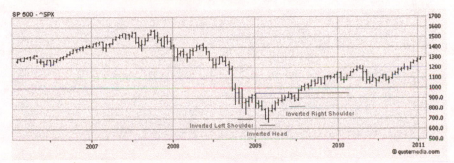

This set up one of the biggest one-year stock market rallies in history. Of course, the market wouldn't have rolled over in 2007 if the fundamentals weren't there to push it over the edge. And the market wouldn't have rallied in 2009 if there wasn't justification for it to do so. But charts can help cut through the clutter and provide sound objective analysis even when fear, greed, and emotions can get in the way. For now, they will serve as bookends, marking the top of the market and the beginning of the financial crisis—and marking the bottom (hope so) and the beginning of the economic recovery.

Summary

Who would've thought a simple chart could pack so much information in it. But it does. And a quick glance at a chart can oftentimes instantly size up the buying and selling sentiment of the market.

Understanding chart patterns can give any trader an extra edge. Even if you only casually look at charts rather than study them for their predictiveness, being able to spot bullish set-ups and bearish set-ups can keep you ahead of the market.

But be sure to combine your technical analysis with proven fundamentals for the best outcome. For instance, a bullish chart pattern in an uptrend with improving fundamentals is more likely to break out to the upside than a chart pattern with deteriorating fundamentals. So getting it right on both fundamentals and technicals helps find the best stocks with the greatest chance for success.

Chapter 14

The Right Tools for the Job

’m one of those do-it-yourself guys. And I'm pretty handy. I've made bookcases before. I put in a pressed tin ceiling (once). I'm a pro at crown molding. In fact, I've taken on enough home improvement projects to know the importance of using the right tools. But I recently learned this lesson all over again, courtesy of a new French door.

I had always wanted a French door in my home office so I decided to put one in. Of course, being a do-it-yourselfer, I decided to do it myself. After picking up the door and getting it home, I immediately got started. After aligning the door and marking it for the hinges, I then ran into my first challenge.

The hinges needed to be recessed into the door so they would be flush. So I had to create a mortise for each hinge. To do that, you should have a chisel. Since I didn't have a wood chisel (I had never hung a door before and didn't know I needed one) I thought I could make do with a screwdriver.

Guess what?—I could. But as I banged away with my rubber mallet and screwdriver, I couldn't help but think how slow and difficult this was becoming. I started thinking about all the doors being hung out there and wondered if they were all this time-consuming and difficult.

After finally getting the mortises carved out and hanging the door, the next step was the door knob. I had the hole-cutting saw and was ready to go. But I knew I had one more mortise to cut for the faceplate. This one required more precision, so I decided to run out and get the right tools, that is, a sharp chisel.

This time, cutting the mortise couldn't have been easier. The chisel went right into the wood with a simple tap. The beveled edge on one side and the straight edge on the other helped me to effortlessly carve out the groove for the faceplate. And the rest of the installation went by in no time at all.

So why do I tell you about my experience in hanging a door? Because it's one of those life lessons that you can get from just living your life. In this case, the lesson was: to do the best job you can, always use the right tools.

Sure, you might be able to get by for a time with the wrong tools, but it will eventually lead to a costly mistake. I was lucky to not have ruined that door. It's the same way for trading and investing. You can try and make do with the wrong tools and inferior research, but it's a lot harder and it may not work out as well as you had hoped. So make sure you have a good screening tool to narrow the universe of stocks to a manageable watchlist, a proven rating system, and a program to test your ideas to make sure they work before you put your money into the market.

Don't invest without the right tools at your disposal. With the right tools, you'll find that managing your money is easier and you'll be happier with the results. And in this chapter, we'll take a look at some of the best tools out there.

A Good Ranking System

There is at least one common theme you've seen me use over and over in my screens, and that's the use of the Zacks Rank. Not only do I use the Zacks Rank in the screens in this book, but I use them in my own trading in real life. It's one of the keys to my success. And it can be yours, too. Simply put, it's one of the best stock ranking systems out there with a 22-year track record of success.

The Zacks Rank is also available to anyone. Granted, it's not free. But membership to the Zacks.com website is worth it. (Go to page 287 for free trial details.) With or without the Zacks Rank, the trading strategies in this book can give any investor an advantage. But as you've also seen, by including the Zacks Rank, it improved the performance in a meaningful way. For anyone seeking an edge over the market, it's definitely something to consider.

Regardless of which stock ranking system you use, the idea that earnings estimate revisions are the most important thing that impacts stock prices is a fact that you can use all on your own. Other sites on the Web will make these estimate revisions available as well. True, nobody packages them up like the Zacks Rank does and puts them in order of best to worst. But the earnings estimates and the earnings estimate revisions are readily available on many websites and brokerage platforms. So if there's at least one takeaway from this book, it's the importance of earnings estimate revisions.

Screeners and Backtesters

Next to a good stock ranking system, it's important to find a good screening and backtesting program. Some are available on different websites. Others are made available through the brokerage company you trade with. There are also software programs you can buy as well. And they all cater to one important goal: to help you screen for the best stocks and uncover the most profitable opportunities to make money in the market.

The screening and backtesting program that I use is the Research Wizard. In fact, all of the screens and trading strategies presented in this book were all made possible through the use of the Research Wizard. And anyone can take a free trial to the program and watch the video tutorials that come with it. (Go to page 287 for free trial details.)

There are plenty of other screeners out there as well. Zacks has a free screener on its website that's quite capable. And if you become a premium member, you can access it with the Zacks Rank included. You'll also find that most big name financial sites and brokerage companies offer screeners as well.

The first thing you want to do is take a quick inventory of the data items. Does the tool offer the data items you're looking for? They will all likely have P/E ratios. But do they have P/E ratios using EPS actuals, and P/E ratios using the F1 estimates? You'll need those to calculate your price targets.

What about the PEG ratio? Or the Price to Book ratio? Or Price to Cash Flow? Or my favorite, the Price to Sales ratio? These are important valuation metrics that you'll definitely want to have available.

Data Items

At the very least, you'll want your stock screening and backtesting tool to include the following data items:

- Company Descriptors that give enough information about the Company's size.
- Price and Price Change data to measure a stock's performance.

- Ratings information such as the Average Broker Rating, Rating Upgrades and Downgrades, and of course the Zacks Rank if possible.
- EPS information including EPS Surprises, EPS Estimate Revisions, actual Earnings, and the EPS Estimates.
- Same thing for Sales, which includes Sales Surprises, Sales Estimate Revisions, actual reported Sales numbers, and Sales Estimates.
- Earning and Sales Growth: Quarterly and Yearly, and past and projected.
- Different ratios like Return on Equity and Return on Assets. Leverage information like the Debt to Equity ratio and Debt to Capital or the Current Ratio. And don't forget Dividend Yields.
- Other needful items are Profit Margins, Income Statement items, Balance Sheet items, and more, in order to dig deeper into a company.

Operators

One of the most defining things between different stock screeners are the operators, e.g., the greater than sign (>) the less than sign (<) the equal sign (=), and so forth.

All screeners will have the basics. But the more sophisticated ones will included ways to define ranges (inclusionary and exclusionary), finding the top or bottom values in a set (#'s or %'s), or applying the criteria to a Sector or an Industry or to the whole of the market itself. And some will allow you to search more specifically within a group to find the best stocks within them.

Fast and Easy to Use

At the most basic level, a stock screener is simply a database of financial information. So the screener has to be able to access this information and be as flexible as possible, so you can query the data in as many different ways as you'd like.

But first it has to be easy to use. Let's face it, if something is difficult or time consuming, you're likely to put if off or simply not do it. That's fine if the task at hand is cleaning the garage. Not so much if the task at hand is managing your portfolio. A smart interface that's easy to use is important to keep you coming back. No need to fight with your tool. Save that for the market. It's also important that data be returned promptly. Forgetting about screeners for a second—we've all been on websites (just regular old websites) that take forever to load. Frustrating isn't it? In fact, we've probably all at one point, left a website or clicked off of a video or whatever, because it took forever to come up. That's the problem with some online screeners. So to ensure that you'll get the most out of it, make sure the screener you use is fast enough as well. If it's not easy enough to use or fast enough to use, you'll ultimately find a reason to not use it. The best screener is the one you'll use.

Saving and Editing

Some screens are easier to set up than others. But regardless, having the ability to save your screens once they are complete is more than a convenience. I consider it a necessity. Screeners are supposed to help you access the data you're looking for quickly and easily. There's nothing quick about having to constantly rebuild your screens every time you want to run them.

Make sure you can edit your screens on the fly as well. There's no reason why you should have to delete an item that you added to your screen just because you've decided that you want a different value instead. If you want to change the way you define that item, you should have the ability to edit the item's value without having to start from scratch.

Reporting

Once you've built your screen, it's now time to see the results. Once again, speed is an issue. If the results don't pop out, get a better screener. Once the report comes up, you should have the ability to choose how you want your data to appear. And make sure you can access other useful information like charts and analysts reports and news stories. And don't forget exporting data to Excel so you can work with that data even more.

This may sound like a big wish list, but it's actually the bare minimum that I would require from a stock screener if someone was serious about their investing.

Backtesting

You also need a way to test your screening strategies to see how well they work. Yes, past performance is no guarantee of future results. But as we mentioned before, what else do you have to go by? If it's between guessing and hoping or actual testing with empirical stats to go by, I'll take the testing every time.

For backtesting, you simply need a way to determine how your stock picking strategy has performed in the past. This will include a deep enough historical database so you can test your strategies over a multitude of market environments.

Getting a healthy mix of bull markets, bear markets, sideways markets, and everything in between, over a decade's worth of trading and economic ups and downs is, quite frankly, what you need—assuming you want to build winning strategies with a high probability of success.

You'll also want to test your strategies using different holding periods. Some strategies work better with shorter holding periods and others with longer holding periods. Even if you know a strategy does better using a one-week holding period but, for whatever reason, you know you won't be able to keep up with that—testing it over a longer holding period is important to see if it will still give you the returns you're looking for.

Take a look at the stocks it's picked in the past as well. It's one thing seeing how the portfolio as a whole would have done. But what about the actual stocks? Get a feel for the kinds of stocks it picks. And see how the individual performance of each one has contributed to the portfolio.

A backtest report will produce a lot of data, especially if you're rebalancing a seven-stock portfolio once a week for 10 years. Make sure the program is able to provide you with an instant analysis. A performance chart showing the equity curve will instantly show you if your screen has any merit. And then a summary of statistics that will display the percentage gain (total and annual), the win ratio (how many times you won or lost), the number of stocks you'll be holding in your portfolio each time (and its turnover), and the risk and volatility (maximum drawdown) you'll have to be comfortable in assuming to trade it.

Any capable backtester should have at least these things and more. So you need a good screener: capable, flexible, fast, and easy to use. And you need a good backtester to test your strategies and produce detailed and useful reports. With a tool like that, you'll be on your way to becoming a better trader.

Research Wizard: A Complete Research Tool

The Research Wizard stock screening and backtesting program is indeed a complete research tool.

It's a stock screener and a ranker. You can generate alerts, customize reports, create portfolios, and access charts. Perform detailed industry and peer analysis. And best of all, you can backtest your stock picking ideas and trading strategies.

The program comes loaded with over 8,500 stocks in its universe. More than 650 different database items to pick and choose from. There's a calculation expression feature to create your own items. (A user can create his own customized items, e.g., compare one item to another item, combine different items together, even compare an item's value to its value from a different time period.) And there's access to over 10 years of historical data to screen on, research with, and to backtest over.

The program also comes loaded with over 50 predefined screens that Zacks has already created, including all of the screens laid out in this book and many others.

Figure 14.1 shows a screenshot of the main page.

FIGURE 14.1   Research Wizard Main Page

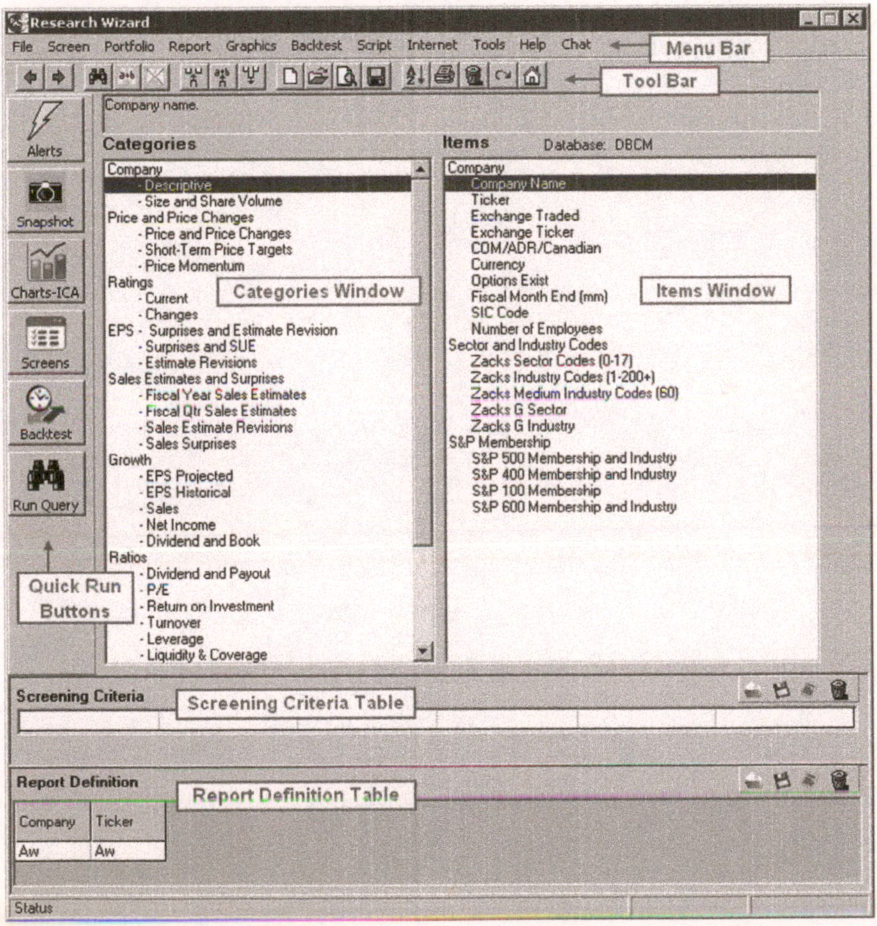

At the top is the Menu Bar, and beneath, there is the Tool Bar. On the left-hand side you have your Quick Run Buttons, also known as the Access Buttons. In the middle there are two big windows labeled Categories and Items. All of the data within the Research Wizard is organized within these two windows. Beneath there is the Screening Criteria Table and the Report Definition Table.

What's interesting is I have found that half of the Research Wizard customers use the program for the proven trading strategies that come with it. And the other half uses the program for the tool that it is: to screen and research stocks on their own and test it all to make sure it works.

Of course, the "strategy guys" also find themselves using the tool. (Who wouldn't want to put their ideas to the test?) And the "tool guys" find themselves using our strategies either as defined or modified to their own preference. Either way, the program is as versatile as it is powerful. And whatever level trader or investor you are, it can help take your stock picking and trading to the next level.

Chapter 15

Getting Started Screening and Backtesting

You already know the importance of screening and backtesting after reading Chapter 1. And you also know what kind of trader you are or what kind of trader you want to be, especially after seeing all of those great screening strategies and stock picking ideas. There's something very exciting about each and every one of them.

So now what? The first step is getting started screening for stocks. And it doesn't have to be complicated.

Screening for Stocks

Screening for stocks is like putting together a shopping list. Think about what you want and write it down. Start with the basics:

- **Price:** Do you want cheap stocks under $5? Or do you want higher-priced stocks? Simple question. But whatever the answer, put it into your screen. Why waste time looking at stocks under $5 if you have no intention of buying any of them? Same thing with high priced stocks. If you're not interested in high priced stocks, exclude those from your screen too. (By the way, if a stock's price is high, that does not tell you anything about its value, only about the price it costs to buy it. So don't shy away from high priced stocks because you think they might be overvalued. A stock's price will not tell you that.)

- **Volume:** The stock has to have enough volume to trade it. Even if you're a smaller investor, you still want enough participation in your stock. But if you're managing a lot of money, you'll want to pay extra attention to this. You can plug in a share amount the stock needs to trade on average each day for it to be considered. Or you can use the dollar volume item, which is price times volume. This will show you how much money is exchanging hands each day on the stock. We used both in our screening examples earlier. Make sure the stocks coming through are stocks you can trade.

  Those items (price, volume, etc.) are not throw-away items. They are just as important as any other item when it comes to finding stocks you want and can and will trade.

- **Ratings:** If you're using the Zacks Rank, decide what Zacks Rank you want your stocks to have. Same thing with the average broker rating. What about the average broker rating change? We saw how important that can be in Chapter 11. Maybe the rating is unimportant to you at the moment. If so, don't get hung up on it. Move on to the next item. You can always add stuff in later.

As you can see, it's just about going down the list of what kinds of characteristics you want your stocks to have. Since there are over 10,000 stocks out there to pick and choose from, you're allowed to be as choosy as you want. In fact you owe it to yourself to be picky. A screener can help you find exactly what you're looking for. Let's keep going:

- **Surprises and Estimate Revisions:** Do you want your stocks to have had a positive surprise in the past? What about a positive sales surprise? As you know, stocks that have just surprised have a tendency to surprise again in the future. This is good to know and good to have in your screen if you're inclined. But it's up to you. If having a positive surprise isn't that important, but excluding negative ones is, put it in there.

What about earnings estimate revisions or sales estimate revisions? Same is true for these items. Stocks receiving upward estimate revisions are likely to receive even more upward estimate revisions. If they're getting downward revisions, they're likely to get even more.

- **Growth:** Are you looking for growth stocks or value stocks? Momentum or growth and income? Your style decision will impact how you search this criteria. There's plenty in this category to choose from: EPS (historical and projected), sales (historical and projected as well), net income, and more.

   Remember to be realistic with what you're looking for. And plug in values consistent with your desired style. As a rule of thumb however, you don't want to be too high. Nor do you want to be too low. If you're unsure, look for stocks doing better than the market or better than its Sector or Industry.

- **Ratios:** There are even more items to consider in this category. You've got all of your various P/E ratios. And all of the other valuation items like P/S, PEG, P/CF, P/B, and more.

   If you're a value investor, these items will play an important part in how you define them.

   As with the growth items already mentioned, when in doubt, compare your picks to their Sector or Industry or even to the market. It's hard to go wrong when doing a relative comparison. But be sure to use some of the statistical guides we presented in Chapter 9. Knowing where the advantage exists can help you further narrow down your list when you're ready.

   The Ratio category will also house the Return on Investment measures like the ROE, ROI, and ROA. Important items. Once again, using a relative measure is a good way to go.

   Other considerations to make in your screen will be a company's debt, its liquidity, and even whether or not they pay a dividend.

For me, once I get a few meaty items in my screen, I'll want to quickly run a backtest to see how that set of criteria has performed. Am I heading in the right direction or am I heading in the wrong direction? A quick backtest will let me see how these items are working together so far. This is important because while some items may do great alone or with other item combinations, they may not perform that well with a different set of items. That's why it's so critical to make sure you know whether the items you're adding to your screen are helping or hurting.

Take note that it's quite easy to fill up your screen with so much information that no stocks qualify. Yes, it's your right to be as selective as you want to be. And you should. But your main goal is to find good-quality high-probability stocks to trade in. Not to exclude every stock because it's not perfect. There are no perfect stocks. So don't bother trying to find them. But put in enough to find the best possible ones. As you add in more parameters, be cognizant as to how that's narrowing down your list.

This is your time to determine what kind of characteristics you'd like your stocks to have. Do you want stocks with increasing profit margins or decreasing profit margins? Of course, you want increasing profit margins, but did you tell that to your screener? If you specifically want something, add it in.

Are there any specific Income Statement or Balance Sheet items you want to add? Then do so. And don't forget, if you're using a capable screener like the Research Wizard, you can create your own customized items. Do you want to compare one item to another? Combine different items together. What else would you like to see in the stocks you're picking? This is your opportunity to define it.

Screening is not rocket science. But it does take some thought.

If you're looking for a good place to begin, you may want to research some of your best stocks in the past. What kind of characteristics did they have? Were there any common denominators? What if you put those winning characteristics into your screen?

And no need to worry if your first few attempts don't produce the greatest results. A lot of it is trial and error. But of course, with a backtesting tool, you can significantly cut down on the error part. By seeing what works and what doesn't, you'll be closer to finding the best strategy for you.

You probably noticed in my screening examples there were certain items and themes I came back to over and over again. Although, I added different items for different purposes and plugged in different values at different times, you'll soon find a core set of items that work and that are right for you. But don't be afraid to experiment. The R-Squared EPS Growth has proven to be a fantastic item for me. It's hardly a commonly used item. And you'd be hard pressed to find it in many screeners. But after experimenting with different items, I "discovered" a great one that has served me well.

That also hits on a good point. You can get inspiration from a great tool.

I would never have thought about the R-Squared EPS Growth Rate item had it not been staring at me in the face. In fact there are a lot of great screening strategies and techniques I would never have come across had it not been for the capability of the program.

We've all heard people say that when they golf with a better golfer it raises their game. That's true not just for golf but any sport. Or when they work with a talented co-worker it makes them perform better. The same is true for the tools that you use.

> **You can get inspiration from a great tool. We've all heard people say that when they golf with a better golfer it raises their game. The same is true for the tools that you use.**

By seeing what a tool is capable of, it allows you to think about what you could be capable of. How can I use these different items to pick better stocks? What kinds of studies could I run to determine what works best? What are the different ways I can use all of this data to make a breakthrough?

A powerful program can indeed inspire you to become a better trader. Not to mention give you the tools to make better decisions.

Backtesting Your Screens

While there are plenty of screeners out there, only a small fraction of them have backtesting. But backtesting is essential to knowing what works and what doesn't before you put your money at risk. If you're not backtesting, you're just guessing.

I've already gone over why backtesting is so important and why it should be included in your screening process. So now let me show you how to set up a backtest and how to read a backtest report.

The first thing you want to do, however, is to understand what kind of screen it is you want to test. Are you screening to generate a watchlist of stocks to do additional research on, or are you trying to create a trading strategy? If the latter, the number of stocks the screen generates is very important.

Why?

Because if you're building a screen that you hope to trade as a trading strategy, you need to make sure you can trade all of the stocks it tells you to trade.

If let's say you have a strategy that makes a 100% return a year, but you have to buy 60 stocks every month to do it – if you can only buy 10 stocks, don't trade that 60 stock strategy, because you'll never recreate those returns. The very moment you don't buy all those stocks is the exact moment you're no longer trading that strategy.

If on the other hand, you're simply trying to generate a list of stocks that have merit so you can do additional research on it, then the size of the list no longer really matters that much. But these are important things to know.

Reading a Backtest Report

While the different backtesting programs out there are all designed to do the same thing (i.e., show how good or bad a screening strategy has performed in the past), the reports each program will generate will likely be different. So I'm going to focus on the backtest reports the Research Wizard generates to illustrate the kind of information you'll see when you run a test.

After you've selected the screen you want to test (we'll test the Filtered Zacks Rank 5 screen), then determine the holding period you want to apply to it (we'll use a one-week holding period) the time span you want to run your test over (for this example, we'll do it over 2009), and the benchmark you want to compare it to (we'll compare it to the S&P 500), you're ready to run your test.

Once the backtest is finished, your backtest report is ready to view (see Figure 15.1).

FIGURE 15.1 Backtest Report

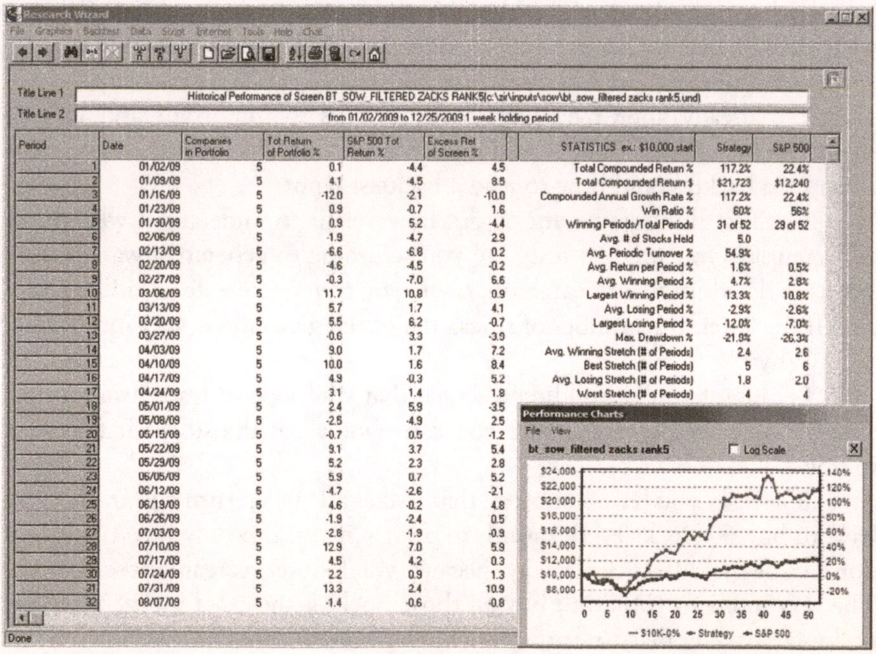

Period	Date	Companies in Portfolio	Tot Return of Portfolio %	S&P 500 Tot Return %	Excess Ret of Screen %
1	01/02/09	5	0.1	-4.4	4.5
2	01/09/09	5	4.1	-4.5	8.5
3	01/16/09	5	-12.0	-2.1	-10.0
4	01/23/09	5	0.9	-0.7	1.6
5	01/30/09	5	0.9	5.2	-4.4
6	02/06/09	5	-1.9	-4.7	2.9
7	02/13/09	5	-6.6	-6.8	0.2
8	02/20/09	5	-4.6	-4.5	-0.2
9	02/27/09	5	-0.3	-7.0	6.6
10	03/06/09	5	11.7	10.8	0.9
11	03/13/09	5	5.7	1.7	4.1
12	03/20/09	5	5.5	6.2	-0.7
13	03/27/09	5	-0.6	3.3	-3.9
14	04/03/09	5	9.0	1.7	7.2
15	04/10/09	5	10.0	1.6	8.4
16	04/17/09	5	4.9	-0.3	5.2
17	04/24/09	5	3.1	1.4	1.8
18	05/01/09	5	2.4	5.9	-3.5
19	05/08/09	5	-2.5	-4.9	2.5
20	05/15/09	5	-0.7	0.5	-1.2
21	05/22/09	5	9.1	3.7	5.4
22	05/29/09	5	5.2	2.3	2.8
23	06/05/09	5	5.9	0.7	5.2
24	06/12/09	5	-4.7	-2.6	-2.1
25	06/19/09	5	4.6	-0.2	4.8
26	06/26/09	5	-1.9	-2.4	0.5
27	07/03/09	5	-2.8	-1.9	-0.9
28	07/10/09	5	12.9	7.0	5.9
29	07/17/09	5	4.5	4.2	0.3
30	07/24/09	5	2.2	0.9	1.3
31	07/31/09	5	13.3	2.4	10.9
32	08/07/09	5	-1.4	-0.6	-0.8

STATISTICS ex.: $10,000 start	Strategy	S&P 500
Total Compounded Return %	117.2%	22.4%
Total Compounded Return $	$21,723	$12,240
Compounded Annual Growth Rate %	117.2%	22.4%
Win Ratio %	60%	56%
Winning Periods/Total Periods	31 of 52	29 of 52
Avg. # of Stocks Held	5.0	
Avg. Periodic Turnover %	54.9%	
Avg. Return per Period %	1.6%	0.5%
Avg. Winning Period %	4.7%	2.8%
Largest Winning Period %	13.3%	10.8%
Avg. Losing Period %	-2.9%	-2.6%
Largest Losing Period %	-12.0%	-7.0%
Max. Drawdown %	-21.9%	-26.3%
Avg. Winning Stretch (# of Periods)	2.4	2.6
Best Stretch (# of Periods)	5	6
Avg. Losing Stretch (# of Periods)	1.8	2.0
Worst Stretch (# of Periods)	4	4

Performance Chart

Figure 15.2 shows a snapshot of a backtest performance chart.

FIGURE 15.2 Performance Chart

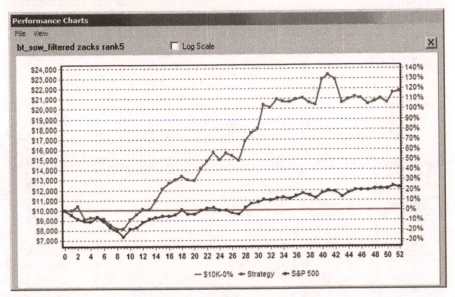

The first thing you'll notice in the backtest report is the performance chart. This will instantly show you how the strategy has performed and if your strategy is worth looking into any further. Clearly, this one looks pretty good.

You can also display the information as a bar chart (not shown) rather than as a line chart.

The rest of the report is broken down into two sections: the main backtest report and the statistics table.

Main Backtest Report

Figure 15.3 shows a snapshot of the first six columns of the main backtest report. Let's take a closer look at what's in each of these sections:

1. Displays the annualized returns for your backtest report.

2. Indicates the number of up and down periods seen by the market (i.e., the benchmark selected—in this case the S&P 500), during your test period.

In this example, there were 29 one-week periods when the S&P was up. And 23 one-week periods where the S&P was down. This

FIGURE 15.3 Main Backtest Report

| Title Line 1 | Historical Performance of Screen BT_SOW_FILTERED ZACKS RANK5(c:\zir\inpu |
| Title Line 2 | from 01/02/2009 to 12/25/2009 1 week holding |

Period		Date	Companies in Portfolio	Tot Return of Portfolio %	S&P 500 Tot Return %	Excess Ret of Screen %	
4	29	07/17/09		5	4.5	4.2	0.3
	30	07/24/09		5	2.2	0.9	1.3
	31	07/31/09	**5** 5	13.3	2.4	10.9
	32	08/07/09		5	-1.4	-0.6	-0.8
	33	08/14/09		5	4.0	2.2	1.7
	34	08/21/09		5	-1.0	0.3	-1.3
	35	08/28/09		5	-0.2	-1.2	1.0
	36	09/04/09	**6**	5	1.2	**7** 2.6	**8** -1.5
	37	09/11/09		5	0.6	2.5	-1.9
	38	09/18/09		5	-2.1	-2.2	0.1
	39	09/25/09		5	-0.9	-1.8	0.9
	40	10/02/09		5	12.2	4.6	7.6
	41	10/09/09		5	1.9	1.5	0.4
	42	10/16/09		5	-2.0	-0.7	-1.3
	43	10/23/09		5	-10.1	-4.0	-6.1
	44	10/30/09		5	1.8	3.2	-1.4
	45	11/06/09		5	1.2	2.3	-1.1
	46	11/13/09		5	-0.7	-0.2	-0.6
	47	11/20/09		5	-2.9	0.0	-3.0
	48	11/27/09		5	1.4	1.4	0.1
	49	12/04/09		5	1.2	0.1	1.1
	50	12/11/09		5	-1.7	-0.3	-1.4
	51	12/18/09		5	4.7	2.2	2.5
	52	12/25/09		5	0.5	-1.0	1.5
Average				5.0	1.6	0.5	1.2
Up Markets	**2**		29	5.0	**3** 4.4	2.8	1.5
Down Markets			23	5.0	-1.8	-2.6	0.8
Annualized					**1** 132.0	26.7	83.6

will show you if your test period was predominantly bullish or predominantly bearish.

(Of course, the benchmark's returns will show you how bullish or bearish the market was as well. But the more granular view broken down by periods also provides some very useful information.)

3. Specifies the average return of your strategy and the benchmark during your test period, including the average return when the market was up and the average return when the market was down. It also includes other summary statistics such as the average number of stocks held, and etc.

4. Lists the individual holding periods in your test along with the corresponding start dates.

5. Specifies the number of stocks that passed your screen in each period.

   In this example, this screen was designed to always pick five stocks. But if the screen generated different amounts of stocks in different periods, it would display that as well as provide an average at the bottom.

6. Displays the strategy's periodic returns.

   For example: in period 29, this shows that had you run the screen at that time, 5 stocks would have qualified your screen. Had you bought all of those stocks in an equal dollar weighted manner and held onto those stocks for the duration of the holding period (in this case, one week), the portfolio would have increased by 4.5%.

7. Indicates the benchmark's periodic returns.

   The S&P during that same period would have gained 4.2%.

8. Lists the excess returns (or deficit returns) of the strategy compared to the benchmark.

   This shows the strategy outperformed the S&P by 0.3% during that period.

Statistics Table

The next section of the report is the statistics table. This displays the return and risk metrics. (See Figure 15.4.)

The table includes:

- **Total Compounded Return %**—performance for the test period.

- **Compounded Annual Growth Rate %**—a measure that translates performance into a yearly return.

  If the test period is for an entire year (as this one is), the Total Compounded Return and the Compounded Annual Growth Rate will be the same. If the test period was for more than a year (five years for example), or less than a year (five months for example) the Compounded Annual Growth Rate would show the annual return (i.e., how the five-year total return breaks down into annual returns or how the five-month return would look on an annual basis if the same type of results continued for the rest of the year).

- **Win Ratio**—winning periods divided by the total number of periods in the test. (This shows how often your strategy's portfolio wins and how often it loses.)

FIGURE 15.4   Backtest Report Statistics Table

STATISTICS ex.: $10,000 start	Strategy	S&P 500
Total Compounded Return %	117.2%	22.4%
Total Compounded Return $	$21,723	$12,240
Compounded Annual Growth Rate %	117.2%	22.4%
Win Ratio %	60%	56%
Winning Periods/Total Periods	31 of 52	29 of 52
Avg. # of Stocks Held	5.0	
Avg. Periodic Turnover %	54.9%	
Avg. Return per Period %	1.6%	0.5%
Avg. Winning Period %	4.7%	2.8%
Largest Winning Period %	13.3%	10.8%
Avg. Losing Period %	-2.9%	-2.6%
Largest Losing Period %	-12.0%	-7.0%
Max. Drawdown %	-21.9%	-26.3%
Avg. Winning Stretch (# of Periods)	2.4	2.6
Best Stretch (# of Periods)	5	6
Avg. Losing Stretch (# of Periods)	1.8	2.0
Worst Stretch (# of Periods)	4	4

- **Winning Periods/Total Periods**—number of winning periods out of the total number of periods in the test.
- **Avg. # of Stocks Held**—average number of stocks held in the portfolio each period.
- **Avg. Periodic Turnover %**—percentage of turnover (stocks sold and new stocks bought) in the portfolio each period.

  For example, if the portfolio held on average of six stocks each period and you replaced on average of three stocks each period (sold three stocks for three new ones), the percent of turnover would be 50%. In this example, the periodic turnover is 56.9%.

  This is a good time to point out that just because you're rebalancing your portfolio every week that does not necessarily mean you're turning over your entire portfolio every week. The weekly rebalance simply means that it's checking the criteria each week (running the screen each week) to see what stocks qualify. If the stocks from last period still qualify, you'll hang onto those stocks for another period. If they no longer qualify, you'll sell those stocks and replace them with the new stocks that qualify for that period.

- **Avg. Return per Period %**—average return for the portfolio on a periodic basis.

- **Avg. Winning Period %** and **Avg. Losing Period %**—average win or loss on a periodic basis.

- **Largest Winning Period %** and **Largest Losing Period %**—largest win or loss in a single period.

- **Max Drawdown %**—the maximum drawdown, i.e., the largest drawdown in equity from a historical peak.

    This can be a single period or a series of losing periods (and not necessarily in a row). To further define it, it's the largest equity pullback from a previous equity peak. In short, it measures how much an investor might have seen his equity drop if he had traded the strategy during that time period. This could mean a drop in profit or a drop in starting equity, depending on when you began.

    If in one period the strategy was −3%, and the next period the strategy was −3%, that's a total of −6%.

    If the strategy then gained 2%, the total is now only −4% (and the maximum drawdown at this point would be recorded as −6%, since that was the largest pullback up to that time).

    But, if the next period was −3%, and the strategy then hit a winning streak, the maximum drawdown would be recorded as −7%.

    Final calculation: −3% + −3% + 2% + −3% = −7% total. And that would be your maximum drawdown.

    (The exact number would be slightly different than this simple illustration as a 2% increase from a lower level would not completely erase a 2% decrease from a higher level. But the illustration (aside from a tenth of a percent) was to show that the losses do not need to be in a row to determine the maximum drawdown.)

    This is a good statistic to know so you can decide whether or not this risk level is an acceptable risk level for your trading.

    In this example, the Max Drawdown is −21.9%. The S&P's was −26.3%.

Other good risk measurements are:

- **Average Winning Stretch** (# of Periods)
- **Average Losing Stretch** (# of Periods)

- **Best Stretch** (# of Periods)
- **Worst Stretch** (# of Periods)

These measurements illustrate the number of consecutive Winning Periods or Losing Periods.

Note that these measurements are helpful in identifying the patterns of winning periods and losing periods as well. If your strategy happens to go through a losing period, you can see the historical "norm" and the probability of success for the next period or periods.

Details Window for Individual Periods

You can also view the backtest period details for each period.

By selecting one of the periods, you can call up a Backtest Period Details window (see Figure 15.5.)

FIGURE 15.5 Backtest Period Details Window

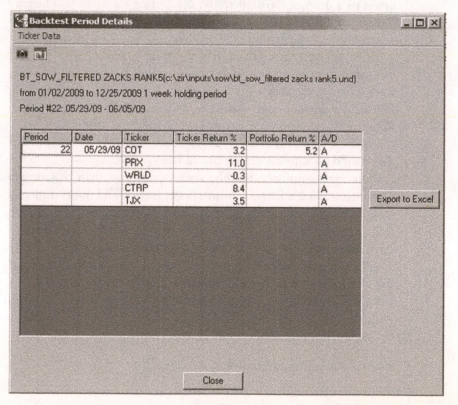

In this window, you can see which stocks qualified in each historical period as well as how the stocks performed individually.

Also, by clicking on any one of the tickers, it'll show you how often that stock came through your screen during the test period and if any of them were in consecutive periods. (See Figure 15.6.)

FIGURE 15.6   Backtest Period Details / Ticker View

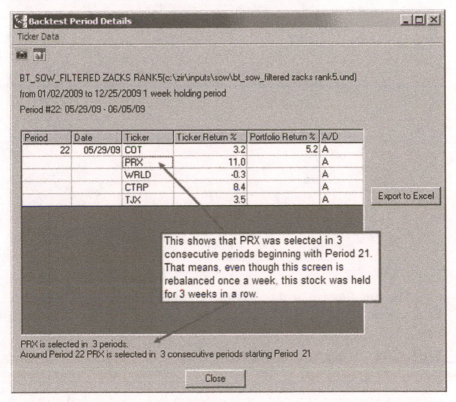

Details Window for All Periods

The Backtest Period Details window can be displayed for each period separately, or you can pull up a Details window with all of the periods in it.

By selecting the annualized return number (as illustrated previously in Figure 15.3) in the main Backtest Report, you can call up a Backtest Period Details window with all of the periods displayed. (See Figure 15.7.)

FIGURE 15.7 Backtest Period Details Window with All Periods Displayed

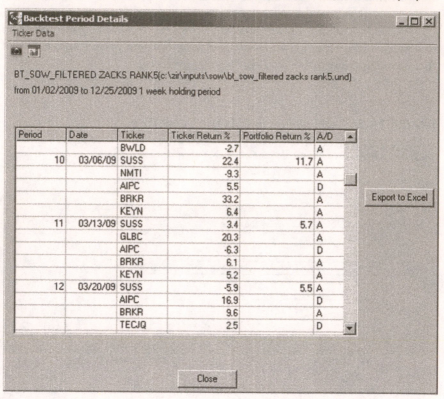

You can also export this data to Excel by clicking on the Export to Excel button.

Stop Guessing and Start Knowing

Virtually everything you want and need to know about your stock picking strategy is now right at your fingertips. Seeing how good or bad a strategy has performed in the past is an invaluable insight. Of course, this does not guarantee that it will do that in the future. But as we've talked about already, I'd definitely be more inclined to trade a strategy or to pick stocks from a screen that has proven to be a winner in the past rather than one that has been a loser.

But all of the information you get a chance to see through these reports is there to help you decide if this is a strategy that's right for you. If this is a strategy that's consistent with the kinds of stocks you want to be in: from the returns to the risk, and from the win ratio to the turnover rate along with everything in between.

Whether you plan on using your screen simply as a way of putting high probability stocks on your watchlist to pick and choose from, or whether you plan on using it as an actual trading strategy (i.e., buying and selling all of the stocks on a periodic basis), being able to see how successful it has been in picking profitable stocks can give your trading an edge.

You'll also remember I talked about periodically running a backtest during your screen-building process. By doing this throughout the construction of your screen, you can quickly see what's working and what isn't. As I mentioned before, this cuts down significantly on the trial and error part of building a screen, helping you come up with better screens in a shorter amount of time.

Advanced Screening and Backtesting

For those wishing to take their screening efforts to the next level, you can do more advanced screening and backtesting. This will not only save you time but it will also allow you to create and test your screening strategies in many different and powerful ways.

Three advanced backtesting techniques we'll highlight are Automated Robustness Analysis, Multi-Strategy Backtesting, and Optimum Valuation Testing.

Automated Robustness Analysis (Best Case / Worst Case Analysis)

Fancy name. But what does it mean? And why should I use it?

Backtesting is an integral part of the screening process. Putting a bunch of your favorite ingredients in a bowl does not necessarily mean you'll create a gourmet dish. And sticking a bunch of your favorite items into a screen does not necessarily mean you'll come up with a great screening strategy. The chef will test and retest the combination of ingredients to perfect his recipe. And the screener needs to do the same. Test how those items work together and if they're picking the right kinds of stocks you're looking for (i.e., profitable ones). If not, it's back to the drawing board.

Backtesting is one of the only ways to see how successful your trading strategies are *before* placing a trade. And testing your strategies over many different time periods is critical to making sure your strategies are robust enough to make money in all market conditions—no matter when you start using it.

So far in this book, we've gone over trading strategies that are to be rebalanced once a week, others every two weeks, and still others every four weeks and 12 weeks.

When you're rebalancing your strategies once a week, you'll essentially be participating in every week it picks new stocks. But what if you're using a two-week holding period or a four-week holding period, or longer? If your strategy, for example, is to buy stocks at the beginning of each month and hang onto them for the remainder of the month, it would be a good idea to see what would happen if you picked your stocks in the second week of the month or the third week or the fourth, and held onto those picks for a different set of four-week periods.

In other words, how does your strategy perform if you buy your stocks at the beginning of the month and hold onto them until the end of the month? Then, what would happen if you bought your stocks on the second week of the month, and held onto them until the second week of the next month? Or bought them on the third week of the month and held onto those until the third week of the next month, and so on?

This is important because (depending on when you run your screen) your strategy could pick a different list of stocks. The list might be slightly different (or meaningfully different) each week you run your screen. These different lists will then be held over different sets of four-week periods.

Therefore, if your strategies do well no matter what and when, you know you've got something special—a proven, profitable, and repeatable way to pick winning stocks. You haven't stumbled over some coincidental performance result, but instead, you have identified a truly robust trading strategy.

Much of this can be done individually through just regular backtesting. But running your screen through an automated robustness check saves time by allowing you to test your strategy over multiple start dates with only one click of the mouse, instead of setting up separate tests for each new start date you want to test over.

This is great for the casual screener and backtester who simply wants to see how something has done over time as quickly and easily as possible. And it's also perfect for the advanced strategy builder who needs answers fast, as different screens and ideas are constantly being tested and re-tested to find advantages over the market.

Let's take a look at one of the strategies we rebalanced using a four-week period to see how this can help your screen analysis. For this example, we'll use the R-Squared EPS Growth Rate. Once you're done setting up the backtest—same as before, but this time including a Robustness Analysis check—you'll see a similar backtest report but with a few key differences (see Figure 15.8).

FIGURE 15.8 Backtest Report / Robustness Analysis

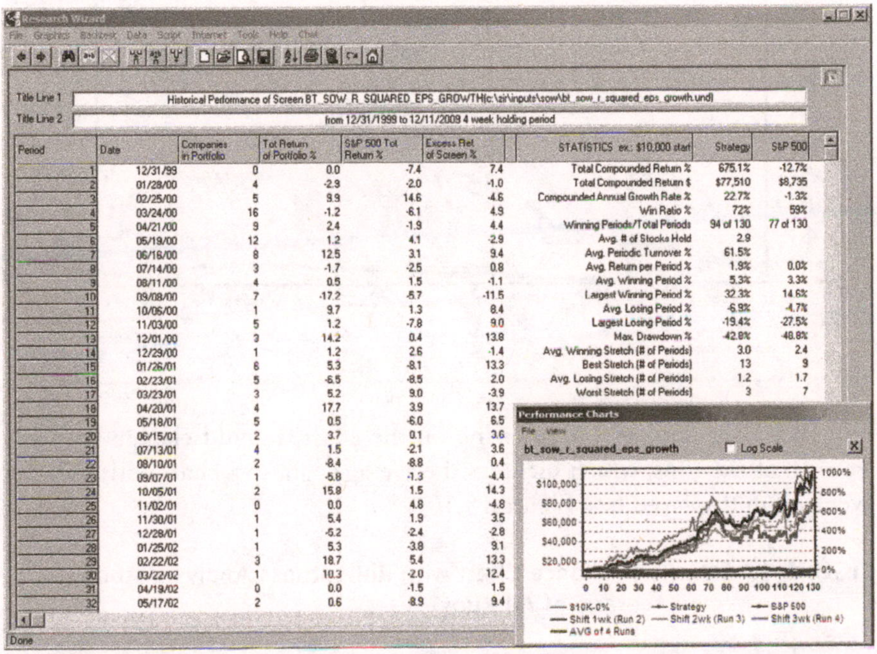

Period	Date	Companies in Portfolio	Tot Return of Portfolio %	S&P 500 Tot Return %	Excess Ret of Screen %
1	12/31/99	0	0.0	-7.4	7.4
2	01/28/00	4	-2.9	-2.0	-1.0
3	02/25/00	5	9.9	14.6	-4.6
4	03/24/00	16	-1.2	-6.1	4.9
5	04/21/00	9	2.4	-1.9	4.4
6	05/19/00	12	1.2	4.1	-2.9
7	06/16/00	8	12.5	3.1	9.4
8	07/14/00	3	-1.7	-2.5	0.8
9	08/11/00	4	0.5	1.5	-1.1
10	09/08/00	7	-17.2	-5.7	-11.5
11	10/06/00	1	9.7	1.3	8.4
12	11/03/00	5	1.2	-7.8	9.0
13	12/01/00	3	14.2	0.4	13.8
14	12/29/00	1	1.2	2.6	-1.4
15	01/26/01	6	5.3	-8.1	13.3
16	02/23/01	5	-6.5	-8.5	2.0
17	03/23/01	3	5.2	9.0	-3.9
18	04/20/01	4	17.7	3.9	13.7
19	05/18/01	5	0.5	-6.0	6.5
20	06/15/01	2	3.7	0.1	3.6
21	07/13/01	4	1.5	-2.1	3.6
22	08/10/01	2	-8.4	-8.8	0.4
23	09/07/01	1	-5.8	-1.3	-4.4
24	10/05/01	2	15.8	1.5	14.3
25	11/02/01	0	0.0	4.8	-4.8
26	11/30/01	1	5.4	1.9	3.5
27	12/28/01	1	-5.2	-2.4	-2.8
28	01/25/02	1	5.3	-3.8	9.1
29	02/22/02	3	18.7	5.4	13.3
30	03/22/02	1	10.3	-2.0	12.4
31	04/19/02	0	0.0	-1.5	1.5
32	05/17/02	2	0.6	-8.9	9.4

STATISTICS ex.: $10,000 start	Strategy	S&P 500
Total Compounded Return %	675.1%	-12.7%
Total Compounded Return $	$77,510	$8,735
Compounded Annual Growth Rate %	22.7%	-1.3%
Win Ratio %	72%	59%
Winning Periods/Total Periods	94 of 130	77 of 130
Avg. # of Stocks Held	2.9	
Avg. Periodic Turnover %	61.5%	
Avg. Return per Period %	1.9%	0.0%
Avg. Winning Period %	5.3%	3.3%
Largest Winning Period %	32.3%	14.6%
Avg. Losing Period %	-6.9%	-4.7%
Largest Losing Period %	-19.4%	-27.5%
Max. Drawdown %	-42.8%	-48.8%
Avg. Winning Stretch (# of Periods)	3.0	2.4
Best Stretch (# of Periods)	13	9
Avg. Losing Stretch (# of Periods)	1.2	1.7
Worst Stretch (# of Periods)	3	7

Performance Chart

Figure 15.9 shows a snapshot of a robustness analysis performance chart.

The performance chart will look different in that it now shows several more performance lines on it. Each line represents a different start date with one of the lines showing the average performance of the combined start dates.

In this chart, the performance lines are all relatively close together. This means the performance of this particular strategy is pretty robust. Regardless of which date it was started on (the first week of the month, or the second week of the month, or the third week or the fourth—there are four possible start dates in a four-week holding period), the results were largely the same. And ideally, that's what you'd want to see.

FIGURE 15.9   Performance Chart with Robustness Analysis Study
                  (All Runs Displayed)

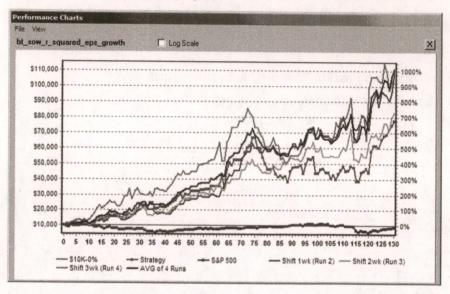

If I were to change the setting on the chart, I could change the view from all of the runs, which includes the average run, to a chart with *only* the average run displayed (see Figure 15.10).

FIGURE 15.10   Performance Chart with Robustness Analysis Study
                    (Average of All Runs)

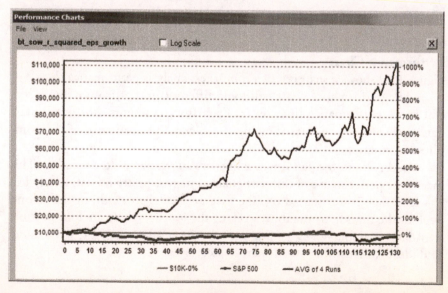

I can also change it to one with only the four start dates displayed (see Figure 15.11).

FIGURE 15.11   Performance Chart with Robustness Analysis Study (Four Start Dates Displayed)

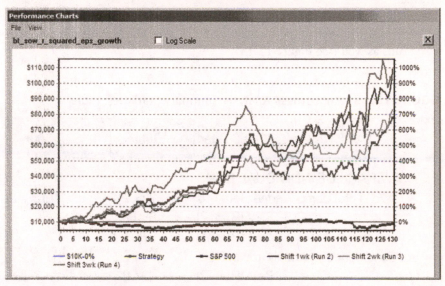

Then, I can change it back to the chart with all of the runs including the average run displayed (see Figure 15.12).

FIGURE 15.12   Performance Chart with Robustness Analysis Study (All Runs Displayed)

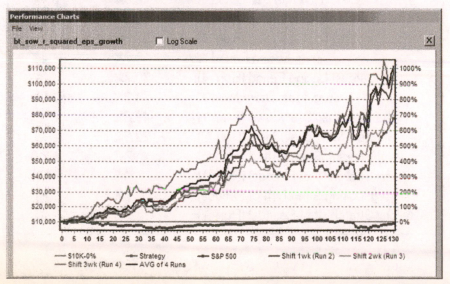

Main Report and Statistics Table

You can also analyze your strategy through the backtest report that's generated. Like the standard backtest report, it will give you a breakdown of all the stocks in all the periods, run by run, so you can see how they performed.

The statistics table does the same thing, but also provides a summary showing you the average performance of the runs along with the best and worst runs as well (see Figure 15.13).

FIGURE 15.13 Robustness Analysis Summary Statistics Table

STATISTICS ex.: $10,000 start	Strategy	S&P 500
AVERAGE OF INDIVIDUAL RUNS		
Avg. Total Compounded Return %	829.7%	-10.1%
Best (Run 2)	990.6%	
Worst (Run 1)	675.1%	
Avg. Compounded Annual Growth Rate	24.9%	-1.1%
Best (Run 2)	27.0%	
Worst (Run 1)	22.7%	
Avg. Win Ratio %	67%	58%
Avg. # of Stocks Held	2.9	
Avg. Periodic Turnover %	63.0%	
Avg. Return per Period %	2.0%	0.1%
Avg. Winning Period %	5.8%	3.3%
Largest Winning Period (Run 4)	52.9%	
Avg. Losing Period %	-5.7%	-4.4%
Largest Losing Period (Run 4)	-30.7%	
Avg. Max. Drawdown %	-34.2%	-50.6%
Largest Max. Drawdown (Run 1)	-42.8%	
Smallest Max. Drawdown (Run 2)	-23.9%	
Avg. Winning Stretch (# of Periods)	2.7	2.5
Best Stretch (# of Periods) (Run 1)	13	
Avg. Losing Stretch (# of Periods)	1.4	1.8
Worst Stretch (# of Periods) (Run 1)	3	

In this summary statistics table, it can be seen that the average compounded annual growth rate was 24.9%. Additionally, it shows the best run (Run 2) being 27.0% and the worst run (Run 1) being 22.7%.

And it'll do the same for the maximum drawdown as well. As you can see, the average maximum drawdown was −34.2% in comparison to the markets −50.6%. The largest maximum drawdown (Run 1) was −42.8%. And the smallest maximum drawdown (Run 2) was −23.9%.

If someone were contemplating trading this as a trading strategy, you can see that regardless of when you start it, the returns look meaningfully the same with approximately the same drawdowns.

Furthermore, it can also give the user a bit of confidence to know that if he happened to get started on the worst possible start date (why does that always happen to people), the returns won't look much different than if he got started on the best start date.

Other Scenarios

What if the returns were actually quite different? Instead of the returns all coming in roughly the same, what if the returns had a significant variance between one start date and the next?

For one, I'd have to give this a closer look to see if I could discover what the cause was for the variance. Is there a noticeable difference among all of the runs or is there just one outlier? Second, I'd want to take a look at the worst possible start date along with the other runs as well. If all of the runs performed well (variance notwithstanding) and if the absolute worst start date still did pretty well, I would at the very least, continue to work on this strategy and possibly still consider using it.

However, if the worst possible start date was something I would not be comfortable with, I would not use that strategy. Why? Because that worst performance could easily wind up becoming my performance. Do not kid yourself into thinking that couldn't happen to you because it could. And if there's only four possible start dates (four in a four-week period) that means there's a 25% chance the worst case scenario could become your scenario. Don't risk it. Only use a strategy if you're comfortable with the worst case scenario.

If on the other hand, you are comfortable with the worst case scenario, and for whatever reason there happens to be a larger difference between runs, you can always try and synch up with the best start date and implement it that way. But it's important to know that just because one start date happens to be the best start date for a particular year, does not mean it'll be the best start date forever. And that is all the more reason to get comfortable with the worst case analysis in your backtest. This way, if the worst case scenario happens in your real life trading, you were prepared for it. If, on the other hand, the best case scenario unfolds and the returns are higher than what you had expected, then all the better.

However, you might still prefer to participate in every start date. And as we went over in a previous chapter on how to trade the strategies (Chapter 6), you could run the screen each week, picking up all the different stocks that come through and rebalancing each week's picks every four weeks.

How would that translate to the R-Squared Growth strategy that we just looked at? The average number of stocks per period is 2.9 (i.e., 3 stocks). The average turnover is 63%, which means you'll get between 1-2 new stocks each week you run the screen. If on your first week you got 3 stocks, and in each of the following weeks you got 1-2 more stocks, that means by the end of the first month, you'll have approximately an 8 stock portfolio. From that point forward, you'll be rebalancing about 2 stocks a week.

The more you know about your strategy, the more informed trading decisions you can make.

Multi-Strategy Backtesting

Multi-Strategy or Combo-Strategy backtesting lets you test multiple strategies together, which is perfect for incorporating different screening styles into one portfolio. You may have a great Momentum style screen or Aggressive Growth screen, but not want your portfolio filled with only those types of high-fliers. You might want some classic Value picks in there and maybe some dividend paying stocks as well.

By testing these different strategies together in your portfolio, you can see how they would do as a whole. This kind of backtesting is different than putting all of your parameters together into one screen. The parameters for a Deep Value screen and the parameters for an Aggressive Growth screen would likely cancel each other out if put into one big screen, leaving you with no stocks coming through at all. But if you backtested a portfolio of screens, you'd now see how these different styles could complement each other in the grand scheme of a fleshed out portfolio.

The next figure shows how two different strategies (the New Highs Momentum screen and the R-Squared Value screen) look together in the same portfolio (see Figure 15.14).

The chart will display the combined performance line, that is, how the New Highs strategy and R-Squared strategy performed together as a portfolio. It will also produce a backtest report complete with a statistics table showing you the profit and loss profile together.

FIGURE 15.14 Combo Screen Performance Chart

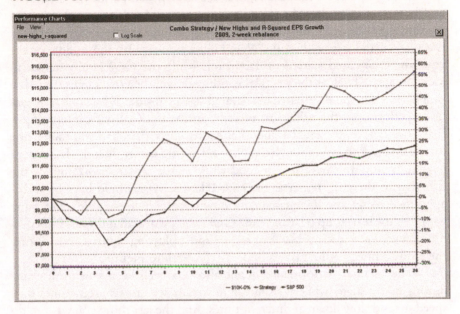

But you can also change the chart setting to show you how each individual strategy performed on its own (see Figure 15.15).

FIGURE 15.15 Combo Screen / Individual Strategies Displayed

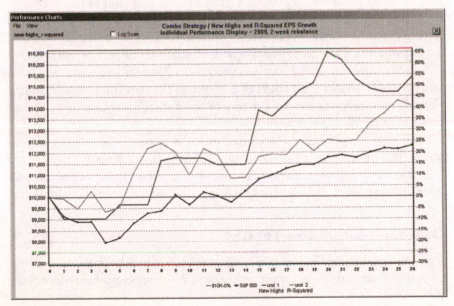

Now you can see how each individual strategy has performed separately and how they contributed to this combo strategy. In this example you can see that the R-Squared Growth Rate strategy started the year off better than the market and better than the New Highs strategy. By the middle of the year, the R-Squared started to flatten out while the New Highs started to kick into gear. Then as the year was winding down, the New Highs started to pull back while the R-Squared accelerated to the upside. While one style was underperforming, the other was picking up the slack. What's interesting is that, together, they created a smoother equity curve than had you traded one vs. the other. And even though the New Highs did better than the R-Squared overall, it wouldn't have felt so good while it was underperforming for the first part of the year, nor near the end. Likewise, you would have been disappointed to see the R-Squared cool down at the halfway point, but quite happy to see it heat up near the end. Each strategy overall did well. But combined, they produced an excellent return and a pleasing equity curve making the entire strategy quite easy to trade. (Refer back to Figure 15.14.)

The steadier performance might also very well keep you from abandoning one strategy while it's slowing down. As we can see, sometimes they speed up and slow down at different times. And the last thing you want to do is abandon the one that's slowing down right before it starts picking up, and hopping on the outperformer just as it's getting ready to pull back. Don't think that doesn't happen to traders, because it does—all the time. They call that "chasing performance," but it's really like chasing your tail.

By being able to test your strategies together, this also means you may not have to choose one style over the other or one screen over the other. See how they act together and if the performance is better combined rather than separately.

Of course, not every combination of strategies will be a winner. Some will do worse. In fact, they could all go down at the same time. But by testing them in this way, you can get a chance to see if there's any benefit or synergy by combining multiple strategies together.

By the way, if there's a stock that makes it through two or more of your screens that make up your Combo screen, the backtester won't buy it twice or put a double weighting on it, and neither should you. It'll only buy a duplicate pick once for that period, thus always maintaining an equal dollar-weighted portfolio.

Optimum Valuation Testing

You can also use the Combo backtesting technique in other ways as well, one of which is testing for optimum valuations. And this is probably how I use it the most.

For example, in Chapter 11, I showed how the top 50% of the Zacks Rank Industries outperformed the bottom 50%. I've included it here again for quick reference (see Figure 15.16).

FIGURE 15.16   Top and Bottom Industry Analysis Using the Combo Strategy Backtest

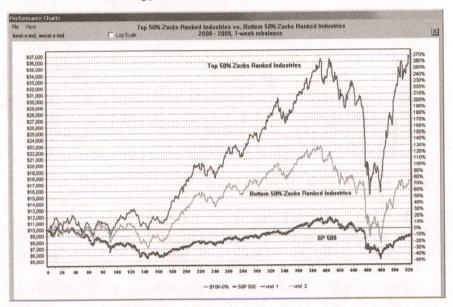

By setting up a Combo backtest with these two screens (top 50% of Industries and bottom 50% of Industries) it generated a chart that instantly showed me how those two screens performed and the magnitude of the difference over the entire length of time. While I still ran the individual strategies separately and recorded the returns; seeing a chart with one screen overlaid on top of the other can oftentimes provide a more meaningful observation than looking at them one by one or just looking at the numbers and data.

I'll also do this type of testing on individual items as well. As I've said before, there can be a lot of trial and error in screening. But by testing which valuation ranges produce the best results, I can start applying those values to my screens, instead of guessing what might work best.

FIGURE 15.17 Optimum Valuation Study Using the Combo Strategy
Backtest (Study: P/E Optimum Range Analysis 0–50+)

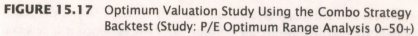

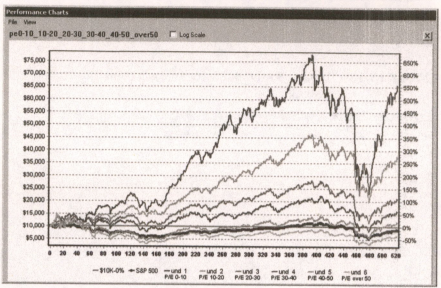

In this example (see Figure 15.17) I set up a Combo screen with six different individual screens inside, each with a different P/E range: 0–10, 10–20, 20–30, 30–40, 40–50, and greater than 50. (I ran this test as part of the P/E study we did in Chapter 9.)

By running the Combo backtest I can instantly see which valuation ranges work the best. If this was a new study for me and I was discovering this for the very first time after wondering which P/E ratio to use; with this information, I could then, at the very least, start experimenting with the values in the range that should likely give me the best results. And this type of testing can be done on virtually any kind of item.

Lastly, I like using this type of backtesting to see the impact of what the screen would look like if I changed a value or added or removed an item. I wrote earlier that the Price to Sales ratio was an important item in the Big Money Zacks Momentum strategy. I know this because I tested it. And by creating a Combo screen of two strategies; one Big Money screen with the P/S ratio and one Big Money screen without it, I could instantly see the impact of removing that item (see Figure 15.18).

This of course works on any screen and can instantly show the importance of an item. Moreover, by seeing how important an item is in one screen, you might try experimenting with it in others as well.

FIGURE 15.18 Item Impact Analysis Using the Combo Strategy Backtest (Study: BMZ Strategy vs. BMZ with P/S Ratio Removed)

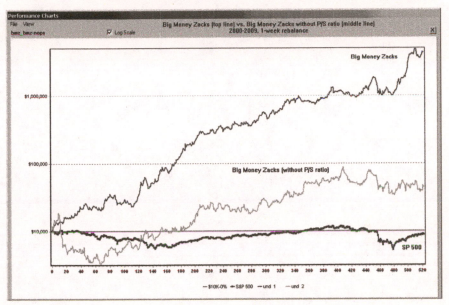

Summary

We've all heard the old adage: knowledge is power. It's a great saying because it's true. And that saying couldn't be truer than when it comes to investing.

There's no better way to improve your trading than to know what works and what doesn't before you get into the market. Knowing what works will lead to picking better stocks. Picking better stocks, of course, involves screening. And the only way to know if your screening strategy picks winning stocks is to backtest it.

Screening and testing your strategies can be fun if you're getting results. And isn't that why we invest in the first place? The next time you run a screen and you're wondering if it's any good or not, backtest it and know. You'll soon find yourself building better screens and becoming a more profitable trader.

Chapter 16

Short Selling Strategies for Bear Markets

U p to this point, we've focused primarily on bullish screens. But, of course, the market does not always go up. And while we all want winning stock screens that will make money no matter what the market does, sometimes the best way to make money is to be a short seller.

In this chapter, we'll go over two short selling strategies and examine what items are best for helping to single out stocks ready to tumble.

Keep in mind, however, short selling isn't for everyone. Not only do you have to specifically set up your account for this and be approved to do so, you also have to want to as well. There are unique risks involved that are different than those incurred when simply buying a stock. And each investor has to determine if it's right for them.

But even if you're not planning on actively shorting stocks, knowing how to spot the ones that are ripe for a fall can save an investor money by getting out before it does.

Let's take a look at our first bearish strategy called Toxic Stocks.

Toxic Stocks

The year 2008 was one of the worst bear market years in recent history. And there was almost no place to hide. Sure, we had a few strategies that managed to stay positive, but overall it was a brutal sell-off and almost nothing was safe.

However, the short-sellers cleaned up. And while the easy money on the short-side hopefully is behind us (until the next bear market), there is always an opportunity to make money on both sides of the market.

Here's a screen I was running in 2008 and early 2009 looking for short-selling candidates.

Parameters and Methodology

The main theme of this screen is to find overvalued companies. Granted, even undervalued companies were getting hammered then (not to mention downright great companies too), but usually the best candidates for short-selling are stocks that are overvalued on valuations, underperforming on growth, and are receiving downward earnings estimate revisions.

- **Price >= $5**

  I prefer to short stocks at higher prices, but I know that low-priced stocks can get clobbered too. So the line is drawn at $5. But $7, $10, $15 stocks are on the table as well as $50, $70, and $100 stocks too.

- **Average 20-Day Volume >= 100,000**

  The volume minimum makes sure that there's at least a fair amount of trade activity each day. Bear markets (whether for the overall market or individual stocks) can be prone to sharp bear market rallies. So make sure there's enough trade activity to be fairly treated if you need to get out fast.

- **Projected Growth Rate F(1)/F(0) < the Median for its Industry**

  This puts companies in the bottom half of their industry on an underperforming radar screen. Nothing sacks a company more than a poor growth outlook. Actually, there is one other thing: falling earnings estimates. And that's in this screen too. Wait for it.

- **P/E using F(1) Estimate > 50**

  Yes, I pulled out my statistical analysis we went over in Chapter 9 and went with the best odds of success. With P/Es over 50 clearly doing the worst out of the test ranges we looked at, searching for companies with P/Es over 50 made the most sense and gave me the highest probability of success.

- **Debt/Equity Ratio > 2 × the Median for its Industry**

  The Debt to Equity ratio shows how much of a company's assets are financed through debt. The bigger the number, the more debt financing it has. In 2008, with credit tightening, debt was becoming harder to come by. Simply put, companies relying too much on debt are more vulnerable. And quite frankly, bull market or bear market, any company that relies too much on debt is more vulnerable. For this screen, we looked at companies with Debt to Equity ratios twice that of its industry.

- **% Change in F(1) Earnings Estimates (last 12 weeks) < 0**

  Stocks receiving negative revisions are prone to receive even more negative revisions. And statistics have shown that companies receiving downward earnings estimate revisions are more likely to go down in price as well.

- **% Change in F(2) Earnings Estimates (last 12 weeks) < 0**

  This put the odds in your favor again by requiring the negative outlook by analysts to extend out more than just the current year. By seeing F(2) get downgraded as well, this seems to show a greater conviction on their reduced outlook.

- **Zacks Rank >= 3**

  This means there are 3s (Holds), 4s (Sells), and 5s (Strong Sells) up for consideration. But don't expect a company with the above criteria to stay in a 3 spot for long. In the meantime, the Zacks Rank 4s and 5s zero in on the worst ones.

- **Zacks Rank Top # 7**

  In fact, this item specifically has the Zacks Rank zeroing in on the worst ones by narrowing the list down to the seven stocks that meet all of the above criteria with the worst Zacks Rank.

All of these parameters combined, make for a less than ideal picture for a stock, which of course makes it perfect for a potential short sale.

Results

So how did it do? In 2008, this strategy, using a four-week rebalancing period, produced an average compounded return of over 120% while the market plummeted nearly −40% (see Figure 16.1).

FIGURE 16.1   Toxic Stocks / Bear Market Strategy (2008, 4-week rebalance)

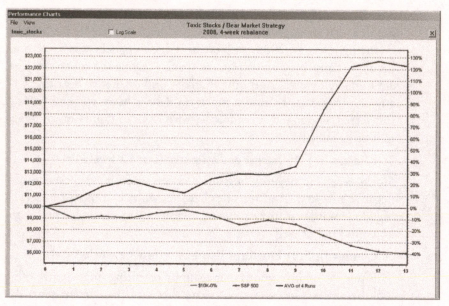

In fact, even if you didn't start trading this strategy until the official beginning of the bear market, which began in July of 2008 (a bear market isn't officially called until it goes down by −20% or more), the strategy still produced an average annual return of over 70% (see Figure 16.2).

Short strategies work best in bear markets. My experience has been that even the best short selling strategies will have a rougher go in a bull market.

I pointed out the official start to the bear market because that would have been the most appropriate time to start using a bear strategy. So when is it the right time to stop using a bearish strategy? Once an official uptrend is called, which came in the second quarter of 2009.

However, I still run this strategy regularly to find stocks on the decline. And while the wholesale bear market has been over for nearly a year and a half at the time of this writing, there's still plenty of uncertainty out there and new short-selling candidates pop up all the time.

FIGURE 16.2   Toxic Stocks / Bear Market Strategy (July 2008–Dec. 2008, 4-week rebalance)

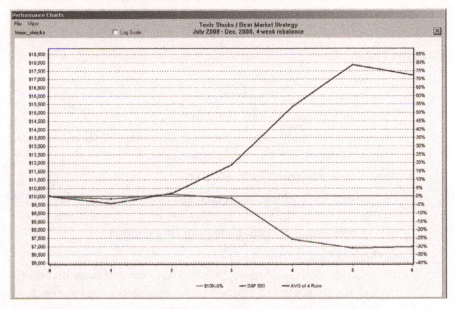

Decreasing Earnings Two Years Out

Another screen I like running for finding potential stocks to short looks at decreasing earnings two years out. I touched on it in the previous screen with the downward F(2) earnings estimate revisions. But this screen takes it a step further.

One of my favorite things for finding stocks to short is to find companies with earnings that are projected to be lower than last year *and* earnings for next year that are projected to be lower than this year. In other words, we're looking for decreasing earnings for the next two years.

It seems simple enough, but you'd be surprised at how many companies are projected down one year but up the next. (Of course, expecting to be up and actually being up are two totally different things.) But finding companies whose difficulties are clearly in front of them and for the foreseeable future leaves little reason to buy and plenty of reason to sell.

One of the reasons I like this concept is because most analysts seem to take an optimistic view of the future. I like to call this the Chicago Cubs effect. What's the old adage after the Cubs blow it every year? "Wait 'til next year." (I'm allowed to say this since I'm a Cubs fan. And a Sox fan for that matter.)

But what if these analysts sour even more on the companies' prospects? That's not a good sign. And if you still believe the views are a bit optimistic, then there's likely even more pain in store than what's forecast.

Parameters

In this screen we're searching for:

- **This Year's Projected EPS (F1/F0) < 0**

  Things are not going so good this year. Of course, anybody can have a bad year, especially when the market is bad.

- **Next Year's Projected EPS (F2/F1)**

  But a negative outlook two years out is pretty rough. Either the industry is going through a tough time or it's just the stock itself having problems. Or both. Either way, it's not good.

- **Zacks Rank >= 4**

  These are the Sells and Strong Sells and have some of the worst short-term outlooks. Combine this with the longer-term negative outlook on the EPS projections, and it makes for a good combination.

- **% Change in F1 Est. over 12 weeks < 0**

  We used this one in Toxic Stocks. We want this year's earnings estimates going down.

- **% Change in F2 Est. over 12 weeks < 0**

  Next year's earnings estimates are going down as well.

- **Current Price >= $10**

  Higher threshold than Toxic Stocks.

- **Average 20-Day Volume >= 100,000**

  Same volume requirement.

These are not the kinds of companies I'd want to be long. But they're at the top of the list of ones I'd want to short.

Additional Comments

I also particularly like to combine short-selling strategies with technical analysis. This includes lower volume when these weak stocks manage an up day and more volume on their down days.

Moreover, I like to see them trading below their moving averages. Ideally, if they have cracked the 50-day or 200-day moving average, those are great stocks to look at. A lot of trend followers and trend traders look at those numbers closely and will likely be selling when those levels are breached. And if you start seeing institutional liquidation, not to mention new short positions being taken, that can sink a stock quite dramatically.

I know it's a fantasy of short-sellers (myself included) to sell it at the tippy-top for a no-worry trade. However, those don't come around that often. But don't be afraid to sell a stock just because you missed the top. Think about it, we buy stocks all the time after we've missed the bottom. This is no different.

But again, a word of caution: make sure you have the trading experience and the temperament to do it. If you're new at it, it can feel different losing on a short-sale than a purchase. I'm not sure why that is. Is it that theoretically, there's unlimited risk? Maybe. Even though I've never seen a stock go to infinity. Is it because when your shorts are losing it's often when the market is going up and the news stations are all euphoric with good news, making a short-sale loss a little more painful? Maybe it's a little of that, too. It can feel like everybody is making money on that day but you. But whatever it is, put it in check or don't bother shorting. And I definitely recommend using stop losses. I'll talk about that a little later.

Summary

Having a good bearish strategy at your disposal is a nice tool to have. What you do with it, is up to you. Whether you plan on incorporating short-selling opportunities in your portfolio regularly, or whether you just want to make sure the stocks you're holding never show up on it, being able to identify bearish stocks can come in handy even for the long-only investor.

But when that next bear market hits—whenever that may be—you don't want to be scrambling to find something that works. You want to be fully prepared and ready to take action.

Let's hope that's a long way away. In the meantime, you can keep your bearish skills sharp by running these screens as often as you'd like and staying familiar with the kinds of stocks that are coming through.

Managing Risk
and Cutting Losses

What's a discussion on trading without talking about risk management? And when talking about risk management, the discussion naturally leads to using stop losses (i.e., an automatic order to sell (or buy) a stock at a set price). Stops are typically used to limit losses to a predetermined amount. They can also be used to lock in gains. In this chapter, we focus on the use of stops to limit one's losses.

First, let me say that all of the performances from all of the different strategies that we've looked at so far have all been done without the use of stop losses or any other type of risk management or money management rules.

And I think this shows just how solid some of these strategies are. Nonetheless, stop losses can be very useful, so let's take a closer look.

Using Stop Losses

Nobody ruins their portfolio when the market is going straight up. It's when the market goes down that people get into real trouble.

But ironically, it's when the market is going up that a lot of these bad habits are created. The problem is that even bad decisions are oftentimes rewarded in a bull market. But when the market is going down, there's no mercy for bad decision makers. Sitting on losses in hopes of them coming back can ruin your portfolio as they grow bigger.

And that's where stops come in. Some people don't use stops at all. Others, however, use very close stops, or tight stops as they're called. I'm not a fan of overly tight stops. You don't want to be kicked out of a position due to an insignificant move.

As for not using stops at all, I think it's fine if you're going to trade a proven profitable trading strategy that has been backtested through and through without the use of stops. Because it's likely that if there's a problem with a stock it's going to be kicked out of that screen soon enough at the next rebalancing period.

But personally, I like to use stops and I like to set them at 10% below my purchase price. The reason why I like the 10% rule is because it's kind of like a tit-for-tat, if you will.

If you lose −10% on a trade, you really only need to make a little bit more than 10% (11.11%) on your next trade (or trades) to get that money back. And if you're running an excellent strategy with great returns and a big win ratio, you're probably going to be in good shape because it shouldn't be that hard to do.

But if you lose −30% on a trade, now you are going to need a nearly 43% gain on your next trade to get it back.

Worse, if you get hit for a −50% loss. You'll now need to pick up a 100% winner on your next trade to get that money back. And like I always say, if you're that good where you can pull a 100% winner out of your hat, why did you just get clobbered for a −50% loss?

So I like keeping losses small.

Plus, I know that if I was in a stock that was down −15% or −20% or more, I would want to pull the plug. And since I would have to pull the plug at those more painful levels, why not just pull the plug at the relatively less painful area of −10% without doing any real damage to my portfolio?

One thing about stop losses is that some people worry that if they get out and the stock goes back up, they're going to miss out on some of the move.

Yes, if you get out and it immediately goes back up, you will miss out on *some* it. But the solution is to give yourself permission to get back in. If the stock goes back up and a big move ensues, that 10% you gave up won't matter.

Of course, don't get right back in the moment it goes one tick above where you were stopped out at in the first place. Give it some proving room.

An easy method for getting back in after you've been stopped out (assuming there's a reason to get back in) is if it qualifies your screen again the next period. Some will even wait until it goes back to the original purchase price. (Unless it goes meaningfully lower than where you were stopped out at, making it now an even greater bargain.)

So does using stops increase your returns and lower your risk? I definitely believe that cutting your losses is a winning approach.

And anecdotally, for some, it can help them stay focused and not get gun shy on their next trade. Nothing can ruin your trade psyche quicker than a big loser.

Plus, getting out at a planned percentage loss takes the emotion out of it. You don't have to beat yourself up or take it personally.

Now, I don't want to say I like getting stopped out, because that would be silly. But I can honestly say that when I do get stopped out on occasion, I feel empowered because I was able to effortlessly make a decision that most people struggle with. And I can then look forward even more to my next trade.

It's up to you whether you use stops or not. But it's definitely something to consider. And it's a great way to *not* ruin your portfolio.

Diversification and Portfolio Weighting

Another way to manage your risk is to make sure you're properly diversified and you're not overly weighted in any one group or stock.

Being in the right sectors and the right industries and the best stocks within those industries is what every investor wants. But having too much of a good thing can work against you when those groups inevitably turn around. (Just ask the tech investors back in 2000. Or even the overweighted energy guys in 2005 and again in 2008.)

A diversified portfolio is critical for reducing unsystematic risk (sometimes referred to as unsystemic risk), which is the risk to your portfolio due to one stock (or a group of related stocks).

Systemic risk (also known as market risk) is attributed to the whole of the market. Systemic risk can't really be diversified away.

But unsystematic risk (also known as specific risk) can be lessened with proper diversification and proper stock weighting.

For the sake of this discussion, let's say that the right number of stocks to hold in a portfolio is no less than 5 and no more than 20. (Investors and money managers with very large portfolios will usually be forced to hold a much larger number of stocks for many reasons, not the least of which is the sheer amount of money they're trying to fit into the market. But let's put that topic beyond the scope of this example for the moment.)

So let's say between 5 and 20 stocks is the right number to have in a portfolio, with 10 being the ideal for many. This means that no one stock will ever account for more than 20% of a portfolio and never any less than 5%, with the goal being approximately 10% for each stock.

Let's also say that no one sector or industry ever represents more than 20% of your holdings (e.g., 20% of your stocks are utilities, 20% are tech, 20% are aerospace, etc.).

Here's where some people get confused.

If you've got a 10 stock portfolio and 2 of your stocks are in oil; that would appear to be fine on the surface. Any more would increase your specific risk (which is the type of risk/volatility people try to avoid).

But if 50% of your money is tied up in those 2 stocks, with tiny portions allocated elsewhere, you've missed the point. So if 20% of your stocks are allocated to energy, that means no more than 20% of your funds should be in energy—no more.

It's good to get into the habit of making sure your stock buys are equally dollar weighted. I've mentioned this quite a bit throughout this book. But again, that means you buy the same *dollar amount* of shares for every stock.

For instance, back in October of 2005 (I'm going all the way back to 2005 because I'm already tired of going back to 2008 for every bearish example), many oil stocks dropped by −20% or more within just a few weeks.

If you had just 2 oil stocks in a larger 10 stock portfolio with everything equally dollar weighted, and both of those stocks each went down −20%, then it would have represented only a −4% loss for the portfolio as a whole.

For example: on a $20,000 portfolio, each stock would get $2,000 (10%). A −20% drop in each oil stock would be a −$400 loss in each (or a loss of −$800 total). And an $800 loss represents only 4% of the $20,000 portfolio.

However, what if you had 25% in each of your oil stocks? Now that loss (which would be −$2,000 total in this instance) would represent a −10% loss for your portfolio. The scenario gets worse the more unbalanced it gets.

Now let's say some of the other stocks in your portfolio were winners. Just remember, the more you have over-allocated in one stock, the more under-allocated you are in another.

If the 2 stocks out of your 10 stocks represented 50% of your portfolio (25% each), that means each of the other 8 stocks only represents 6.25% each.

So let's say the 2 oil stocks each lost −20% for a total loss of −$2,000. But now let's say 2 other stocks each gained 20%. However, since the other stocks had only a 6.25% weighting, the gains are only $250 for each (or $500 total). Your gains haven't offset your losses, and you're still down −$1,500 or −7.5% overall.

However, if you were equally weighted, the gains would have completely offset your losses.

If you're using a proven, profitable trading strategy, you'll typically be purchasing your stocks in an equal dollar weighted format. And a good strategy will usually have a high win ratio of 60% or even higher. And if your strategy is typically finding good, solid stocks, you'll often see those stocks coming from the best sectors and industries.

So don't put the bulk of your money (and never ever all of it) in just one sector or industry. Diversify your portfolio over several good sectors and industries. And again, make sure all of your stocks are equally dollar weighted.

If you want to make sure you're diversified over enough groups, you can specifically screen for that as we've demonstrated in some of the previous strategies.

Remember, diversification doesn't mean compromise as long as you're doing so over the best stocks and the best industries. And proper diversification can mean less risk and volatility and actually superior returns.

Summary

Keeping a close eye on risk is an instrumental part of successful trading. Unfortunately, too many investors overlook this part or even dismiss it. Only when a damaging loss is seen do they pay attention to risk, but by then it's too late.

Sure it can be tough selling a loss sometimes. And equally as hard to not load up on a stocks that are doing great. But exercising this kind of discipline is what sets apart a good trader from a great trader.

If you're losing less money, that means you have more money to invest. We all know 2008 was a terrible year. But imagine for a moment that you lost 10% *less* money than what you actually did. It feels good just to think about it. Now imagine having that much more money in the market when it turned around in 2009. Then calculate how much more money you could have made on the way up doing nothing different than what you did. The only difference being that you simply had more money in the market.

Too bad we can't go back in time. But you can start losing less and making more right away. Just decide to better manage your risk. And with all of the great stock strategies we've covered, the upside will take care of itself.

Know Your Options

S creening for better stocks is more than half the battle to becoming a better trader. But how you trade those stocks and the vehicles you use to do so can also give you an advantage as well.

In fact, one of the key advantages with options is the opportunity to make money if a stock goes up, down, and depending on your strategy, even sideways, all while assuming less risk while doing so. And with some strategies you can even be wrong on the underlying stock's direction and still profit.

Let's take a look at options and how this can fit into a well-rounded portfolio and how your stock screening strategies can uncover the best opportunities.

The Option Is Yours

Did you know that, in spite of all the turmoil in the financial markets (or maybe partly because of it), the growth in options trading has continued to rise?

In fact, for the last seven years in a row, the volume of options contracts traded has steadily increased, with 2009 setting an all-time high of 3.59 billion contracts. More and more people are now including options in their investments as a smart way to get ahead of the market.

Most people know that options offer many advantages, not the least of which is a guaranteed limited risk when buying calls and puts. They also offer a great deal of leverage while using only a fraction of the money you would normally have to put up to get into the actual stocks themselves.

But as we said at the top, one of the best advantages of options is flexibility: the ability to make money if a stock goes up, down, or sideways, as well as to simultaneously provide ways to reduce your risk and increase your returns.

Before we go over some of the different strategies, let me first go over a few definitions.

Call Option: A call option gives the buyer the right (but not the obligation) to buy a stock (typically 100 shares) at a certain price within a set period of time.

Put Option: A put option gives the buyer the right (but not the obligation) to sell a stock (100 shares) at a certain price within a set period of time.

Premium: The amount paid (if buying) or collected (if writing) for the option.

Strike Price: The price on an option contract at which you can exercise your right to buy or sell the stock.

In-the-Money (ITM): For a call option, an in-the-money option is a strike price below the current price of the stock. It's said to be in-the-money because it has intrinsic value.

If a stock was trading at $50 a share, a call option with a strike price of $45 would be in-the-money.

For a put option, it's a strike price above the current price of the stock. If a stock was trading at $50, a put option with a strike price of $55 would be in-the money.

At-the-Money (ATM): For both a call and a put option, it's a strike price that's at the same current price of the stock.

Out-of-the-Money (OTM): For a call option, it's a strike price above the current price of the stock. This option has no intrinsic value and is only comprised of time value or extrinsic value.

If a stock was trading at $50, a call option with a strike price of $55 would be out-of-the-money.

For a put option, it's a strike price below the current price of the stock.

If a stock was trading at $50, a put option with a strike price of $45 would be out-of-the-money.

In-the-money options have greater deltas and out-of-the-money options have smaller deltas.

Delta: This is the percentage the option will increase or decrease in value in relation to the underlying price movement of the stock.

A delta of .60 for example, means the option will move (or change in value) equal to 60% of the underlying stock's price change, meaning a $1.00 rise in the stock should see a 60 cent rise in the option premium. The delta changes as the stock rises and falls.

Intrinsic Value: The difference between an option's strike price (that's in-the-money) and the current price of the stock.

For example: if a stock was trading at $50, and a $45 call option with 30 days of time left on it was selling for $6.50 (or $650, which is $6.50 × 100 shares), that option would have $5 (or $500) of intrinsic value.

[$50 (stock price) − $45 (strike price) = $5 (intrinsic value)]

Time Value (or Extrinsic Value): The amount of the premium that is not comprised of intrinsic value. This part of the premium is said to be your time value.

Using the same example as above, that same option would have $1.50 or $150 of time value or extrinsic value.

[$6.50 (premium) − $5 (intrinsic value) = $1.50 (extrinsic value or time value)]

Expiration: This is the last day an option contract can be traded. At expiration, an option's only worth is its intrinsic value. Since there's no time left to hold your option to buy or sell, there's no more time value or extrinsic value left, and at-the-money and out-of-the-money options would expire worthless.

Exercise: The time in an option's trade (usually at expiration) when the underlying stock is assigned to either the buyer or the writer, based on the rights and obligations of the transaction. Exercise usually takes place for in-the-money options. Most brokerage companies will automatically exercise in-the-money options at expiration unless notified otherwise.

The expiration date for most options is effectively the third Friday of the month of the option.

If you're unfamiliar with any of these terms, you can use this list as a reference as you go through the chapter.

Buying Calls and Puts

Buying calls and buying puts is one of the most common ways investors trade options. If you believe the price of a stock will go up, you can buy a call option on it and make money as it goes higher. If you believe the price of a stock will go down, you can buy a put option on it and make money as the price goes lower.

> **If you believe the price of a stock will go up, you can buy a call option on it and make money as it goes higher. If you believe the price of a stock will go down, you can buy a put option on it and make money as the price goes lower.**

Buying Calls

Options give an investor tremendous amounts of leverage, allowing someone to speculate on a stock without putting up a lot of money. For the option buyer, this also comes with a guaranteed limited risk, which is confined to the buyer's purchase price (or premium) plus any applicable commissions and fees.

Let's take a look at how buying a call option works.

Example

Let's say you were interested in a stock that was trading at $90 per share. Buying $100 shares of a $90 stock would require a $9,000 investment.

But instead, you might be able to buy a $90 at-the-money call option for an $8.00 premium (which means $8 × 100 shares or $800). That's a significantly smaller investment with a guaranteed limited risk.

If for example, the price of the stock fell −$20 (from $90 to $70 a share), your stock investment would have lost −$2,000.

However, at expiration, the maximum you could lose on your option investment would be only- $800 (plus your commission and fees).

The option gives you great upside as well. A $20 move up in the stock price to $110 would mean a $2,000 increase in your stock investment.

However, at expiration, that $90 call option would be $20 in-the-money, meaning it has $20 of intrinsic value and is now worth $2,000. And $2,000 less your $800 premium is a $1,200 profit or 150% gain. The $2,000 gain on your $9,000 investment represents a 22% gain.

Now, let me say that options aren't a panacea. Too many people use options recklessly by loading up on cheap out-of-the-money options that ultimately expire worthless. And even though they have a limited risk (limited to what you put in), if you put everything in there you run the risk of losing it all. But smart options trading has a respectable place in an investor's portfolio. Only invest in an option what you absolutely can afford and would be willing to lose if your assumptions on the market are incorrect.

Before we move on, let's take a closer look at that call option example. Once again, the stock is trading at $90 and you decide to buy a $90, at-the-money call option, with three months of time on it, for an $8.00 premium (which means $8 × 100 shares or $800).

At expiration, the stock needs to be over $98 in order to show a profit above your investment premium. Why? Because you paid $8 for the right to buy 100 shares of stock at $90. If it goes to $98, that's an $8 move. At expiration, a move to just $98 would mean the $90 call option would be $8 in-the-money making it worth $800, which would result in a breakeven trade (less trading costs).

$$8 \times 100 \text{ shares} = \$800$$

That's what you paid for the option in the first place, giving you neither a profit nor a loss. You would need to see a move above $98 to make a profit. The higher it goes, the bigger your gain. A move from $90 to $110 for instance is a $20 move.

$$\$20 \times 100 \text{ shares} = \$2,000$$

$$\text{less } \$800 \text{ premium} = \$1,200 \text{ gain}$$

You can either sell the option at that higher premium, or you can exercise it and purchase the underlying shares at the agreed upon strike price. Please remember, that if you do not sell your in-the-money option at expiration, your brokerage company will likely automatically exercise it for you.

If at expiration, the stock is above $90 but below $98, you will have a loss of *some* of your investment premium but not all of it. Why? Because your option still has some intrinsic value. The amount your option would be worth would be the difference between the strike price ($90) and the stock price.

For example: if the price of the stock was trading at $96.50, your option would be worth $6.50 or $650.

$$\$96.50 \text{ (stock price)} - \$90 \text{ (strike price)} = \$650$$

$$(\$800 \text{ premium} - \$650 \text{ value} = -\$150 \text{ loss})$$

If, at expiration, the stock is below $90, you will have a loss of *all* of your investment premium. Why? Since there's no more time left, there's no time value. And since there's no intrinsic value either, the option would expire worthless.

The benefit is that's all you can lose. No matter how low the market goes, you can only lose the amount you paid for the option, plus your trading cost. Never any more, unlike a stock, where your losses will get bigger the lower the stock falls. Of course, with a stock purchase, there's no time limit as to how long you can hang onto it though.

I should also mention that you don't have to hold onto the option until expiration. It is completely liquid and you can sell it at any time before it expires. Doing so will let you benefit from both intrinsic value (if there is any) and time value as well.

Buying Puts

Buying puts works the same way except you're profiting if the market goes down.

Example

Let's say a stock is at $100 and you buy a three-month, $100 put option, for a premium of $10 (that is, $10 × $100 a share = $1,000). At expiration, the stock needs to fall below $90 in order to show a profit beyond your investment premium. That's because you paid $10 for the right to sell 100 shares of stock at $100. If it goes to $90, that's a $10 move. At expiration, a move to just $10 would result in a breakeven trade (less trading costs).

$$\$10 \times 100 \text{ shares} = \$1,000$$

That's what you paid for the option in the first place, giving you neither a profit nor a loss. You would need to see a move below $90 to make a profit. The lower it goes, the bigger your gain. A move to $70 for example is a $30 move.

$$\$30 \times 100 \text{ shares} = \$3,000$$

$$\text{less } \$1,000 \text{ premium} = \$2,000 \text{ gain}$$

You can either sell the option at that higher premium or you can exercise it and sell the underlying shares at the agreed upon strike price. Please remember, that if you do not sell your in-the-money option at expiration, your brokerage company will likely automatically exercise it for you.

If at expiration, the stock is below $100 but above $90, you will have a loss of some of your investment premium but not all of it. Why? Because your option still has some intrinsic value. The amount your option would be worth would be the difference between the strike price ($100) and the stock price.

For example: if the price of the stock was trading at $93, your option would be worth $7 or $700.

$$\$100 \text{ (strike price)} - \$93 \text{ (stock price)} = \$700$$

$$(\$1,000 \text{ premium} - \$700 \text{ value} = -\$300 \text{ loss})$$

If at expiration, the stock is above $100, you will have lost your entire investment premium. Since there's no more time left, there's no time value. And since there's no intrinsic value either, the option would expire worthless.

The benefit is that's all you can lose. No matter how high the market goes, you can only lose the amount you paid for the option, plus your trading cost. Never any more, unlike a stock, where your losses will get bigger the higher the stock goes up. Of course, with stocks, as we've said before, there's no time limit as to how long you can hang onto it though.

Once again, you don't have to hold onto the option until expiration. It's completely liquid and you can sell it at any time before it expires. Doing so will let you benefit from both intrinsic value (if there is any) and time value as well.

Another benefit to buying put options is that it's a great alternative to short-selling. Some people simply do not want to short sell a stock or can't, either because they are simply uncomfortable doing so, or their account is not set up for margin, or they are in a qualified account (i.e., retirement account) and can't, or their brokerage can't borrow the shares to facilitate a short sale.

Either way, all these conditions make buying put options a great alternative for betting that a stock will go down.

Tip: Buy In-the-Money Options

Both the call example and the put example used at-the-money options for easy illustration. However, when buying options, I strongly recommend buying in-the-money options. They will give you a higher probability of success.

You may spend an extra few hundred dollars on each option you buy that's in-the-money, but at expiration, it's worth it. Why? Because at expiration your option's only value is its intrinsic value. Since there's no time left, there's no time value.

Let's take a look at two examples: one that's in-the-money and one that's out-of-the-money and compare them.

In-the-Money Example

Let's say a stock was trading at $50. A $45 call option with a premium of $6.50 (i.e., $650) would be comprised of:

- $5 of intrinsic value (or $500)
- $1.50 of time value (or $150)

At expiration however, if the stock was still trading at $50, the option would be worth $5 or $500. Why? Because once again, at expiration, there's no time left and the only value is the intrinsic value, which is the difference between the stock's price and the strike price that's in-the-money.

At-the-Money/Out-of-the-Money Example

Let's now say instead of a $45 call option, you had a $50 call option. That $50 call might have a premium of $4.00 or $400. If so, it would be comprised of:

- $0 of intrinsic value ($0)
- $4 in time value ($400)

At expiration, if the stock is at $50, the $50 call would be worth nothing. Why? Because there's no intrinsic value, and with no time remaining, there's no time value. Now let's go back to the beginning.

Someone might decide that buying the $50 call was the better proposition since it was only going for $400 versus the $45 call that was going for $650. In fact, someone might conclude that the $55 call was the better bargain because it would be even cheaper, and they might actually be able to get two of them for what it would cost to get one in-the-money call.

But at expiration you can see that the cheaper options (out-of-the-money options) were the worse investment because at expiration, they lost all of their premium (which was comprised solely of time value and which had expired) whereas the in-the-money still had its intrinsic value left.

The other benefit to buying in-the-money options is that they'll have bigger deltas. A delta of .70 or 70% for example means it will move 70% of the underlying stock's move. So a $1.00 move in the stock means the option will move 70 cents.

Out-of-the-money options have smaller deltas, making it harder to profit.

And while option deltas change as the price of the underlying stock changes (the delta increases as the option gets closer to the money/in-the-money—and the delta decreases as the option gets further away from the money/out-of-the-money), giving yourself the best chance for success right from the start, is the smartest way to go.

As I mentioned earlier, too many people will load up on cheap out-of-the-money options in hopes of seeing an extraordinary move and cashing in. The problem is that, the majority of the time, that won't happen. And when it doesn't happen, they forfeit everything they put into it. By focusing on the right options, you can tilt the odds of success in your favor.

Tip: Buy More Time

Many investors will also skimp on time in hopes of saving a couple of hundred dollars on their purchase price. But in reality, this savings can be costly.

Example
Let's look at three hypothetical options all at the same strike price:

- There's a two-month option going for $5.00 (or $500).
- A four-month option going for $7.00 (or $700).
- And a six-month option going for $9.30 (or $930).

Some simple math will quickly show you which options are the better bargain.

For the two-month option, divide the premium ($500) by the amount of time remaining (two months). That means each month of time costs the investor $250.

Now take the four-month option; divide that premium ($700) by the amount of time remaining (four-months) and you'll see that the investor would only be paying $175 for each month of time he/she gets to hold onto that option.

The six-month option is even better ($930 divided by six months) because you're only paying $155 per month of time in this case.

Using the preceding examples, the six-month option is the better bargain because you're paying less for each unit of time than the others. Of course, if you really don't think you want (or need) that much time, the four-month option would still be the better bargain than the two-month option. So while you don't need to buy excessive time, as a general rule, it's usually a good idea to get a little extra time. This is true for two major reasons:

1. If you run out of time, it's game over on that option. And sometimes the difference between making money and losing money in options comes down to just a little extra time.
2. Time value shrinks (time decay) at its most rapid pace within the last 30 days or so prior to expiration.

The simple act of getting a little extra time can keep you out of that time-value-crunch red zone.

Straddles and Strangles

A straddle or a strangle involves buying both a call and a put at the same time.

As discussed earlier, you buy a call if you expect the market to go up. And you buy a put if you expect the market to go down. A straddle or a strangle is a strategy to use when you're not sure which way the market will go, but you believe something big will happen in either direction.

> A straddle or a strangle is a strategy to use when you're not sure which way the market will go, but you believe a big move will happen in either direction.

For example, let's say it's earnings season and you expect a big move to occur, either up or down, based on whether the company reports a positive surprise or a negative surprise. With these strategies, you can make money in either direction without having to worry about whether you guessed correctly or not.

What's the difference between a straddle and a strangle?

- A **straddle** is when you have both a call and a put, with the *same* strike price (both at-the-money), and with the same expiration dates.

- A **strangle** is when you have both a call and a put option, with *different* strike prices (both out-of-the-money), and with the same expiration dates.

Both strategies are used to position oneself on either side of the market in an effort to take advantage of a potentially big move, in either direction.

Once again, this could be before an earnings release, or a key announcement, or a big report, or maybe the charts are suggesting a big breakout could be getting ready to take place in one direction or another. Whatever the reason, this is generally when someone would implement this type of strategy.

Example
Let's say a stock was trading at $100 a few days before their earnings announcement. So you decide to put on a straddle by buying:

- the $100 strike call
- and the $100 strike put

Since you only plan on being in the trade for a few days (to maybe a few weeks), you decide to get into the soon-to-expire options. But isn't getting more time usually better? And why the at-the-money options? Aren't in-the-money options better, too? Yes to both, in most cases, when buying a call *or* a put.

But when playing both sides of the market simultaneously, for an event you expect to take place in the near immediacy, the opposite is true. Why? Because at expiration, your profit is the difference between how much your options are in-the-money minus what you paid for them. So if you don't need a lot of time, this keeps the cost down and your profit potential up.

If you paid $150 for an at-the-money call option that will expire shortly and another $150 for an at-the-money put option that will expire shortly, your cost to put on the trade was $300 (not including transactions costs). If that stock shot up $10 as a result of a positive earnings surprise, that call option that you paid $150 for would now be worth $1,000. And that put option would be worth zero ($0).

So let's do the math: if the call, which is now $10 in-the-money, is worth $1,000, then subtract the $150 you paid, and that gives you an $850 profit on the call. The put, on the other hand, is out-of-the-money, and is worth nothing, which means you lost −$150 on the put. Add it all together, and on a $300 investment, you just made a profit of $700. Pretty good—especially for not even knowing which way the stock would even go.

However, if you paid more for each side of the trade, those would be extra costs to overcome. But by keeping each side's cost as small as reasonably possible, that leaves more profit potential on the winning side and a smaller loss on the losing side.

Moreover, if the stock stays flat (in other words, the big move you expect to see happen doesn't materialize, thus resulting in both sides of the trade expiring worthless), your cost of the trade was kept to a minimum.

So buying a straddle or a strangle, by their very nature, should be looked at as a short-term trade. If the outcome of the event that prompted you to get into the straddle or strangle in the first place now has you strongly believing that a continuation of the up move or down move is in order, you could then exit the straddle or strangle and move into the one-sided call or put and apply the *in-the-money* and *more time* rules for that, as discussed earlier.

Spreads

While straddles and strangles are strategies that incorporate buying both calls and puts simultaneously, spreads involve buying and selling multiple calls *or* multiple puts and with different strike prices and/or expiration dates. These can be put on for either debits or credits. And you can both buy spreads or write them.

There are many different kinds of spread strategies out there. But the most popular ones are buying bull call spreads and buying bear put spreads. This involves buying the nearby strike price and selling the farther out strike.

One thing to keep in mind however, is that while buying spreads can typically be put on quite inexpensively and with limited risk, they also give the investor a limited profit potential.

Example

Let's say a stock was at $40. If you were mildly bullish on the stock, you might consider a bull call spread.

- I could buy a $40 call at a premium of $4.00 (or $400).
- And I could write a $45 call for a premium of $2.50 (or $250).

If I spent $400 and collected $250, my net outlay was $150.

My maximum profit comes in between the two strike prices minus the cost to put it on.

Let's take a look at four different scenarios using the example we just outlined and see how our bull call spread would fare.

Scenario 1

If the stock at expiration were to go up to $45, my $40 call would be worth $500 because it's now $5 in-the-money. That's a $100 profit on that call.

The $45 call that I wrote would be now be worth $0, which means I keep the entire $250 collected. That's a $250 profit for me. Add those both together and that's a $350 profit—on just a $150 investment.

Scenario 2

If the stock at expiration were to skyrocket higher, let's say to $60; the $40 call would be worth $20 or $2,000 because it's now $20 in-the-money. That's a $1,600 profit on that call.

However, the $45 call would now be worth $15 or $1,500, which means I would have a loss of −$1,250 on that one. Add those together and it still comes out to be $350.

The call that I write limits my gains on the one that I buy, capping my upside. Because of this, bull call spreads are not advisable if you're expecting a significant move to occur because you'd be limiting your profit potential. But if you have a milder bullish outlook, this is an excellent strategy to use. Essentially, you're benefiting from the time decay of the farther out-of-the-money strike price.

Scenario 3

If the stock at expiration were to stay flat at $40, the $40 call would be worth $0, which means I would've lost −$400 on that call.

The $45 call would also expire worthless, meaning I would keep the entire $250 collected as my profit on that one. Add those together and you get a loss of −$150. Your risk is limited to what you paid for the spread.

But if the stock went to $41 for example, the $40 call would now be worth $100. Since I paid $400 and it's now $1 in the-money, it's now worth $300. So instead of a loss of −$400, the loss is only −$300 on that call.

Once again though, the $45 call would still expire worthless, meaning I would keep the entire $250 collected for my profit on that one. Add those together and now the loss is only −$50.

In this example, at $41.50, I'd break even for a scratch trade (0% gain or loss). And anything above it would be a proportional profit. My maximum profitability would come in at $45 or higher.

Scenario 4

If at expiration, the stock went down to $35 for example (or even lower), the $45 call would be worth $0 for a loss of −$400.

And the $45 call would also be worth $0, meaning I would keep the entire $250 collected. Add those together (−$400 + $250) and that equals a loss of −$150.

Once again, no matter what, my loss is always limited to what I paid for the spread. As you can see, options have lots of flexibility and different ways to make money. Strategies for up moves or down, big moves and small, fast markets or slow, even strategies if you have no idea which way the market will go.

Covered Call Writing

Covered call writing (writing calls on a stock you own) is an excellent strategy to use in both up, down, and sideways markets. This is a strategy used to reduce risk and generate income. In fact, you can even execute a strategy like this in many retirement accounts.

So let's review: Buying an option gives you the right but not the obligation to purchase 100 shares of a stock at a certain price within a certain period of time.

The price you pay, let's say $500, is the premium. In general, if the stock goes up, the call option will increase in value. If the stock goes down, it will decrease in value. But your risk is limited to what you paid for the option. Even if the stock went to zero, you could never be on the hook for more than you paid for the option.

If you write an option, you're collecting that premium. Someone else is buying the right to own 100 shares of a stock at a certain price within a certain period of time. If that stock goes down and the option expires worthless, the buyer of the option loses −$500. But the writer of the option makes $500.

For a covered call strategy, this is who we're going to be—the writer.

So let's say you have 100 shares of stock at $110 for instance. For every dollar the stock goes up or down, your investment will increase or decrease by $100. Now let's say you wrote a four-month, $125 call option for a premium of $6.50. (You stand to collect $650.)

Let's go through five quick examples to see how you can make money and offset risk. And while writing a call against a stock you own will not increase your risk, it can limit your upside if there's a big advance in the stock.

Example 1

If the stock goes down $6.50 to $103.50, between when you wrote the option and expiration, you've just offset $6.50 or $650 worth of your downside risk. How? Because if the stock went down $6.50, your stock position just declined by $650. But, at option expiration, you've gained $650 on the option you wrote, essentially losing nothing, even though your stock position declined by $650.

$110 (stock buy price) − $6.50 (decline to $103.50) = −$650 loss on stock

You collected $650 (premium) for writing option = $650 gain on option

−$650 stock loss + $650 option gain = $0 (or breakeven)

The maximum profit zone is $103.50 to $131.50. The higher you are in the zone, the more profitable your trade becomes. Below $103.50, your trade starts to lose money as the loss in your stock becomes greater than the downside protection the covered call provided. But if you're worried about downside risk in your stocks, this is a great way to hedge some of it away and potentially make money at the same time.

Example 2

Now let's say the stock stays flat. It doesn't go up or down. Just stays at $110. You haven't made anything or lost anything on that stock. But at expiration, that $125 call option you wrote for $650 would expire and be paid to you. So even though the stock didn't budge, you still made $6.50 or $650.

How? Because if the underlying stock at option expiration ended unchanged from where you purchased it, that means the stock neither made nor lost anything. However, you also collected (kept) the entire $6.50 premium or $650 from writing the $125 call option, resulting in an overall gain of $650 on the trade (less trading costs).

$110 (stock buy price) − $0 (stock price still at $110) = $0 change collected

$650 (premium) for writing option = $650 gain on option

$0 change in stock position + $650 option gain = $650 gain on trade

Once again, your maximum profit zone is between $103.50 and $131.50. The higher up in the zone, the more profitable your trade becomes. The lower you are in the zone, the less profitable your trade is. If the market enters into a period of sideways action, this is a great way to generate returns if your stocks get stuck in a sideways pattern as well.

Example 3

Now let's say the stock goes up instead. It rallies all the way up to $125. That's even better. You've just made $15 on your stock and that $125 call you wrote will expire worthless, and you'll pocket $650. Your grand total is now a $21.50 gain or $2,150 on a $15 move.

How? Because the stock increased in price by $15 for a $1,500 gain. And at option expiration, you'll end up keeping the entire $6.50 premium or $650 you collected for writing the option. Even though the stock only increased by $15, you would end up making $21.50 in total, as both your stock and option made money, resulting in maximum profitability on the trade.

$110 (stock buy price) to $125 = $15 increase or $1,500 gain on stock

collected $6.50 (premium) or $650 for writing option = $650 gain on option

$15 stock gain + $6.50 option gain = $21.50 or $2,150 gain on trade

As in the previous examples, the maximum profit zone is $103.50 to $131.50. If the market goes up, you can profit on both the stock movement and the options income.

Example 4

In this example, let's say the stock rallies to $131.50. Your profit is still $21.50 or $2,150 in total on the trade. But the way you arrive at that point of maximum profitability is a bit different than the previous example.

Why? Your stock increased from $110 to $131.50 for a $21.50 gain. But you're now giving up your option premium gain of $6.50 on the $125 call you wrote. At expiration, that $125 call is now $6.50 in-the-money, which means that option is actually worth $650, which would go against your gains.

(Remember, when you're the purchaser of an option, you want the premium to increase in value. As the writer or granter of an option, you want the premium to go down. An option that expires worthless represents the maximum loss for the buyer, but it also represents the maximum gain for the writer.)

As the option writer, you are obligated to deliver that stock at $125, even though it's at $131.50. That represents a loss of −$650. In this example, since you collected $650 for writing the option in the first place, you're essentially giving it all back, either by getting the stock called from you at $125 even though it's now at $131.50 or by buying the option back at $650, thus avoiding having your stock called away from you. So while you didn't really lose anything on the option, you also didn't gain anything either.

Scenario 1

As the option writer, you're obligated to sell that stock at the strike price you wrote (in this case $125), even though the price of the stock is at $131.50. This means you're essentially buying the stock at $131.50 and selling it for $125, for a loss of −$6.50 or −$650. This is offset by the premium you collected of $650, making the option portion of the trade a wash.

Scenario 2

You can also choose to buy the option back before the stock is called from you. But the dollar result is the same. With the option now $6.50 in-the-money, you'd have to pay $6.50 or $650 to offset your obligation on the call you wrote. If you collected $650, but then paid $650 to exit the trade, that's a net result of $0 (less transaction costs).

Note that most people don't get their stock called away from them. Usually they'll simply buy that option back before it expires.

You have the same maximum profitability in this overall example going to $131.50 as in the previous example (Example 3) where it went to $125. But this time, your profit on the trade is coming from just the stock increase and not from the option.

$110 (stock buy price) to $131.50 = $21.50 increase or $2,150 stock gain

wrote the $125 call option for $6.50 (premium)
at expiration with the stock at $131.50, the option is $6.50 in-the-money
= $0 gain/loss for the writer

$21.50 gain + $0 gain/loss on the option = $21.50 or $2,150 gain on trade

If the price goes above $131.50 (above your maximum profit range), the option portion of the trade will preclude you from profiting any more on higher prices (see Example 5).

Example 5

In this example, let's say the stock goes above $131.50 to $140. No further gains can be made above $131.50. As we illustrated earlier, while your stock continues to gain the higher it goes, your option will begin to lose money commensurately.

Why? Your stock increased from $110 to $140 for a $30 gain. But you're now not only giving up your option premium gain of $6.50 on the $125 call you wrote, but you're now also losing money above and beyond that as well. For every additional $1 rise in the stock, you're losing an additional −$1 on the option. At expiration, that $125 call is now $15 in-the-money (or is $850 above the $650 premium collected), which means that option is actually worth $1,500, which would go against your gains.

As the option writer, you are obligated to deliver that stock at $125, even though it's at $140. That represents a loss of −$1,500 less the $650 premium collected for a net loss of −$850. Or you can buy that option back instead for $1,500, which is $850 more than you collected for it for a loss of −$850. Either way, this will result in a loss of −$850, which will go against your stock gains.

Once again, you have the same maximum profitability in this overall example at $140 as you do at $131.50 or even $125; and that is $21.50 or $2,150. But above $131.50, precludes you from any further gains.

$110 (stock buy price) to $140 = $30 price increase or $3,000 stock gain

wrote the $125 call option for $6.50 (premium)
at expiration with the stock at $140, the option is now $15 in-the-money
= $850 loss for the writer

$30 gain − $850 loss on the option = $21.50 or $2,150 gain on trade

Essentially, when you write an option, you're reducing your downside risk by a set amount, but you're also potentially giving up some upside if the stock goes above the strike price that you wrote. Sometimes this will happen. Although, you can simply roll your option up by buying back the original strike price and writing another one further out, thus opening up your profit opportunity.

You can even buy a call option, which would give you additional upside potential as well. But stocks won't always go straight up. And while sometimes you may lose out on some upside potential, you'll likely find yourself consistently collecting premiums on your covered calls over and over again.

This is a wonderful strategy, and it truly is a shame more people don't know about it. But now you do (if you didn't already).

Uncovered Call Writing

Uncovered call writing (writing calls on a stock that you don't own), works the same mechanically as writing covered calls. But there are different risks given that you don't own the stock. This strategy is also known as naked call writing.

Once again, writing calls can be profitable in mildly bullish markets, sideways markets, and bearish markets. However, while writing calls presents the investor with limited gains (limited to what you collected in premium for the option), in theory, the risk is open. This is where naked call writing and covered call writing essentially differ.

Again, in a covered call, if the stock price goes up past your strike price, you'll start losing on the short call, but you're also offsetting it with the gains on the stock. In other words, you have a limited risk.

However, with the naked call write, if the stock goes up above your strike price, your option will lose money, but with no offsetting gains from being long on the underlying stock; that is what makes the trade have unlimited risk.

Of course, you can buy the option back and exit the trade whenever you want as the option is just as liquid as a stock. But it's important to understand the differences in risk before deciding on one strategy or another.

You'll win, if at expiration, the stock is at or below the strike price. This is because the option would be worth $0, which means the buyer would lose what he paid for the option and the writer of the option (that's us) would keep the premium collected for a profit.

You'll draw, if at expiration, the stock price was above the strike price plus an amount commensurate with what the writer collected for the premium. In this case, the stock could actually go against you and still not lose any money.

For example, if you wrote an $85 call option for a premium of $5.00 or $500—if at expiration, the stock was at $90; that means the $85 call would be $5 in-the-money. As the writer of the option, you'd either have to deliver 100 shares of stock at $85 (and be down −$500, since it's now at $90) or simply buy back that option for $500, meaning the $500 you collected in premium you'd have to use to exit the trade resulting in a scratch ($0 gain or loss).

You'll lose on this trade if the stock goes up past the strike price plus the amount collected in premium.

However, once the stock looks like it's breaking out above your strike price, you should consider buying that option back to limit your loss (or depending on where you are in the trade, you might just be lessening your gain).

Alternatively, you could always buy an option above it, thus capping your loss to a specific amount or just buy the stock.

But the preferred action is to simply exit the trade by buying the option back and moving on.

Once again, this strategy can be profitable in mildly bullish markets, sideways markets, and bearish markets. And as described earlier, this strategy turns time decay (the very thing that works against most options investors) and puts it to work for you.

To increase your odds of success with this strategy, concentrate on out-of-the-money options. Those have a greater likelihood of expiring worthless, which is what the writer is hoping for. This is true because of the dynamics of how options work. But also, if you write options that are out-of-the-money, it means the stock will have to make a larger move to reach your strike price in order for your written call option to lose. So the further out-of-the-money you go, the better your chances of success.

Of course, you'll have to balance how far out to go with how much premium you can collect for the risk. But when done right, this can be a strategy with a high rate of success.

Put Option Writing

If writing call options is a lesser known strategy, then writing put options is probably one of the least known strategies. But this a great strategy and another great way to generate income, not to mention a way to potentially get into a stock you'd like to own at a much cheaper price.

You will need full option privileges to do this in your account, so check with your brokerage firm to see if you qualify.

Here's how it works. As you know, if you buy a put option, you're buying the right to sell a stock at a certain price within a certain period of time. The buyer pays a premium for this right. He has limited risk—which is limited to the price he paid for the option.

However, the writer is taking the other side. He's obligated to buy the stock at a certain price within a certain period of time. As in the call example we went through earlier, the option writer collects a premium. We're going to be the option writer.

So the benefits are: If you write an out-of-the-money option on a stock you wouldn't mind owning if it went down, you might just get the chance to own it at a cheaper price than it's currently trading at if it does go down.

If however, it never gets to that level, you've collected the premium for writing the option and taking the risk that the stock would be put to you at that price. But again, if you wouldn't mind owning it if it did go lower, you've still won if it was put to you, because now you've got that stock at a better price. Let's look at some examples.

Example 1

Let's say a stock is at $110 and you wrote a four-month, $95 put option, for a premium of $6.00 or $600.

If you'd like to own that stock, but would like to buy it at a cheaper level, you can either put in a buy stop at $95 and hope one day it gets hit. Or you can write the $95 put option instead.

If it never goes down to $95, you'll keep the entire $600 at expiration. This is better than a buy stop that never gets hit, because there's no reward if it doesn't hit you. But with the put writing, you're collecting a premium.

Example 2

Let's say it does go down to $95 this time. If it does, the option could be exercised and you'd now be obligated to buy that stock for $95 a share. Options can be exercised (the shares put to you) at any time. Of course this would only make sense if the price fell below the strike price.

Note that most options do not end in exercise, but instead are bought and sold until expiration.

At expiration, you could now be obligated to buy that stock for $95 a share. At expiration though, that at-the-money option has no intrinsic value and is worthless to the purchaser, which means you (the put writer) have pocketed the full $600.

It's unlikely that the at-the-money option would be exercised as there's no financial incentive for the holder or buyer to do so. But even if it was, you were paid the full $600 premium that you were hoping to receive, and you also got the stock you wanted at the price you were comfortable in owning it at. You can then happily hold the stock or sell it. It's just as liquid as if you bought the stock on your own.

Of course you don't need to hold onto that written option until expiration if you don't want to. You could buy that option back right before expiration at virtually nothing and be done with it, locking in your gains.

Example 3

This time, let's say it goes down to $85. You'd now be obligated to buy that stock at $95 even though it's selling at $85.

So you're now down −$1,000 on the stock that was put to you. But you also collected $600 premium for writing that put option in the first place. So your capital loss on owning that stock at $95 is currently −$1,000, but this is offset by the $600 premium that you took in for a net loss of only −$400 for owning that stock at $95.

This is a better deal than simply putting in a buy stop on that stock you were interested in owning, because if your buy stop did get triggered, you would have gotten your stock at $95, but you would not have gotten any offsetting premium that you could have collected for writing a put.

Your capital loss in that case would be −$1,000 as opposed to only −$400 for writing the put option as in the example.

Note that in this example, $89 would represent how low the stock could go without losing any money on the trade, that is, the breakeven point where there's no gain or loss on the trade.

wrote the $95 put option for $6.00 (premium) or $600

if stock falls to $89 (that's $6 below my strike price)
stock will be put to you at $95
$95 stock purchase price − $89 market value = −$6.00 or −$600

$600 gain on premium for writing the put, − $600 loss on the stock
= $0 gain/loss

If you thought the stock could fall below your strike price and even below your breakeven point, and you didn't want the stock to be put to you at the strike price that you had, you could do what's known as rolling down your option before expiration. This is done by buying back your current put option and writing a new put option with a further down strike price.

Of course, the money spent on buying back the nearby strike price would be greater than the premium received for writing the further out strike price, but your full purchase price of the stock if it were put to you at a lower price would now be less expensive.

You would have to work out the math to see if it would make sense for you. And you'd have to review your outlook to determine your interest in still owning that stock.

In a bear market, for example, you better be very sure that you're okay with owning a falling stock if it's put to you. But if you're interested in owning a stock, although only at a lower price, this is a great way to generate income and potentially get the stock you want.

Of course, you don't have to want to own the stock to use this strategy. If you have a belief that a certain stock simply won't go down below a certain price, then writing a put option is one way to make money, especially if you believe there's more upside risk than down.

In general, I prefer to write puts on stocks I wouldn't mind owning because there's less stress involved if you see the stocks move lower.

Example 4

Let's look at an actual trade I did for a real life example. On December 3, 2008, I decided to write a put option on Apple Computer, stock ticker AAPL. I chose the April, out-of-the-money, $70 put option at a price (premium) of $8.35 or $835.

AAPL was selling at approximately $93 at that time, and I believed that AAPL would go up, or at least not go down much below $70. At the time, I didn't have enough conviction that APPL would go straight up, so I didn't want to commit $9,300 to get long 100 shares of AAPL.

But I also didn't want to miss out on an opportunity to make money in AAPL because I thought I had correctly identified its general range and wanted to profit from that. Also, I thought that if it did go down to $70, I wouldn't mind owning AAPL shares at that price. And even if it never got there, I'd still get paid a premium in the meantime. So on December 3, I wrote the April $70 put at $8.35. Figure 18.1 shows what the chart of AAPL looked like on December 3, 2008.

FIGURE 18.1   Apple Chart on December 3, 2008

If AAPL stayed above $70 at expiration (the third Friday of April), I'd keep the full $835 I collected. And potentially get to own AAPL at $70.

If the market went below $70, to even as low as $61.65, I still wouldn't lose anything. (If you need to review why the stock could fall this low and not lose any money, go back and reread Example 3.) Only if AAPL went below $61.65, would I start to lose on the trade.

Between the time I placed that trade on December 3 and the expiration date on April 17, the price of AAPL got as low as $78.20 and as high as $124.25.

That AAPL option has since expired worthless, which means I kept the full $835 premium I collected, less my commissions and fees of $10.75, for an $824.25 gain, or a 98.7% return.

Figure 18.2 shows what the chart looked like on April 17, the last trading day before expiration.

FIGURE 18.2 Apple Chart on April 17, 2009 (Last Trading Day Before Option Expiration)

Here's some additional insight on my thoughts on that trade. As the option expiration got closer and while the price of AAPL climbed higher, I simply chose to let the option expire worthless, because I didn't feel my profits were in danger at that point. Plus, by doing so, I didn't have to pay another $10.75 in exit costs.

But it should be noted that, in general, when the option is literally worth only a few dollars, getting out at such a ridiculously low price is smart since you've now locked in that profit and no longer have any risk on the trade.

And in this example, that option was priced at less than $10 (and even as low as just $1; that's only a 1 cent premium) for many weeks before it expired. In hindsight, with AAPL trading at over $124 at the time of the option expiration; had I got in at $93, I would have been up $31 or $3,100.

But between December 3 and April 17, before AAPL traded as high as $124.25, it got as low as $78.20 while the bear market was still raging. This means, if I bought the stock at $93, I would have been down as much as −$1,480 from my purchase price. And I would've had to have made a decision about whether I would've gotten out or not when it was falling. And since that represents nearly a −16% loss, it's likely I would have gotten out of that trade at a loss and potentially missed the chance to be in on the run up.

But with the written put option, the trade remained profitable virtually every day from its inception, even when the market was down. In fact, at worst, the option might have increased in value a couple of hundred dollars max, which means I never had to second guess the trade once.

And again, even if it fell all the way down to $61.65, I still wouldn't have lost any principle. This is in stark contrast to potentially being down −$1,480 if I had the stock from $93 to $78.20 and as much as −$3,135 if the stock went down to $61.65. What a difference.

That trade turned out to be virtually picture perfect. And I'll likely continue to do this again and again, every few months.

Summary

As you can see, there are many different ways to make money in options. And the ones in the preceding sections are just some of the many different option strategies that you can use to make money in the market, no matter what. And there are many, many more. But the ones I just covered are my favorites.

If these are new to you, take the appropriate amount of time to research each one of these before you attempt to place one on your own. Start slow.

After you've put on any of the discussed options trades and see it in your account, it'll make even more sense to you. And you'll be able to feel what it feels like to have one of these positions on and see how it fits with your trading style.

Now let's see how to find the right kinds of stocks for these different option strategies.

Stock Screening for Options

When you're considering these different options strategies, remember to consider their Zacks Rank. The Zacks Rank 1s and 2s are Strong Buys and Buys. The 4s and 5s are Sells and Strong Sells. The 3s are a Hold or Market Perform.

If you're expecting a Zacks Rank 1 stock to blast off, you probably shouldn't be writing a call against your long stock position. Likewise, you may not want to be in such a hurry to write a put option on a stock that's just been Ranked a 4 or a 5. You might want to give it some time to see if it'll go any lower first.

Here are some practical guidelines for picking the right stocks to go with the right option strategies.

Buying Calls on Momentum and Aggressive Growth Stocks

Momentum style strategies and Aggressive Growth style strategies are probably the best ones to use with outright call buying. Remember, these are stocks on the move with some of the most explosive upside potential.

When buying calls or puts, you need to be right on direction as well as time. I still advocate getting plenty of time (a quick rule: however much time you think you need, try and get at least an extra month or more). But these are the likeliest candidates to profit with this strategy.

Buying Puts on Short-Selling Screens

We went over several screens to find stocks to short. We also looked at several technical analysis screens to find stocks headed lower. This is the first place to begin for finding stocks to buy puts on.

I've seen people throw money into puts the moment a stock hits a new 52-week high, as if somehow because it made a new high, it must be ripe for a fall. Don't do it. We've already seen how stocks making new highs have a tendency of making even higher highs.

The goal is to put the probabilities of success on your side. Find the overvalued stocks that shouldn't be trading where they are. Find the stocks under their important moving averages. And concentrate on the ones with downward earnings estimate revisions. This is where you'll find your edge with puts.

Note that puts can also be used as a hedge. When doing so, make sure you recognize where your profit and loss zones are. But if you're really expecting a stock to tumble, determine if you wouldn't simply be better off getting out of that stock altogether or simply using a stop loss order instead.

Straddles and Strangles

The best stocks for this option strategy are:

- **High beta stocks**
  These are stocks that move and can move big, and that's exactly what you need to see happen with this kind of strategy. A small move or medium sized move won't cut it.

- **Stocks ready to report earnings or an important announcement**
  In order for a stock to move, there usually needs to be a catalyst. One of the most reliable catalysts out there for big moves (up or down) are earnings reports. For some reports, you'll want to get long in front of them. For others, short. But there are those where you don't believe there's an edge one way or the other and that it really could go in either direction—and sharply. These are great opportunities for straddles and strangles.

- **Stocks at key technical levels**
  This means pulling out your technical analysis hat. Consider stocks that are right at, or have just pierced, their 50-day or 200-day moving average. Why? Because those levels will either act as a support or resistance and send the stocks back into the direction where it came, or the stocks might breakout and put great distance between itself and those moving averages as a new trend starts to develop.

- **Stocks with certain chart pattern set-ups**
  Some charts patterns have clear advantages when traded from one side or the other. But there are some that can be explosive in either direction. I'm referring to the Head and Shoulders and Inverted Head and Shoulders. As we illustrated in Chapter 12, the Head and Shoulders and Inverted Head and Shoulders failures can be great patterns to trade. For example, if a Head and Shoulders formation, which has put in all the requisite price action to be identified as such, starts heading back to the right shoulder (for whatever reason), usually one of two things will happen:

  1. It will get repelled right back and move toward the neckline for the expected breakout.

  2. It's going to fail and breakout sharply through the plane of the right shoulder and likely past the head and more. Since this pattern can result in big and fast price moves when it fails, this is a pattern to look at when it starts acting out of the ordinary.

Either way, a big move is needed to profit on this strategy. So be sure there are ample catalysts out there that could trigger such a move.

Spreads

You can be bullish or bearish on these. But usually you're not expecting something to be explosive. Instead, you expect a move in a particular direction, but you understand that it may be slower going. Buying calls or puts are fine, but if it moves too slow or doesn't move enough, the call or put won't profit as expected.

Spreading lets the options trader benefit from time decay. So while the stock is moving in the hoped for direction, the slowness of it, while eating away at the time decay on the one you bought, will also eat away at the one you wrote, thus allowing you to benefit from a slower moving, but correctly called, directional trade.

Value style screens and even Growth and Income screens can produce some good picks for a bull call spread strategy, particularly stocks expected to move higher for example, but not with a big splash.

As for put spreads on stocks you expect to move lower, the short screens are fine, but you should decide if you wouldn't be better off with a long put instead. The Zacks Rank 3s that come through could also be good candidates. Weak enough fundamentals to qualify a short stock screen, but still good enough to hang onto its #3 Zacks Rank.

Writing Calls

If you're writing calls on stocks you own, look for the ones that you think may be cooling off or headed for a pause or a bit of consolidation. Or even ones where a pullback could be seen. Not enough to get out, but enough to see the benefit of writing calls on your stock and collecting premium while its upward trajectory is on hold.

As for uncovered calls, I'd look for stocks with a little less bullishness. In other words, not stocks you're likely to want to own at those levels.

For these, you're essentially taking a neutral to bearish stance. I'd focus on Zacks Rank 3s and higher. Stocks that are clearly showing fatigue. And stocks that may be showing up on your sell screens. Writing calls can make money on all of these scenarios, but it does have a limited gain (limited to the premium collected) and an unlimited risk (meaning if the stock goes up, the option can continue to lose money as long as it keeps going against you.)

I also like to get a little technical analysis confirmation on these stocks, too. I'm not so quick to jump at stocks at their peak as we've discussed earlier, but rather stocks that have clearly lost the upward momentum and are even trading below their important moving averages. In addition, looking for stocks that are in bearish chart formations or that have already broken through them can put good call writing stocks onto your consideration list.

Writing Puts

For me, as a rule of thumb, I'll only look to write puts on a stock I wouldn't mind owning. But you don't have to want to own it to take advantage of this strategy.

Virtually any neutral to bullish strategy where you don't think a stock is going to go down will work with this. But if you're trying to maximize your gains, there are other strategies besides writing puts that could give you a better payout, given the fact that the put writer only has a limited profit potential.

Value style screens are good candidates for writing puts, especially if you're writing the puts on out-of-the-money strikes. In effect, you would be looking for the stocks to trade at even more of a discount than it already is, thus allowing you to potentially buy the stock at a true bargain, and if not, you'll at least get paid while you wait.

In fact, value screens are an ideal stock selection for this because they essentially let the investor determine the discount he's willing to pay. Some value stocks are good buys, but maybe not good enough for you yet. But if the stock were to fall to $X, making the P/E and P/CF for example, trade even lower, then you'd love it. Problem is, many value investors have seen their value stock opportunities pass them by because they never got down to a deep enough discount for them. But with put writing, you can finally profit from those instances. If you wish that value stock were a bit lower before you bought it, write a put on it and win, no matter what.

Summary

I have had far greater success screening for option trades using a stock screener than an option screener. Since options are simply instruments to trade stocks with, using stocks as your starting point is the smartest thing. And once you understand the stock's trade characteristics (i.e., direction, magnitude, time element, etc.), you can then determine the correct option strategy for that stock.

True, sometimes you'll find a stock and have the perfect option strategy in mind, only to find that the option has virtually no volume or the option prices are way out of whack (excessively large bid/ask spreads). In those cases, move on. There are too many good trades to pick from rather than trying to make do with one that's posing difficulties at the onset.

But learn how to use these different option strategies as yet another set of tools to gain an advantage over the market. And it all starts with screening for the right stocks.

Investing in ETFs

Another great way for investing in the market is with Exchange Traded Funds (ETFs). These are essentially baskets of stocks that trade like an individual stock.

ETFs were first introduced back in 1993 with the Standard & Poor's Deposit Receipts ETF, ticker symbol SPDR. The "Spider" (as it's often called because of how it's spelled) was designed to track the S&P 500, while offering the convenience and liquidity of a stock.

Since then, the number of ETFs and the kinds of ETFs available has grown tremendously as their popularity exploded. You too can include ETFs in your trading. And you can use a stock screener to find the best opportunities at the right time.

ETFs for Any Market and Any Direction

ETFs can be used for virtually any market and in any direction. There are now ETFs on the Dow Jones, newer ones of the S&P 500, the Nasdaq, and the different Russell Indexes.

In addition, there are ETFs on many different sectors and industries such as:

Financials

Oil and Gas

Basic Materials

Consumer Goods

Real Estate

Healthcare

Technology

Telecommunications

Utilities

And so many more.

There are even ETFs on currencies and treasuries, gold and silver, and international market ETFs representing the indexes in China and Japan, to name a few.

But the innovation of the ETF business doesn't stop there. Investors can actually buy ETFs that will make money (rise in price) as the market or a specific industry falls.

As we discussed in the options section, buying put options has often been used as an alternative to going short a stock. Since shorting stocks requires a margin account, there are some who can't short because of the type of account they have, and others who simply don't want to. And while options offer a great alternative, they are not for everybody. But many of these investors would still like a way to profit if prices go down.

Short ETFs (i.e., inverse ETFs) do just that. Let's say you believed that the S&P 500 was going to go down. One of the easiest ways to trade this idea would be to buy (or go long) a short S&P 500 ETF such as the ProShares Short S&P500 ETF, ticker symbol SH. A short ETF will correspond inversely (or opposite) to the daily changes in the S&P 500 index (before fees and expenses).

For example: If the S&P 500 was down −3% one day, the short ETF that you bought would increase by 3%, giving you an easy way to profit from a market decline without any special setting-up in your account.

And since it trades like a stock, you can get in and out at any time during the market you want. In addition to short index ETFs, there are also short sector and industry ETFs among others.

Let's say you thought Financials were headed for another fall. You could buy a Short Financial ETF, such as the ProShares Short Financials, ticker symbol SEF, which would correspond inversely to the daily price movement of the Dow Jones Financials Index, which holds companies such as JP Morgan, Bank of America, Citigroup, Goldman Sachs, and more. As those companies fall and the financial index goes down, your stock would increase in value commensurately.

Making money on the downside has never been easier—unless, of course, you're using the Ultra Short ETF products.

Ultra Shorts work much the same way as the regular short ETFs, but instead, correspond inversely to twice the daily return of the underlying Index or Sector. So if you're exceptionally bearish or want to leverage your investment dollars to their fullest amount, you can buy an UltraShort ETF such as the ProShares UltraShort QQQ, ticker symbol QID. This ETF corresponds inversely to twice the daily price change in the underlying Nasdaq 100 Index.

A −5% decline in the Nasdaq 100 for example, would equate to a 10% increase in your UltraShort Nasdaq ETF, QID. These UltraShort ETFs are also available for the Dow Jones, the S&P 500, different market-cap and Style Indexes, as well as various Sectors and Industries.

These types of products are ideal ways to make money if you believe stocks are headed for a fall. And they are great ways to hedge an existing portfolio. Plus, with the extra leverage available with the Ultra ETFs, you won't have to tie up a lot of money to do so.

Of course, the Ultra ETFs are also available on the long side, too. Even a small 5% or 10% rise in the market could add up to a 10% or 20% gain. (And even more with the new triple leverage ETFs.) But a word of caution: don't over-leverage yourself or put too much money into any one of these Ultra ETFs in an effort to make a big score. Get comfortable with seeing your position rise or fall twice as much as the underlying market or Sector you're participating in.

Sure, a 10% gain on a −5% down day for the market is exciting. But a −10% loss on a 5% up day for the market may push you out of your risk to reward comfort zone. So take it slow and feel how it feels to have this additional leverage.

Screening for the Right Sector and Industry ETFs

A good screening strategy can make it easy to determine which Sectors and which Industries are poised to perform the best (or the worst).

As we've covered in the previous chapters, you can run a Sector or an Industry screen to see which groups have the best average Zacks Rank (Zacks Industry Rank), or which groups have the highest percentage of stocks trading within 10% of their 52-week highs. In fact, virtually any item that you could add to a stock, you could apply to an industry for a broader assessment.

As we've demonstrated, it's easy to do and you'll instantly know what the top (or bottom) groups are. And as you know, research has proven that the best groups outperform the worst groups by a significant margin.

Stocks screeners are light years ahead of most ETF screeners. But that's okay. In fact, all one needs is a simple list of ETFs that you can grab from the Internet or your online brokerage. Once you know which Sectors and which Industries are worth paying attention to through the use of a capable stock screener, picking an ETF that corresponds to that group is a snap.

Take note however, some ETFs don't always perform as expected. When the real estate market got hammered in 2008, the ProShares UltraShort ETF, ticker SRS, instead of being up twice what the market was down, it was actually down itself for the year and even more than the Index it was tracking. How can an inverse ETF (and two times the magnitude no less) lose money when the group it's tracking is down? The short answer is that it has to do with how they rebalance their portfolio of instruments, which is daily. And they freely disclose this by saying that the return over periods other than one day will likely differ in amount and possibly direction from the target return over the same period. Quite frankly, I'm still not sure I understand the "why" behind that. And I'm even less interested in the long answer.

But for this discussion, it doesn't really matter. Why? Because those opposite performances are the exceptions and not the norm. And all one has to do is go to the company's website and see if the ETF is responding as you would imagine it should. What should you look for? Look at the YTD return and the 1 Year return and see how it compares to the performance of the Index it's tracking. If it's performing in line with what you would expect (daily rebalancing mumbo jumbo notwithstanding), you should be alright. If it's way off, look for a different one.

Remember, these are not supposed to be long-term holdings that you can get into and forget about. Although, I have held ETFs for weeks and even months. But eventually, the move you were looking for has either happened or it hasn't and it's time to move on.

Aside from that caveat, ETFs are a great way to make a directional play on a group, or an Index or even a foreign market with all of the simplicity and convenience of trading a stock. And you can take full advantage of all of this with a stock screener and the right screening strategies.

20

Putting It All Together

We've covered a lot of ground in this book. And it's been fun. Every time I pick up a new book, I think to myself: If I can learn one new thing or have something I already knew reaffirmed in some different way, then I'm happy. I hope this book has done that — and many times over.

Whether you're a beginning stock screener or a seasoned stock screening pro, I hope the information in this book has encouraged and motivated you to use screening even more in your trading. Learning new and better ways to pick more profitable stocks is one of the quickest ways to becoming a better trader, no matter what level of trading success you've already achieved.

It really all comes down to three things:

1. Identify: The first step is to identify what kind of trader you are or what kind of trader you want to be. And what kind of style suits you best. Whether it be Momentum or Aggressive Growth, Value or Growth and Income, Technical Analysis or even just "stuff that works," decide who you are as a trader first and foremost. And what goals you're hoping to accomplish with your trading. This is all part of the identification process.

2. Analyze: The second step is to analyze. You don't have to turn yourself into an analyst. But you do have to screen for stocks and analyze

which trading strategies work and work best for you. This is actually the easiest of the three steps. Because once you've identified what kind of trader you are, it's easy to find stocks with those types of characteristics with a good screening strategy.

3. Manage: The third and last step is to manage your risk and to pay attention to your portfolio. Some people think they're too busy or they don't have time. Sure you do. Keeping track of your investments doesn't have to be difficult or time consuming. And it isn't with the right tools. In fact, managing your investments is really just about common sense. Getting rid of losers before they ruin your portfolio. Taking profits before you give them back. And making sure the reasons you bought a stock in the first place still apply.

I said this at the beginning and it's worth saying it again: Your investments are probably the largest, most important chunk of money you will ever be responsible for in your entire life. And if it isn't now, it likely will be one day. You owe it to yourself to take care of it the very best you can.

Start with screening and backtesting. And if you remember to always **I**dentify, **A**nalyze, and **M**anage your investments, you will be able to say, "**I AM** a better trader."

Disclaimer

The performance calculations for the strategies throughout this book were done with the backtesting feature of the Research Wizard using the DBCMHIST database and consist of the total return (price changes + dividends) of an equal weighted portfolio. Returns are calculated on a specified periodic basis (most often one or four weeks) and assume no transaction costs. The portfolio is rebalanced at the start of each new period. Returns can be stated as either annualized or compounded.

Stock trading/investing involves risk, and you can lose some or all of your investment. Hypothetical or backtested results may not always be duplicated in the real world. Backtesting can at times produce an unintended look-ahead bias. Results can also at times be over or understated due to the possible exclusion of inactive companies. In addition, hypothetical trading does not involve financial risk, and no hypothetical trading record can completely account for the impact of financial risk in actual trading, not the least of which is the ability to withstand losses or to adhere to a particular trading strategy in spite of trading losses. These are material points that can also adversely affect actual trading results. The Research Wizard program has been aligned, to the extent possible, to eliminate look-ahead bias. Zacks, however, cannot make any guarantees in regard to this or any other possible limitation. For more information on backtesting, please go to: www.zacks.com/performance.

The performance of the Zacks Rank portfolios for annual and year-to-date periods are the linked monthly total returns (price changes + dividends) of equal weighted hypothetical portfolios, consisting of those stocks with the indicated Zacks Rank, assuming monthly rebalancing and zero transaction costs. These are not the returns of actual portfolios. The hypothetical portfolios were created at the beginning of each month from January 1988 forward based on the values of the Zacks Rank available to Zacks' clients before the beginning of each month. The portfolios created monthly from 1988 through September 2006 exclude American Depository Receipts (ADRs) and are comprised of stocks that have the indicated Zacks Rank and were covered by at least two analysts at the time of the stocks, inclusion in the portfolio.

Starting in October 2006 and going forward, the portfolios are comprised of all stocks with the indicated Zacks Rank and do not exclude ADRs, which is more reflective of the list of stocks that customers will find on the Zacks web sites. The Zacks #1 Rank performance numbers have been independently audited from 1996 through 2007 by Virchow, Krause & Company, LLP.

The S&P 500 Index (S&P 500) is a well-known, unmanaged index of the prices of 500 large-company common stocks selected by Standard & Poor's. The S&P 500 includes the reinvestment of all dividends, no transaction costs, and represents the gross returns before management fees.

Free Trials and Other Resources

For the past two decades, Zacks Investment Research has been helping investors beat the market with independent analysis, innovative products and services, and, of course, the Zacks Rank. Because of this, Zacks' research is among the most widely used research on the Web.

Try the following products and services at Zacks.com to see if any of them are right for you.

Research Wizard Free Trial

All of the screens, trading strategies, and studies found in this book were created and tested with the Research Wizard stock screening and back-testing program.

If you'd like to take a free trial to the Research Wizard to follow along with the book, or if you'd like to put your own ideas to the test, just go to the link below to begin your free, no-obligation trial.

You'll soon discover that the Research Wizard is one of the most powerful tools available to the individual investor but remarkably easy to use. Give it a try and see how it can help you improve your own stock picking abilities. Go to: www.zacks.com/rw1.

Zacks.com and Zacks Premium

With Zacks.com, you can access our unique market insights, free daily stock picks from each specific trading style, and our free daily newsletter. You can also take it to the next level buy trying Zacks Premium, which gives you full access to the Zacks Rank, our Zacks Equity Research, comprehensive Industry Analysis, and our new Zacks Mutual Fund Rank. For a free 30-day trial, just go to: www.zacks.com/pfp1.